Gendering the Reader

Gendering the Reader

edited by

Sara Mills

 HARVESTER
WHEATSHEAF

New York London Toronto Sydney Tokyo Singapore

First published 1994 by
Harvester Wheatsheaf
Campus 400, Maylands Avenue
Hemel Hempstead
Hertfordshire, HP2 7EZ
A division of
Simon & Schuster International Group

Introduction, Chapter 1 and Conclusion © 1994 Sara Mills
Chapter 2 © 1994 Chris Christie
Chapter 3 © 1994 Barbara Bradby
Chapter 4 © 1994 Zoe Wicomb
Chapter 5 © 1994 Joanna Thornborrow
Chapter 6 © 1994 Lynne Pearce
Chapter 7 © 1994 Julia Hallam
Chapter 8 © 1994 Kay Boardman
Chapter 9 © 1994 Imelda Whelehan

Typeset in 10½/12½ Goudy Old Style
by Hands Fotoset, Leicester

Printed and bound in Great Britain by
BPCC Wheatons Ltd, Exeter

British Library Cataloguing in Publication Data

A catalogue record for this book is available from
the British Library

ISBN 0-7450-1130-6 (pbk)

1 2 3 4 5 98 97 96 95 94

Contents

Illustrations

Acknowledgements

We would like to thank the following people for discussions which helped in writing this book: the members of the feminist research group and staff and postgraduate research group in the Department of English and Drama at Loughborough University; members of the Women's Studies Centre at Lancaster University, especially Jackie Stacey, who, were it not for serious illness, would have been a welcome contributor to this volume. We would like to thank staff, especially Nigel Fabb, Martin Montgomery and Alan Durant, and postgraduate students in the Programme in Literary Linguistics, University of Strathclyde, where discussions around readership in a variety of different contexts developed certain of the ideas which generated this collection of essays. Members of staff in the Department of Cultural Studies, University of Central Lancashire, especially Jane Darcy and Shauna Murray, commented on the book, as did Brian Maidment of Edge Hill College of Higher Education. Tony Brown provided useful comments on specific chapters and general discussion of the ideas in this book, as did Elaine Hobby, Mick Wallis and Bill Overton. We would also like to thank Sally Robertson, who began the analysis in Chapter 5 and provided the two advertisements which form the basis of the analysis. Jackie Jones has been an extremely supportive, encouraging and, most of all, patient editor. Thanks to Susan Rae-Brown, who transformed herself from 'working girl' to 'career cobra' without the assistance of Prince Charming.

PERMISSIONS

Lyrics from 'Material Girl' and 'Into the Groove' reproduced by permission of Warner Chappell Music Ltd/International Music Publications.

The poem 'Blood' by Caroline Douglas is from *No Holds Barred* edited by the Raving Beauties, first published by the Women's Press, 1985. We would like to thank the Women's Press for permission to publish this poem; all efforts have been made to obtain the author's permission.

Dante Gabriel Rossetti's *The Beloved* is reproduced by kind permission of The Tate Gallery, London.

The photograph by Jan Dibbets is reproduced by permission of Rizzoli Publications, New York.

The advertisement for family planning is reproduced by permission of *True Love Magazine*, Drum Publications, Johannesburg, South Africa.

The two advertisements for Filofax are reproduced by kind permission of Filofax Ltd, Ilford, Essex.

Introduction

GENERAL AIMS OF THE BOOK

This book aims to analyse the difficult relationship between gender and reading/viewing/listening.[1] *Gendering the Reader* is a series of essays which constitute feminist analyses of the way that texts address readers, and the way that readers adopt, or are directed towards, positions in relation to texts. It is concerned with the power of the reader in the production of meaning: to what extent s/he can resist the dominant address of the text and adopt and/or construct alternative reading positions. We are particularly concerned with the analysis of the way that texts gender their readership, but recognise the necessity not to resort to a simple binary female/male analysis; we examine the differences within the term 'gender' (that is, differences of race, age, class, sexual orientation, knowledge base/ education, occupation and so on). We are not therefore concerned here with producing a simple analysis of the way that all women or all men read, but rather with examining the way that we as women are sometimes described and addressed as if we were the same, at the same time being mindful of the heterogeneity lurking behind that problematic term 'woman'. As many feminist theorists have shown, the term 'woman' needs to be used to describe oppression, at the same time as its unified nature needs to be called into question (see Fuss 1989; Butler 1990). Theorists such as Monique Wittig have drawn attention to the fact that the terms 'woman' and even 'women' are used to refer to women within heterosexual relations; in order to theorise the gender identity of lesbians, a different term or frame of reference is necessary (Wittig 1992). Many Black feminist theorists have also noted the way that 'woman' tends to be used to refer only to white women in feminist theoretical work, whilst masquerading as a more generic reference (see *Feminist Review*, no. 31). Indeed, it is significant that developments in theories of how gender is implicated in

1

the reading process have depended on a changing view of the gendered subject. The post-1980s feminist assault on essentialism has effectively destroyed our ability to talk unproblematically of 'the woman reader' or 'the woman's text'. But as Modleski states: 'It seems more important to struggle over what it *means* to be a woman than whether or not to be one' (Modleski 1991: 20). Most of us still retain a common-sense belief in the existence of 'women' because we are constantly categorised as such, but it has become much harder as a feminist critic to write about this in a manageable or theoretically stimulating way. What seems important for us is that in widening our focus from an unproblematised notion of 'woman' we do not then go on to slip into the potentially apolitical position which certain approaches to gender seem to encourage, as Modleski states in a critique of certain types of gender studies: 'feminism in this formulation is a conduit to the more comprehensive field of gender studies; no longer is the latter judged . . . according to the contributions it can make to the feminist project' (Modleski 1991: 5). We feel strongly that it is possible to work within gender studies and still produce analyses which will contribute to feminism as a whole. It is clear that radical anti-essentialist positions may lead to the use of the term 'woman', no matter how hedged around with modifications, being disallowed. What many feminist theorists fear is that this type of deconstructive move can lead towards a 'refusal to accept responsibility for one's implication in actual historical or social relations or a denial that positionalities exist or that they matter, the denial of one's own personal history and the claim to a total separation from it' (Martin and Mohanty, cited by Modleski 1991: 19). This debate about gender positionality informs all of the essays in this collection.

The question of the role of the reader in discovering or creating a meaning for a text is one which has been debated by linguists and literary/ cultural theorists for a number of years.[2] Most of this debate has been conducted without interdisciplinary cross-over, and therefore these essays contribute significantly to the field by analysing the positioning of the reader from an interdisciplinary perspective, combining the benefits of both feminist linguistic and literary/cultural theoretical models. It is our aim to develop particular problematics which arise when positioning is seen from this combined viewpoint. Much linguistic work has attempted to consider the way that the language of a text cues responses in the reader; this work is invaluable for anchoring some of the more general theoretical debates which have been raging in literary circles about the positioning of the reader (Fowler *et al.* 1979; Fairclough 1989). However, some of this work simply assumes that all readers will necessarily decode these traces in the text in a similar way; furthermore, this linguistic work remains insufficiently attentive to the role of the reader in determining meaning. It is for this reason that it is necessary to consider some of the theoretical work in literary theory and cultural studies which is more welcoming to the notion of multiple interpretations. However, much of this literary work, including recent post-structuralist work, makes unquestioned assumptions about the nature of 'text' and its role in determining meaning, to the point that the reader is portrayed as a passive dupe. Because of the lack of attention to these two elements *together* – the role of the reader *and* the role of the text – we feel it necessary to construct a range of synthesised positions which have benefited from crossing these interdisciplinary boundaries. We call for a re-evaluation of the relation between reader and text, made possible by combining empirical linguistic study of the features of the text which lead to particular readings, with a literary/cultural theoretical study of the factors, such as race, class and gender, which lead to certain of these potential reading positions being adopted by the reader.

We have grouped these essays under three main headings: ethnographic/ empirical readings linguistic readings and reception-theory/reader-response analyses. Broadly speaking, these groupings, which we discuss below, denote tendencies in the essays towards certain theoretical perspectives rather than others; however, none of the essays rests easily in these categories. And that is the result of efforts on all of our parts to integrate elements of theoretical work done in different fields, rather than simply to restrict ourselves to our own disciplinary boundaries. We have felt it important to produce interdisciplinary work and this has resulted in choices at several levels: firstly, we do not address just literary texts, but a wide variety of texts, ranging from films and pop-song lyrics, to modern poetry, advertisements and magazines; secondly, we have chosen texts from different historical periods and contexts – advertisements produced in present-day South Africa, nineteenth-century British short stories and art, twentieth-century American music; thirdly, we have drawn on a range of theoretical positions and disciplinary approaches. Our aims in doing this are to explore the heterogeneity of the reading process in relation to texts in different contexts, and to combine theoretical perspectives in order to produce new analyses.

We work in disciplines such as linguistics, literary theory, film and media studies, sociology, art history, and in all of these fields the reading process has been analysed in distinctly different ways. Yet, as feminists, it is important for us to produce analyses which combine elements from these fields, which is one of the defining characteristics of a great deal of work in women's studies and gender studies as a whole. We are not aiming to produce a synthesised approach; in fact, we are trying to work critically with the idea that generic differences will necessarily yield theoretical and methodological differences. However, it is clear that each field can learn from the theorising of other disciplines especially through the challenge to long-held preconceptions (see, for example, Bowles and Klein 1983).

Working across disciplinary boundaries presents certain problems, for instance, in the overlap of different theoretical vocabularies for writing about the same thing: where critics working on advertising in cultural studies and following Judith Williamson might refer to a referent system, a literary theorist might prefer Roland Barthes' notion of a cultural code, or a linguist some concept of background knowledge (see Mills, and Thornborrow, this volume). None of these terms is, of course, the exact equivalent of the others (it is important to acknowledge that they have developed separately in different theoretical communities), but there are strong functional similarities that can sometimes leave the interdisciplinary reader wondering which set of terminologies to reach for.

However, interdisciplinary work can help us in tackling theoretical problems. For example, we have found it important to realise that questions around authorship in, say, the analysis of advertisements and films, because of the nature of their process of production, force us to try to develop new theoretical frameworks which can somehow deal with the notion of the text positioning the reader, without having to rely on a unitary author as the source of intelligibility of the text, as in traditional literary approaches. This work on advertising can lead us to formulate different models of authorship in literary analysis. Recent work in film studies has similarly been crucial in offering ways forward in how we can, as feminist readers, understand our pleasure in ostensibly recalcitrant texts (Stacey 1988; Pearce 1991). We have also found it useful to focus on the difference that style and speed of reading will make in terms of analysis. For example, an advertisement is often read in a particular way, usually focusing on images and headlines – a slack reading (see Wicomb, this volume) – whereas a literary text may be read either in a 'slack' way, skimming and skipping pages, or it may be read using close reading techniques, carefully analysing word by word, then rereading sections. Although we are not necessarily invited to read an advertisement using close literary analysis, such analysis can be profitable in terms of uncovering ideological assumptions. Thus, a cross-fertilisation can be usefully achieved across all of these different disciplinary approaches to the question of reading.

As we mentioned above, we have, despite these interdisciplinary concerns, decided to group the essays under several headings, and this is because they do show tendencies towards certain trends within the analysis of reading as a whole. As such, these essays can be seen as attempts to debate, exemplify and work through certain positions. There are certain theoretical problems which these groupings point to, and each of the essays discusses these issues from a different perspective. Let us deal with each of these in turn.

ETHNOGRAPHIC/EMPIRICAL WORK

In many of the essays, we have found it important to base our work on real readers rather than on the way that we felt that readers would respond. Literary theorists have been particularly guilty of making assumptions about what readers or ideal readers think, based on the intuitions of the critic or theorist herself/himself. Even where literary critics have tried to involve real readers in the discussion of readership they have often still seemed to impose their own interpretative schemes onto these readers (see Richards 1929; Holland 1975). In some of the essays, we have attempted to follow the lead of critics such as Janice Radway and Bridget Fowler amongst others who have tried as far as is possible to map out the way that we read by analysing the responses of real readers (Radway 1987; Fowler 1991). By using questionnaires, interviews and group discussions, a number of the essays have tried to analyse the way that gender informs a reading response.

There are a number of practical and theoretical problems with attempting to focus on real readers and their responses. Firstly, it is difficult to bring to consciousness the processes by which we interpret, as Culler has noted: 'we understand very little about how we read' (Culler 1982: 265). Very often the processes by which we form an interpretative framework are ones which are not of our own making and are informed at a deep level by ideological knowledges; these processes may seem to us to be 'common sense' and in that way so self-evidently the *only* way to read that we may not be able to describe what it is we are doing. Secondly, when questioning readers, it is extremely difficult to verify if your respondents are telling you what they think that you want them to produce rather than what they really are experiencing. Whilst this is a problem with all empirical work, with reading it is very difficult to check whether respondents are giving accurate accounts of their reading processes, or whether in fact your questions are steering them into particular responses.

There is also the further theoretical issue that, according to many critics, ethnographic approaches to readership are entirely incompatible with text-based methods of analysis, especially those which postulate universalised models of reception based on psychoanalysis. From this perspective, the empirical data Mills and Bradby draw upon in their chapters in this volume, for example, should exclude them from talking about those same readers in terms of textual positioning, since the latter presupposes a different methodology. The conflict between these two approaches has been most evident among critics working in film and cultural studies, where there has been a split between the film theorists, who have concentrated on the textual positioning of the spectator (e.g. Laura Mulvey 1975), and television critics like David Morley (1986, 1989) and Ien Ang (1989), who have concentrated on setting up new models of audience research. In the battle for the 'true reader/viewer' which has resulted, the film theorists have dismissed the ethnographic approach of the cultural studies camp for its naive empiricism, while the cultural studies critics have been sharply critical of the film theorists' universalism and ahistoricism in constructing a reader positioning which takes no account of the experience of actual audiences.

Jackie Stacey offers a comprehensive overview of this debate (1992) and looks for a way of resolving the methodological crisis caused by this stark polarisation of textual reader/actual reader. One of her most salient points is that the discussion is a red herring to the extent that the audience responses culled by the ethnographic researcher are, themselves, *texts*, whose analysis may be informed by the same narrative or psychoanalytic models as those employed by the 'textual' critics. For Jane Feuer (1986) this restatement of textuality is regarded with irony, but Stacey sees it as a means of mediating between the two approaches. With respect to her research, which is based on a questionnaire of female cinema-goers from the 1940s and 1950s, she argues for a middle way in which the answers of her respondents are regarded as both textual *and* 'authentic', unconscious and conscious:

> Memories of Hollywood stars do need to be treated as texts in so far as they are forms of respresentation produced within certain cultural conventions. . . . I have argued for the importance of seeing my material as narrativized accounts of the past which produced particular 'treasured memories' in which the respondents may have had certain personal investments. However, to take such an approach is not to argue that what my respondents wrote me is fictional, and thus only of relative significance to other fictions. Taking account of the narrative formations of audiences' memories is not to rob them of their specificity, and to treat them as fictional narratives like the films they were watching. This would be to confuse categories of narrative and fiction. To argue that audiences produce narrative accounts of their responses to Hollywood is not to say that they may as well have made them up! (Stacey 1992: 137–8)

Allowing for this degree of textuality in the answers of her respondents, Stacey is able to elide the hypotheses of the film theorists concerning spectatorship with a more factitious approach to her findings: she is able to register the extent to which her respondents' accounts of fascination and identification cohere with psychoanalytic analyses of such processes, while at the same time allowing for their difference and dissent. This is not to say that such a negotiation is without problems (the subtext of Stacey's work is concerned with this), but that such a struggle is inevitable for any critic wishing to keep actual readers/spectators in view: to insist upon the social and historical specificity of the reading process. This is precisely the type of synthesis which the two chapters by Mills and Bradby attempt to address; however, Christie foregrounds this debate more in her chapter arguing that it is practically impossible to maintain a notion of positioning, whilst at the same time examining real readers. Drawing on Sperber and Wilson's linguistic work on relevance, she argues for stress on context, background knowledge and agency. This debate about empirical work is not restricted to these chapters alone: it informs the writing of many of the essays in this collection and for most of the writers it is important to try to refer to the responses of readers when discussing the processes by which we understand texts, at the same time as being aware of the theoretical difficulties which arise when this type of study is embarked upon.

LINGUISTIC ANALYSES

The chapters by Wicomb and Thornborrow within this section concentrate on exemplifying the way in which particular linguistic theories can be of use in understanding the process of reading. Wicomb draws on the work of Michel Pêcheux to analyse the wider discursive context of an advertisement, and Thornborrow uses critical linguistic analysis of two advertisements in order to try to examine in detail the way that advertisements which are targeted at particular gender groups differ in their address. Like Christie's chapter in the previous section, both chapters are concerned with analysing structures and patterns in texts, but not with the assumption that these structures are *located* within the text in any easy sense. These are not simple formalist analyses where linguistic items in a text are located and categorised as having one meaning or one function. Rather they use linguistic models which allow them to see the process of making sense of texts as a complex negotiation between reader, text and the discursive structures within which both are situated. Meaning is not posited, as in some linguistic analyses, as a simple decoding process, as Christie demonstrates, but rather as a series of hypothesis formation on the basis of evidence which is negotiated between the traces in the text and the reader's background knowledge. Both of these essays try to go a stage further than much linguistic research in that they are concerned that features such as gender, race, class and sexual orientation are an integral part of linguistic analyses; these elements, in all of the essays in this book, are not considered to be extra-textual but factors which are an integral part of both the production and the reception of texts. Through close linguistic analyses of advertising texts Wicomb and Thornborrow reveal elements which help to document the process whereby texts 'make sense'; this concern with the language of the text is manifested in most of the other essays in this collection.

RECEPTION-THEORY/READER-RESPONSE ANALYSES

As Elizabeth Freund has noted, once a theorist has changed her focus of attention from a formalist analysis of the text itself to a concern with the reader, many other elements are also forced to change:

> the swerve to the reader assumes that our relationship to reality is not a positive knowledge but a hermeneutic construct, that all perception is already an act of interpretation, that the notion of a 'text' in itself is empty, that a poem cannot be understood in isolation from its results and that subject and object are indivisibly bound. (Freund 1987: 5)

This is indeed a wholesale change of perspective from conventional literary analysis of text.

A dissatisfaction with formalist accounts and with attempts to trace author intentions have led to concerns with the reader. Once the author is considered 'dead' (Barthes 1986), then it seems to be a logical move to try to institute the reader in that position of stability, so that the critic's interpretation can be anchored on firm ground. However, these essays question whether it is necessary simply to become enmeshed within the argument that either the text is dominant or the reader is dominant in the construction of meaning. Most recent work in this field shows that texts are not simply 'open' in Umberto Eco's sense, in that it is not possible simply to read texts in *any* way (see Iser 1978; Eco 1979; Culler 1982). Rather, it would seem that texts must structure the reader's response to

some extent through certain clues and frames which signal to the reader
the range of readings which are possible. However, it is *the extent* to which
the text structures and the reader resists which is of interest here. Most of
the essays in this volume propose that the struggle for meaning is a complex
negotiation between text *and* reader: that the balance of power between
the two is shifting and precarious, hence it is impossible to prescribe strict
rules and limits.

Although reader-response theory within literary criticism is often seen
to have a distinctly Anglo-American pedigree originating with such critics
as Norman Holland and Stanley Fish (Holland 1975; Fish 1980) it is
important to recognise the tremendous significance of Louis Althusser's
work on ideology (especially Althusser 1971) in shifting attention to the
relationship between text and reader. Althusser's synthesis of psychoanalysis and Marxism had a major influence within the whole of literary
theory and criticism in the 1970s and certainly moved the reader/subject
to centre stage. His far-reaching influence is testified to by the fact that
many of the essays in this volume make reference to his work; however,
this is not a passive application of Althusser's theories, but rather a critical
engagement with them. One of the problems now seen with Althusserian
analyses of the relation between texts and readers is that the reader is
conceived of as a passive (indeed captive) recipient of the text's ideology
with little or no room for resistance. According to Althusser, the message
of most texts is univocal, and the reader has no option but to take up the
dominant reader position offered to him/her. The same criticism has also
been made of Judith Williamson's work on advertising, which has been
influential in demonstrating the way in which address systems operate and
may be decoded (Williamson 1978). Her work has been very important in
trying to map out the way in which audiences are targeted very specifically
in certain circumstances, for example, in advertisements; her work has
drawn attention to the way that certain types of texts seem to encourage
the reader to engage in some inferential work whereby they are called upon
to make the necessary 'logical' links between juxtaposed images, for
example, in order to achieve the 'right' reading for the text (see
Montgomery *et al.* 1992 for a discussion of juxtaposition). This has led to
a theorising of the process whereby the reader becomes almost a part of
the text's structure through the inferential work s/he is drawn into
performing; this notion of 'suture', where the reader in making sense of the
text becomes enmeshed in its structures of meaning, has been drawn on
widely in film theory (see Kuhn 1982, and also Boardman, and Hallam, this
volume). This concern with the complex relation of the textual structure
and the reader's work in interpretation has also been a concern in linguistic

work (see, for example, Sperber and Wilson 1986; Fairclough 1989; and Christie, this volume).

A further area in Williamson's work which has been of some importance in theoretical debates has been her analysis of the way that advertisements often work through a reliance on a construction of the presumed male reader's desire for upward mobility and sex. She was one of the first theorists explicitly to relate the positioning of the reader with gender issues. Williamson is not simply concerned with the way that texts act on readers in the somewhat impersonal way that Althusser was; rather she is concerned with the effect the images that we find in advertisements have on us as individuals. This concern is taken up by Dorothy Smith in recent work where she sees texts less as simple determinants of the selves we construct, but rather as a discursive link between people, by which we as individuals mediate our relationship to certain discursive frameworks, such as femininity (Smith 1990; see also Bradby, this volume).

However, although it is clear that texts are constructed out of a range of ideological messages, it is difficult to see that those messages are received by the reader and absorbed by her in any simple fashion. Texts do not just simply reproduce ideologies, since language itself is not so univocal and straightforward, as the essays on linguistic analysis point out. Texts are sites of potentially competing interpretations where several messages may be struggling for precedence, and texts often contain information apart from ideological messages which may work to undercut the dominant ideological themes (see Mills 1991). For example, Kate Millett reads certain male-authored texts as simple presentations of sexist ideology; however, in order to do this she has to omit reference to other material, say in D. H. Lawrence's work, which works in quite a different way, or which challenges that overall message (Millett 1977). And, as Terry Eagleton states, it would be absurd to assume that the reader simply 'took in' these messages and that s/he believed everything she read in an undiscriminating way, since this would mean that the only readers who could 'see through' ideology, were those who had the academic training to do so (Eagleton 1991). Christie and Boardman both interrogate this question in their essays, and both of them discuss the range of positions which are available to the reader and which they may or may not take up depending on factors such as education, class and, as Whelehan mentions in her essay, pleasure. Eagleton puts the issue succinctly when he states:

> to believe that immense numbers of people would live and sometimes die in the name of ideas which were absolutely vacuous and absurd is to take up an unpleasantly demeaning attitude towards ordinary men and women. It is a typically conservative estimate of human beings to see them as sunk in irrational

prejudice, incapable of reasoning correctly; and it is a more radical attitude to hold that while we may indeed be afflicted by all sorts of mystifications, some of which might even be endemic to the mind itself, we nevertheless have some capacity for making sense of our world in a moderately cogent way. If human beings really were gullible and benighted enough to place their faith in great numbers in ideas which were utterly void of meaning, then we might reasonably ask whether such people were worth politically supporting at all. If they are that credulous, how could they ever hope to emancipate themselves? (Eagleton 1991: 12)

Focus has shifted in recent discussions of the reader to ways in which she is able to resist certain messages or appropriate them for her own ends (Fowler 1991). It is clear, however, that not all readers are the same in this and that factors such as education, class, gender and background knowledge have an effect on the way that readers collude with texts or resist their meanings (Boardman, this volume).

Analysis of reader response has been an area of research characterised by a series of polarised debates around a number of issues. Firstly, theorists have discussed at length whether there are communities of readers who agree to certain interpretations of texts or whether each individual comes to a slightly different reading of the text because of her personal history and personality. There is a tendency to see this as an either–or argument: for example, Stanley Fish argues for consensus readings within communities of like-minded readers, whilst Norman Holland considers the way that individuals read texts, analysing the feelings and psychoanalytic histories of responses to texts (Holland 1975; Fish 1980). Secondly, theorists tend either to be concerned to describe the constraints which inform the reading process and interpretation of the text – the conditions of the text's intelligibility (Iser 1978; Culler 1981) – or they stress the indeterminacy of the text, the fact that a seemingly endless plurality of readings is possible (Eco 1979). As we noted in the discussion of empirical versus textual approaches above, there is an apparently irresolvable tension between theorists who tend to characterise the reader as a simple recipient of a reading enforced by the text or they are concerned to posit the reader as an active resister of the meanings which the text attempts to foist on her. For example, Althusser is more concerned with the force of ideology impinging on the reader than he is with the way that the reader herself reacts to that material, whilst Morley is concerned with the way that readers, in this case of television, do not simply passively consume the material that they watch, but rather selectively watch and interact with the material that they are presented with (Morley 1986; 1989). Finally, some theories have tended to characterise the reader as a stable position for the reception of univocal meaning, whilst others have argued for the destabilising of this certainty; for example, Culler states:

once the conscious subject is deprived of its role as source of meaning – once
meaning is explained in terms of conventional systems which may escape the grasp
of the conscious subject – the self can no longer be identified with consciousness.
It is 'dissolved' as its functions are taken up by a variety of interpersonal systems
that operate through it. (Culler 1975: 28)

Thus for Culler 'The reader becomes the name of the place where the
various codes can be located: a virtual site' (Culler 1981: 38).

None of these polarisations of position seem to us adequate to describe
the complex process of reading and it is for this reason that these essays
should be seen as critical engagements with theoretical positions. This
involves, as we mentioned earlier, seeing these essays as debates around
problems in the theoretical work rather than final answers to the problems.

KEY DEBATES WITHIN THESE ESSAYS

All of these essays are part of debates around the issues mentioned above
which derive from different theoretical perspectives. In this section, we
would like to consider some further issues of debate which these essays
interrogate across the disciplinary boundaries.

Control of the meaning of the text

One of the central issues in these discussions is the notion of who or what
ultimately is the determining factor in meaning production. Although the
work which has been undertaken in linguistics and literary/cultural theory
about the way that the reader is addressed by a text has developed some
useful terminology (for example, implied reader, narratee and so on), there
is a sense in which the debate has mainly centred on an opposition as to
who is finally in control: the text or the reader. Is it the text which
determines the way that the reader responds, and therefore the reader is
simply a passive dupe of the ideological messages of the text, or does the
reader have ultimate control of the meanings of the text and simply create
the meaning of the text out of her previous experiences and readings?[3]
There is little sense in much of this work of an awareness that this process
might best be described using a notion of negotiation (see Smith 1990;
Mills 1992). Most of the essays in this collection focus on both the reader
and their context in order to analyse in detail the factors which are brought
into play in the interpretative process. Our aim is not to come to some
final answer to the question of which is more important in the reading

process, but rather to analyse the complexity of that engagement, so that, as we mentioned above, the reader herself is seen to be already inscribed in the discourses which inform the production of the text.

Feminist appropriation of recalcitrant texts

One of the ways in which the notion of the control of the text informs the reading process in feminist analyses is the question of whether it is possible to read and appropriate seemingly resistant texts for our own pleasure. This debate begins with Judith Fetterley's work on American literature (Fetterley 1978). Many feminist critics have noted the problematic position of the female or feminist reader, especially when reading male-authored texts. For some theorists like Fetterley it is necessary for the female reader to undergo a process of dual affiliation, whereby the reader learns to read as a male and then as a feminist she finally learns to read as a woman. In a similar way, Laura Mulvey has described the way that female spectators are forced to identify as male in order to make sense of narratives in Hollywood movies (Mulvey 1975). However, as Deirdre Pribram asks:

> How have we come to perceive all forms of filmic gaze as male when women have always taken up their proportionate share of seats in the cinema? How have we come to understand cinematic pleasure (narrative, erotic and so on) as pleasurable to the male viewer, but not the female? Why have we failed to see our own presence in the audience when women have always watched – and loved – films? (Pribram 1988: 1)

Mills' and Boardman's essays consciously adopt and adapt this notion of the resisting reader to map out the range of readings possible to a reader; but these essays do not simply assume that the resisting position is so easily locatable. Christie's essay is a thorough-going critique of the notion of a simple resisting reader and shows how necessary it is to perform an analysis of the context of reading.

Some of the most interesting work in this area has been undertaken by feminists working in the area of popular romance (see Modleski 1984; Radway 1987; Fowler 1991). Modleski's book, *Loving with a Vengeance* is, for example, ground-breaking in suggesting that, far from being the passive dupes of an insidious ideology, the women who read Mills & Boon type romances are active and questioning and that, far from simply consuming the fiction of the text, they often use it to challenge or develop their own identities and relationships. The notion of the popular text being 'identity-forming' in a positive sense is explored in Jackie Stacey's essay 'Desperately seeking difference' (1988), which presents the fascination of the central female protagonist (Roberta) with Susan (played by a thinly disguised Madonna) as exemplary of the process of identification/transformation played out between the female spectator and the Hollywood star. *Desperately Seeking Susan*, as a mainstream Hollywood movie could, itself, be subjected to far less favourable feminist readings, but Stacey's essay concentrates on how it may be read as both positive and pleasurable. In her chapter on the female spectator and Pre-Raphaelite painting, Pearce also discusses how her own previous work on this area was primarily concerned with the feminist appropriation of recalcitrant texts 'against the grain'. That she, personally, has subsequently discovered a number of ethical and political problems with such a reading practice should not detract from the possibilities for empowerment offered by this type of approach. Although in her book *Woman/Image/Text* (1991), Pearce demonstrates how this may be achieved by the reader liberating oppositional and alternative meanings from the text through a range of 'deconstructive' reading strategies, she concludes that such 'pleasure' can often only be secured by wresting the text/image from the historical context of its production and consumption. In simple terms, this means the feminist reader/viewer must wilfully usurp a male-inscribed reading position and ignore the fact that she is occupying a space never 'intended' for her. While such a manoeuvre may seem, at one level, radical and liberatory, on the other it is in danger of making invisible the gendered exclusiveness of such texts. This is also a question which Thornborrow encounters in her chapter, where in the analysis of advertisements the implied reader of her texts is quite clearly gendered, and where the ideological information which the reader has to 'buy into' in order to make sense of the text, defies a liberatory feminist appropriation. In consequence of this political qualm, Pearce chooses to read Rossetti's painting of *The Beloved* in terms of the *dominant* reading position(s) it offers, and examines her own consequent exclusion as a female/feminist viewer. She suggests that the way forward, for the feminist still wishing to preserve for herself the pleasure of 'reading against the grain', is perhaps to adapt Stuart Hall's (1973) model of the text as a 'hierarchy' of reading positions; there is nothing to stop the reader adopting whatever reading position she chooses, but this cannot displace the text's preferred reading position or its dominant ideological meaning.

Gender

Most of the mainstream linguistic and literary theorists who analyse reading have not considered gender as a factor in reading; they have been more concerned to analyse what they consider to be general characteristics of the reading process. However, this has often led to them assuming that what can clearly be seen as a male-addressed text is in fact a universal or general address. Most of the texts analysed by critics have been mainstream or canonical literary texts, and women's writing has in the main not been considered. This is a question which Whelehan deals with in her essay in some detail, since she foregrounds the danger that academic feminists may encounter when making similar value judgements themselves when they choose texts for analysis or when constructing a syllabus for a course. In this collection we have decided to analyse a range of texts, female-authored texts, male-authored texts and avowedly feminist texts; we have done this so that we can move from analyses which assume that the gender of the author is the only factor in determining the reading position, without losing sight of the fact that women's texts and especially feminist texts are read in particular and often discriminatory ways. As we noted earlier in this introduction, focusing our attention on the reader rather than on the text means that many other assumptions are necessarily overturned. The same is true when we focus our attention then on the question of the gendered identity of the reader. Warhol and Herndl state:

> A feminist reading would be the reception and processing of texts by a reader who is conceived of not only as possibly female, but also as conscious of the tradition of women's oppression in patriarchal culture. The feminist reader . . . is committed to breaking the pattern of that oppression by calling attention to the way some texts can perpetuate it. (Warhol and Herndl 1991: 489)

Both Mills and Christie analyse feminist poems and television programmes to gauge the range of positions which are available to readers when they are interpreted; Boardman and Hallam analyse texts directed specifically to a female audience and Thornborrow analyses two advertising texts which target specific groups of female and male readers. Pearce considers the ways in which male texts can be read by female audiences, particularly when they seem to be presenting material of an overtly ideological nature, and Wicomb considers the case of a supposedly female-directed advertisement which in fact is directed to what she terms a 'surrogate' male reader.

Some of the feminist work in this area has assumed a unified woman reader/spectator, so that for example in Laura Mulvey's early work, there is an assumption that all women respond in the same way to the way that they are positioned as spectators (Mulvey 1975; see also Hallam's discussion of her work, this volume). Similarly in Flynn and Schweickart's (1986) collection of essays, *Gender and Reading*, it is assumed that all women process texts in much the same way (although there is an interesting attempt in Crawford and Chaffin's article to distinguish amongst women and men for sex-typing).[4] This is partly due to the fact that many feminist theorists base their models of reading on psychological and psychoanalytic theories where generalising theories of womanhood appear less problematic. It is essential firstly not to assume that all women will react in the same way to a particular text; there is usually a range of positions which the text holds open for the female reader and the reader can decide to adopt these or to construct further positions for herself. For example, as Bradby shows in her essay in this volume, adolescent girls need to be considered as a specific group of women who will react according to different external pressures which they may categorise as 'adult discourse'. Very often, texts seem to proffer certain types of readings to very specifically targeted audiences; however, other readers may read them in very different ways from the dominant reading.

It is important to note that the male reader also has this option open to him, as Jonathan Culler shows in his article 'Reading as a woman' (1982).[5] Males can choose to adopt the reading roles which the text poses as self-evident for them, and frequently it is in their interest to do so, but they can also choose to read against the grain and read 'as a woman' or 'as a feminist', a position of resistance to the messages of the text. But the reasons for adopting different positions and resisting the readings offered by the text are political ones, and in this context, mainly influenced by feminist work, which many male readers may not be familiar with, as Mills shows in her chapter. The extent to which we can read 'across gender' is a problem for feminist and pro-feminist work in reading (see, for example, Jardine and Smith's collection: *Men in Feminism*, 1987). For many feminists, there is a post-structuralist side of their work which assumes that it is important to deconstruct the notion of a gendered identity; therefore, anyone can 'read as a woman' which entails a disintegration of the notion that there is such an entity as 'woman', as we mentioned earlier in the Introduction; however, at the same time, those same feminists need to retain the notion of women as a specific class/caste or group who are addressed globally by texts in particular ways (see Fuss 1989 and Butler 1990 for discussion; see also Mills, and Thornborrow, this volume). Not all women will want to adopt feminist positions in relation to the text and feminists themselves will adopt different interpretative strategies. There is a lack of address in much feminist work to the fact that there is a wide range of feminist positions. The essays included here do not present a unified feminist line.

This concern with a range of issues centred around gender does not restrict itself to questions of the gender of the author or the reader; for example, as mentioned above, Whelehan analyses the gender implications of decisions made within academic feminism about which texts to study, which texts are valuable enough to be read. She argues that feminist literary criticism retains some unexamined patriarchal prejudices of its own, not least in its construction of an alternative canon of women's 'literature'. She asserts that feminism therefore creates an implied feminist reader of its own, a reader who can identify the boundaries between literature and trash and accepts that trash homogenises female experience, whereas literature deals with the problematics of the female self and its construction. She suggests that only a comparison/destabilisation of both categories can produce a more complex analysis of the gendered reader, and can truly revolutionise a feminist critical practice that dispenses with the sins of its critical forefathers. Feminist cultural criticism has provided a useful lead in this area, particularly in its re-introduction of the role of textual pleasure and complex modes of resistance to narratorial stances. Whelehan does not simply attempt to undermine the extensive contribution made by feminist critics, but rather suggests that the task of radicalising textual practice is one which demands that we constantly change our targets better to resist institutional absorption.

As well as forcing us to analyse the relation between gender and the institution a concern with gender has enabled us to analyse critically certain concepts in mainstream theories which may not benefit the female or feminist reader; for example Fish's notion of a community of readers can be considered by those firmly within the community as a very positive consensus of ideas, but when women are represented in particular ways and when certain ideas are signalled as constituting common sense background knowledge then, as Elizabeth Freund states: 'the appeal to the imperialism of agreement can chill the spines of readers whose experience of the community is less happily benign' (Freund 1987: 110–1; see also Dale Bauer's work on how female readers can or cannot find a space for resistance in particular interpretive communities, 1988).

These concerns with gender force us as readers to consider the factors which make up our gendered identities and therefore the gendered positions that we can adopt in relation to texts. It is clear from these analyses that gender is a space which is intersected by other factors such as race and class, rather than simply being the space accorded to sexual difference when other factors such as race and class have been omitted (Spelman 1988). In all of these essays we address the question of what gender means when it is the site of struggles over definition: for example, when we talk about women, are we referring to white women or black women (see Wicomb, and Pearce, this volume), when we refer to black women are we referring to working-class or bourgeois women (see Wicomb)? It is necessary for us to consider the intersections of determining features such as race, class and sexual orientation, which can often be omitted in discussing the 'woman reader'.

The process of reading

Because of the work on popular culture and audiences by theorists such as Morley and Hall, we have come to realise that the way that literary theorists analyse reading is flawed; most theorists simply see the text as a finished product, the end message of which determines the meaning for the reader (Hall 1973; Morley 1986). We feel that a theoretical approach which is more concerned with the process of reading than with a finished product can describe what happens in reading. Resisting reading can take place at any point in the text and can refuse the final closure which the text tries to impose, as Whelehan shows in her essay. For example, in reading a poem which the reader interprets as sexist and which seems to be trying to force the female reader into collusion by praising the beauty of a female addressee, the reader can resist a simple position of reading the poem as a self-contained statement; she can refer to a wider tradition whereby women are portrayed and referred to as objects of beauty, whose qualities are to be dissected by men. Thus, rather than being restricted to a simple linear reading of the text, she can refer constantly outwards to a set of discursive frameworks which inform both the construction and the interpretation of the text. In this sense, the text is not accorded the simple closure and coherent message which conventional readings of sexist writing have tended to attribute to them (see Boardman on closure, this volume). Similarly, whilst recognising the reading position that she is supposed to adopt, the dominant reading – that position of intelligibility for the text which, by reference to ideological discourses circulating in the wider society, makes sense of the meanings of the text – she can also refuse this position and construct other, less coherent, but ultimately more resisting, positions from which to read. She can even take the dominant reading and turn it from a weak objectified representation of women to an interpretation which sees this as a position of power. Thus, as Boardman shows in her essay, the reader does not simply interpret the information presented by the text at face value; in her analysis of a didactic text which presents alcohol abuse as a degrading and fatal sin, she argues that the wild images of the seemingly degraded woman character have a sexual and inspirational power which the 'good' female character does not inspire in the reader, despite the text's strenuous efforts to force us into colluding with its message. And Hallam also shows in her chapter that in popular films which may not have overtly feminist messages, and which may not have the feminist messages which we as readers would like, there are still pleasures which can be found, even if they are not necessarily in our own 'best interests'.

The context of reading

In many of these essays, the context of the reading process is a crucial determinant of the range of readings. Hallam considers research which has been undertaken in film studies, particularly in relation to the analysis of popular film. Unlike in books and magazines, where the reading experience is usually an individual one, films are almost invariably viewed collectively, either in the cinema or on television. These two areas of film consumption are, however, completely different, not least because of the size and quality of the image when it is shown as a film on the big screen. Cinema audiences have an individual experience of viewing within the darkened collectivity of the auditorium, a situation which has, since Freud's time, led to the analogy that the viewing experience is similar to that of dreaming. In the cinema, we can forget about the world outside and ourselves, and become totally engrossed in the story, a situation that has always worried those who are concerned with the power of popular films to influence the hearts and minds of those who watch them. For many feminists, popular films have mostly been seen as promoting a dominant patriarchal world view that keeps women in their place, a view that tended to coincide with the dominant critical view of the mass audience; that is, that they were a mindless, unthinking mass of undifferentiated subjects who unquestioningly absorbed the meanings of popular film. This high/low cultural divide has been highly influential in film theory, with early feminist appropriation of theoretical models tending to perpetuate the divisions (see also Whelehan's essay, this volume).

From the variety of theoretical problems that this collection of essays ranges over, it is quite clear that we do not intend to attempt to forge one theoretical position which works for a wide range of analyses. Feminist theory now is no longer concerned with achieving a simple consensus; rather, these diverse essays from different disciplines are consciously at odds with each other. Bringing together theorists from different disciplines has the effect of producing the conflict and debate which leads to new theoretical positions. What holds this collection together is a common concern with readers as active participants and a common concern with interrogating our own theoretical positions, so that nothing is accepted at face value. Much theoretical work tries to put forward an image of itself as answering all of the questions; we feel that it is necessary to recognise the diversity of approaches to this subject, when two problematic terms – 'gender' and 'reading' – are brought together, and that debate must therefore be the focus of our attention.

NOTES

1. We will use the term 'reading' to mean the interpretative process in general, whether we are referring to reading per se, viewing or listening.
2. For surveys of reader-response and reception theories, see, for example, Suleiman and Crossman (1980) and Freund (1987).
3. For a good review of some of the discussions around this area see the chapter by Allen on 'Reader-oriented criticism' in Allen (1989).
4. Mary Crawford and Roger Chaffin: 'The reader's construction of meaning: Cognitive research on gender and comprehension', in Flynn and Schweickart (1986: 3–30).
5. Although perhaps it can be argued that Culler is reading as a feminist or as a pro-feminist rather than as a woman.

REFERENCES

Allen, R. C. (1989) 'Reader-orientated criticism and television', in R. C. Allen (ed.) Channels of Discourse, London: Routledge, 1989, pp. 74–112.
Althusser, L. (1971) Lenin and Philosophy, London: New Left Books.
Ang, I. (1989) Watching Dallas: Soap opera and the melodramatic imagination, London: Methuen.
Barthes, R. (1986) 'The death of the author', in R. Barthes, The Rustle of Language, Oxford: Blackwell, pp. 49–55.
Bauer, D. (1988) Feminist Dialogics: A theory of failed community, Albany, NY: SUNY.
Bowles, G. and Klein, R. (eds) (1983) Theories of Women's Studies, London: Routledge.
Butler, J. (1990) Gender Trouble: Feminism and the subversion of identity, London: Routledge.
Culler, J. (1975) Structuralist Poetics: Structuralism, linguistics and the study of literature, Ithaca: Cornell University Press.
Culler, J. (1981) The Pursuit of Signs: Semiotics, literature, deconstruction, London: Routledge & Kegan Paul.
Culler, J. (1982) On Deconstruction: Theory and criticism after structuralism, Ithaca: Cornell University Press.
Eagleton, T. (1991) Ideology: An introduction, London: Verso.
Eco, U. (1979) The Role of the Reader: Explorations in the semiotics of text, Bloomington: Indiana University Press.

Fairclough, N. (1989) *Language and Power*, London: Longman.

Feminist Review (1989) *The Past Before Us: Twenty-five years of feminism*, no. 31.

Fetterley, J. (1978) *The Resisting Reader: A feminist approach to American fiction*, Bloomington: University of Indiana Press.

Feuer, J. (1986) 'Dynasty', paper presented at International Television Studies Conference, London.

Fish, S. (1980) *Is There a Text in this Class? The Authority of Interpretive Communities*, London and Cambridge, MA: Harvard University Press.

Flynn, E. A. and Schweickart, P. P. (eds) (1986) *Gender and Reading: Essays on readers, texts and contexts*, Baltimore and London: Johns Hopkins University Press.

Fowler, B. (1991) *The Alienated Reader: Women and popular romantic literature in the twentieth century*, Hemel Hempstead: Harvester Wheatsheaf.

Fowler, R., Hodge, R., Kress, G. and Trew, T. (1979) *Language and Control*, London: Routledge & Kegan Paul.

Freund, E. (1987) *The Return of the Reader: Reader-response criticism*, London: Methuen.

Fuss, D. (1989) *Essentially Speaking: Feminism, nature and difference*, London: Routledge.

Hall, S. (1973) 'Encoding and decoding the TV message', CCCS pamphlet, University of Birmingham.

Holland, N. (1975) *Five Readers Reading*, New Haven: Yale University Press.

Iser, W. (1978) *The Act of Reading: A theory of aesthetic response*, London: Routledge & Kegan Paul.

Jardine, A. and Smith, P. (eds) (1987) *Men in Feminism*, London: Methuen.

Kuhn, A. (1982) *Women's Pictures: Feminism and cinema*, London and Boston: Routledge & Kegan Paul.

Millett, K. (1977) *Sexual Politics*, London: Virago (first published 1971).

Mills, S. (1991) *Discourses of Difference: Women's travel writing and colonialism*, London: Routledge.

Mills, S. (1992) 'Negotiating discourses of femininity', *Journal of Gender Studies*, 3, 3 (May): 271–85.

Modleski, T. (1984) *Loving with a Vengeance: Mass-produced fantasies for women*, London: Methuen.

Modleski, T. (1991) *Feminism without Women: Culture and criticism in a post-feminist age*, London: Routledge.

Montgomery, M., Durant, A., Fabb, N., Furniss, T. and Mills, S. (1992) *Ways of Reading*, London: Routledge

Morley, D. (1986) *Family Television: Cultural power and domestic leisure*, London: Comedia.

Morley, D. (1989) 'Changing paradigms in audience studies', in E. Seiter, H. Borchers, G. Kreutzner and E.M. Warth (eds) *Remote Control: Television, audiences, and cultural power*, London and New York: Routledge, pp. 16–42.

Mulvey, L. (1975) 'Visual pleasure and narrative cinema', *Screen*, 16, 3 (Autumn): 6–18.

Pearce, L. (1991) *Woman/Image/Text: Readings in Pre-Raphaelite art and literature*, Hemel Hempstead: Harvester Wheatsheaf.

Pribram, D. (ed.) (1988) *Female Spectators: Looking at film and television*, London: Verso.

Radway, J. (1987) *Reading the Romance: Women, patriarchy and popular literature*, London: Verso (first published 1984).

Richards, I. A. (1929) *Practical Criticism*, London: Kegan Paul.

Smith, D. (1990) *Texts, Facts and Femininity: Exploring the relations of ruling*, London: Routledge.

Spelman, E. (1988) *Inessential Woman: Problems of exclusion in feminist thought*, London: Women's Press.

Sperber, D. and Wilson, D. (1986) *Relevance: Communication and cognition*, Cambridge, MA: Harvard University Press, and Oxford: Blackwell.

Stacey, J (1988) 'Desperately seeking difference', in L. Gamman and M. Marshment (eds) *The Female Gaze: Women as viewers of popular culture*, London: Women's Press, pp. 112–29.

Stacey, J. (1992) 'Star gazing: Hollywood cinema and female spectatorship in 1940s and 1950s Britain', unpublished PhD thesis (forthcoming, Routledge).

Suleiman, S. and Crossman, I. (eds) (1980) *The Reader in the Text: Essays on audience and interpretation*, Princeton: Princeton University Press.

Warhol, R. and Herndl, D. (eds) (1991) *Feminisms: An anthology of literary history and criticism*, Baltimore: Rutgers University Press.

Williamson, J. (1978) *Decoding Advertisements: Ideology and meaning in advertising*, London: Marion Boyars.

Wittig, M. (1992) *The Straight Mind and Other Essays*, Hemel Hempstead: Harvester Wheatsheaf.

Part I

Ethnographic/Empirical Readings

Chapter 1

Reading as/like a Feminist

Sara Mills

Much feminist work which has centred on gender and reading has been concerned with the way that women read male-authored texts and construct alternative reading positions for themselves. In this chapter I would like to focus on the way that women read texts written by women, and particularly texts by feminists. This analysis will examine formal features in a literary text in order to test whether these features determine the reading of the text and also constitute the site of resistance to the dominant reading position. In this sense the chapter constitutes a move away from a strictly Althusserian position, which sees language elements as a determining factor in the way that readers interpret the text: here, rather, language serves as both a cue for possible readings and a site from which to resist those readings. Rather than simply performing a language analysis, I have attempted to use real readers, both women and men, by sending out a questionnaire which tries to investigate the process of reading a poem in order to investigate the way that gender impacts on the reading process. My main aim in this chapter is not just to investigate sex difference in reading, but rather to map out the differences within a female audience, especially those differences which are the result of identifying as feminist.

DIRECT ADDRESS/INDIRECT ADDRESS

Most of the work which has considered the notion of a text addressing its reader has been influenced by the work of Louis Althusser (see especially, Althusser 1984). He has influenced linguists and cultural theorists alike in his notion that ideological messages are internalised by people through a process of constant 'hailing' or 'interpellation', that is, you are called upon to recognise yourself as the imaginary self that the text constructs (see Boardman, this volume). The text here takes on an important role in constructing individuals according to social norms. Judith Williamson gives a thorough account of this process of interpellation in her work on advertisements, where she shows that women are called upon to recognise themselves as similar to the representations of women within advertisements, and to construct and shape themselves according to the images which are presented (Williamson 1978; see also Introduction, this volume). This type of work describes the process of direct address as a fairly simple one and assumes that the construction of gendered subjectivity is simply the result of exposure to a range of similar representations.

In an attempt to formulate a more complex mode of analysis based on more strictly linguistic grounds, Martin Montgomery focuses on deixis: the way that a text creates a context for itself, for example, by the use of *I* and *you* pronouns (Montgomery 1986, 1989). He shows that there are many different kinds of direct address which call on the reader; some of them address the reader as a generalised *you* which can be taken to refer to all readers, whereas some texts address only a very specific part of that audience, for example, as Montgomery shows, when in a radio programme the disc jockey addresses only those members of the audience who have a particular star sign in order to read them their horoscope. From this work, it is possible to conclude that rather than a simple and direct 'hailing', a great deal of direct address to the reader is to a specific section of the audience, which is nevertheless 'overheard' by the reader who may not be a member of that group. That is not to say that the reader is unaffected by this type of address, but that even within direct address, there may be a range of mediated positionings for the reader.

Direct address must therefore be analysed in more complex ways to examine how readers process texts which are not specifically directed at them. Furthermore, as I have shown in articles on Althusserian feminist analysis of the reading process, direct address should be considered less important in the process of interpellation than what I have termed 'indirect address', where elements of background knowledge are assumed to be shared and where certain information is posed to the reader as if it were self-evident (Mills 1990, 1992). It is clear that texts do not make sense in themselves, but rather with reference to a body of knowledge which it is assumed the reader will take for granted, or will take as forming part of a cultural code.[1] In that sense, knowledge which is presented in the text only makes sense because of its prior appearance in a wider context. Thus, for example, women's magazines such as *Bella* and *Women's Own* present certain types of statement about women and their interests as common sense; it is assumed that women necessarily wish to know about recipes, relationships, clothes, beauty, horoscopes, problems, stars and so on. This knowledge does not originate in the magazines themselves and in fact has evolved as 'self-evident' through a long process of accretion. It makes sense to the reader in that she assumes that this information should 'naturally' appear in the magazine, because of the long ideological history of women being addressed in certain ways and being presented with certain types of information, not just in magazines, but in many other contexts. It is this larger discursive view of ideological knowledge and the way that readers draw upon it to make sense of texts which I would like to investigate in this chapter (see Thornborrow, this volume).[2]

THE RESISTING READER

In the articles on Althusserian feminist analysis referred to above, in analysing the positions which male-authored and sexist texts offer to female readers, I drew on Judith Fetterley's term 'resisting reader' to describe the process whereby readers can refuse to take up the position offered to them by the text (Fetterley 1978, 1986; see also Boardman, this volume). Fetterley shows that much American literature is written to a male implied reader; she argues that women have two choices when faced with this reading position: they can adopt this 'male' position and agree with information about women which is proffered by the text, or they can resist this position and construct other positions for themselves (cf. Christie, this volume). Fetterley is implicitly describing the notion of the dominant reading of a text which is that which presents itself as self-evidently *the* reading of the text. It is a seemingly coherent message which can be summed up as the message of the narrative. For example, when asked what a story is about, most readers will be able to summarise it. In order to do this, they have, firstly, to omit a great deal of the information contained within the text and, secondly, to impose a coherence on it which is only possible by reference to other narratives of a similar order circulating within their society. As Hayden White has shown, this summarising exercise to determine what a text is about is often a profoundly ideological one, because although the summary may masquerade as merely factual, it is always information filtered through an ideological framework (White 1980). And as Pierre Bourdieu has shown, this recognition of the coherence of the text is the result of a long process of education, both formal and informal (Bourdieu 1984). The readers may not agree with the ideas contained within the summary/dominant reading that they have produced, but they will be able to recognise that their summary constitutes the position from which the text makes sense and which it proffers to the reader.

The notion of a dominant reading has been questioned to some extent in recent theorising, especially since this notion of a reader being proffered a position to read from may be seen as reinstituting a view of the reader as passive and as not having to engage in a negotiation with the text. In using the term 'dominant reading', it is necessary to ask whether, after all, it is so easily recognised, and whether in fact there may be a number of dominant readings within the text. Despite these reservations, however, the notion of dominant reading does seem important to retain, since although readers do negotiate meanings, they clearly negotiate *with* some information which the text proffers them; readers work within the constraints imposed on their reading by the range of discursive structures circulating through society at that time (cf. Pearce, and Hallam, this volume).

Fetterley's notion of the resisting reader is a useful concept but it is clearly in need of some modification, for she does not consider the ways in which language elements may both determine the way that we read and be used in the process of resisting that dominant reading. Thus, Fetterley gives no proof that there is a male implied reader, apart from judicious quoting from the literary texts that she analyses. There is therefore little space for the female reader to resist, or actively to construct a reading, except in the sense of critique. Some of Norman Fairclough's work on critical reading practices may be useful here, in the sense that as a linguist he is concerned with the way that the language of a text may determine the reading outcome; he says

> The producer of the text constructs the text as an interpretation of the world, or of the facets of the world which are then in focus; formal features of the text are *traces* of that interpretation. The traces constitute *cues* for the text interpreter who draws upon her assumptions and expectations . . . to construct her interpretation of the text. (Fairclough 1989: 80)

Whilst it is not necessary to accept such an agented view of text production, the notion that there are language items in a text which cue our reading in some way can be used to make Fetterley's model of the resisting reader more closely tied into an analysis of the language of the text.

Film theorists such as Laura Mulvey have considered this notion of the positioning of the reader as male in more formal and structural ways than Fetterley has, considering, for example, the way that shot sequences can determine the way that a position is constructed for the reader by the film (Mulvey 1975; see Hallam, this volume). It is this attempt to grasp the way that formal qualities of a text or a film may determine to an extent the way that reading happens which interests me here. I am not stating that linguistic elements have one clear function; indeed Deborah Cameron *et al.*'s work on the multifunctionality of language items points to the importance of not assuming that single linguistic items *mean* something, once and for all (Cameron, McAlinden and O'Leary 1988). However, it is clear that language items within a particular dominant reading will be inflected so that they mean in a certain way in that context. In the process of reading, readers hypothesise as they read about what they think the text is about, and in this process they begin to narrow down the possible ranges of interpretation for particular language items. Readers often shift the focus of their hypothesis about the meaning of a text in the light of the evidence they encounter, and this in turn inflects the language items they read. In this process of adjusting their original hypothesis, readers may change their focus on the language items which they have coded as particularly important to the overall meaning of the text. One of the ways in which a resisting reading might be constructed is that the reader may locate and recognise a set of specific inflections which would lead to the dominant reading; then those inflections might be 'translated' into a different discursive framework, to make them 'mean' differently, or different lexical items may be highlighted.

It is necessary to focus our attention on language items in the text which we can submit to some form of empirical analysis, so that the results of our analysis can be replicated, verified and challenged, in order to move away from the content analysis bias of much feminist work on reading so far (see Christie, Thornborrow and Bradby and cf. Boardman, this volume).[3] This is a problem with Fetterley's work, that her analysis of the reading process is not based on any empirical evidence of what actual women readers do when they read. As happens only too frequently in reception-theory work, the definition of the reader and the reader's response is based almost entirely on the responses of the critic. When reading Fetterley's work, I was struck by the way that the complex process of reading was reduced to a simple position where texts address the reader as male, and women have to resist that address. It is clearly the case that not all texts address their readers as male (although it is evident that many texts pose as universal in their address, whilst in fact addressing only males); not all women will resist that address, or even want to resist that address, since not all women are feminists. Furthermore, Fetterley's view of reading seems to be very product-centred rather than process-orientated. By that I mean that, for her, the dominant reading is the coherent product of the text, the end result of the reading; every statement in the text is read and reread in the light of that message. As I have signalled above, I will be attempting to see ways of reading texts in a less coherent way and in ways which attempt to focus on the process of reading itself, the way that we read as women and/or as feminists (cf. Stacey 1988).

WOMEN AS READERS OF WOMEN'S TEXTS

As I stated above, much of the early work around the woman reader was concerned with the way that some women, mainly feminists, have found it necessary to resist the meanings of male-authored texts. The effects of negative and stereotypical representations of women characters on women readers, for example, has been an important focus of debate within feminist theory (see Betterton 1987; Davies et al. 1987; Pribram 1988; Pearce 1991). However, there has been a recent shift to analysing the way that women read texts which address them as women (see Radway 1987; Gamman and Marshment 1988; Fowler 1991; Frith 1991; Pearce 1992). Early feminist theorists describing the reading of female-authored texts by women tended to concentrate on the discussion of role models and identification. For many of these early feminist theorists, if a text describes a female character's experience, that text must be considered to be addressing the female reader rather than the male. Although this notion has some validity, especially given that a large number of the texts which we read do not contain this type of subject matter, there is clearly more to gendered address than a simple inclusion of information about female experiences. There is a similar problematic tendency in this work to consider the depiction of female characters in women's texts as presenting female readers with role models with whom to identify. Identification is a problematic concept in reading: the notion that we somehow align ourselves with a texual representation and form our notion of self with respect to it seems simplistic (see Hallam, this volume). Selves and textual representations are infinitely more complex and there can never be a simple mapping of one onto the other; the self is not a unitary entity and text representations always exceed their limits. Although information contained in texts obviously has some effect on us, it only does so as part of a wider discursive process, which is much more complex and diverse than the simple notion of identification can encompass. We read texts within a context of reading other texts; for example, we face a barrage of interpellations every day from advertisements, the radio, television, newspapers and so on, and when we read, the 'images' which are proffered 'make sense' within the context of all these other contradictory and conflicting 'images'.[4] Thus rather than focusing on identification, we need to consider the ways that texts affect the reader, in relation to other discourses.

Although a great deal of feminist work has centred on content analysis and whether you agree with the ideas expressed in a text, it is important to move further than this as a theoretical position, particularly when considering feminist creative writing. The notion of judging the correctness of a feminist poem seems to be theoretically naive, and a more interesting analysis could focus on the way that readers make sense of a text and the range of possible readings within which they construct readings (see Gamman 1991). There should be a space for resisting the reading positions which are proffered to you by women's and feminist texts, so that it is not necessary to assume that all women's writing will be enjoyable or of the same quality, or give the reader the same pleasures (see Whelehan, this volume).

I aim to question the notion that there is a unified woman's reading position or even that there is a unified feminist reading position. As Gill Frith notes

the female reader is herself a complex and shifting entity: the 'woman who is reading' has to be differentiated both from a historically constituted configuration of the 'female reader', and from the 'female reader' who is constructed by the narrative of any specific text. (Frith 1991: 67)

For example, when I first read the poem that I will be analysing later, I read as a feminist, and felt that I was being addressed as a feminist reader, but the sentiments and feminist position displayed in the text and proffered to me as the dominant position from which to make sense of the text do not match my own politics and concerns (see the poem on p. 35). This does not mean that I reject the poem, nor that I do not like the poem, but that some of its background knowledge and mine are not congruent. As Pearce shows, there is a sense in which not only is there the construction of a shared knowledge between the text and the reader, as I suggested in the discussion of indirect address, but there may be a code or private language which is being developed between the feminist text and the feminist audience, where it is assumed that the reader will be able to decode the language (Pearce 1992). Pearce notes that particularly in texts which address an ideal reader who is lesbian this notion of coded knowledge comes into play. Feminist writing may be considered that writing which contains clear signals to the reader that certain knowledge is shared. In this way, there may be feminist texts which set out to construct their reader as those readers who agree with that particular feminist position. However, that is not to say that simply because readers can decode the language they necessarily agree with or are coerced into agreeing with the positions which the text puts forward.

When considering the way that a text written by a female author addresses a female reader, we need to consider a number of elements which might affect our reading. As readers, we may have different assumptions if we know that the text is female-authored, although this is only a generalised expectation which may often be defeated, since there is little reason to assume that women writers will write in particular ways any more than male writers (see Mills, forthcoming). It should also be borne in mind that the writer herself or the writing position that we can hypothesise from the text is not one which the writer herself is in complete control of. Viewing the production of text from a Foucauldian disourse theory perspective, the writer herself does not create the knowledges which she produces but exists at the point where discourses can be activated and resisted (see Mills 1991). Thus, the fact that the writer is a woman may simply activate certain expectations in us as readers about the type of background knowledge that the text will be assuming – expectations which may well be defeated.

READING AS/LIKE A WOMAN/MAN

Some feminist theorists hold that women share more with each other than with other interest groups.[5] However, a wide range of feminist theorising is currently analysing the very differences within the term 'women' and calling into question the notion of a core gender identity. As Judith Butler states:

> A humanist feminist position might understand gender as an *attribute* of a person which is characterised essentially as a pregendered substance or 'core', called the person . . . [but] a social theory of gender [would] understand gender as a *relation* among socially constituted subjects in specifiable contexts. This relational or contextual point of view suggests that what the person 'is', and indeed, what gender 'is', is always relative to the constructed relations in which it is determined. As a shifting and contextual phenomenon, gender does not denote a substantive being, but a relative point of convergence among culturally and historically specific sets of relations. (Butler 1990: 10)

Thus, the notion of 'woman' becomes less a category of essence, for example, referring to a shared biology, than a category of shifting, constructed relations between people and between people and institutions.

Diana Fuss goes further in exploding the notion of 'woman', since she argues that we cannot classify women as a class on the basis of either 'essence' or the notion of a shared 'women's experience' (Fuss 1990). Fuss examines this problem of categorising women in relation to recent research concerned with reading. She analyses the notion of 'reading like/as a woman/man' which Jonathan Culler, Robert Scholes and Tanya Modleski have debated (Culler 1982; Modleski 1986; Scholes 1987). For Scholes and Culler, their reading of texts is a form of masquerade, for Culler, reading *like* a woman, and for Scholes, reading *like* a man. This distinction between 'like', meaning to read as if you were acting out a particular reading position, rather than 'as' which assumes that you *are* that particular gender position, is a crucial move towards allowing male readers a more productive space in reading female/feminist-authored texts. This type of reading strategy seems one which male theorists in Jardine and Smith's collection *Men in Feminism* (1987) have adopted, in contradistinction to a more mainstream male response to women's/feminist texts which concentrates on the way that they as readers feel excluded or attacked (see Bobo 1988).[6] Male readers sometimes seem to be put in an uncomfortable position by texts which are written overtly for women, since they assume that the address does not include them, unlike the seemingly universal masculine address. Culler tries to consider ways in which men might read as women, but his focus on *women* as readers rather than feminists as readers leads him to assume that the woman reader is simply a construct and that therefore anyone can take up the position. This is a useful move in terms of trying to deconstruct the notion of a unified woman reader, but leads to a destabilising of the very concept of women. This category needs to be maintained for the simple reason that women are still discriminated against *as* women. Modleski perceives these manoeuvres to read as/like a woman as attempts to usurp feminist theory for men, and she suggests that reading as/like a woman should be restricted to women (Modleski 1986). But as Fuss notes: 'I read . . . *like* a feminist; what it means to read as or even like a woman, I still don't know' (Fuss 1990: 26). Perhaps the conclusion which can be usefully drawn from this discussion is that it is important not to assume that there is a simple relation between the text, gender and the reader: thus, not only may men masquerade as women/feminists when they read, but women/feminists may also be considered to perform a similar process of distancing from 'themselves' when they read.

Thus, rather than positing a unified and universal 'woman reader' or 'feminist reader', we need to specify the elements which distinguish between women and which affect the woman reader's processing of the text. For example, one's relation to femininity and masculinity affects reading processes, as Mary Crawford and Roger Chaffin have shown (Crawford and Chaffin 1986). They argue that women and men readers do not necessarily read in ways which are different to a statistically significant degree; however, when they consider the degree of what they term 'sex-typing', that is the degree to which you position yourself on a scale of masculinity and femininity, differences in reading pattern occur. Similarly, the degree to which you identify yourself as a feminist plays a significant role in the way that you read. Your level and type of education (formal, informal/self-educated) and your class position, race, religion, sexual orientation, work and political experience, your past relations with males and females, will all affect the type of reading that you will make. As Diana Fuss asks: 'Can we ever speak . . . simply of "the female reader" or "the male reader", "the woman", or "the man" as if these categories were not transgressed, not already constituted by other axes of difference (class, culture, ethnicity, nationality . . .)?' (Fuss 1990: 28). That is not to suggest that 'woman' and 'man' have no meaning, for it is clear that gender difference is used for the purposes of discrimination; indeed some theorists such as Monique Wittig have argued that 'woman' is a category *of* heterosexual oppression (Wittig 1992). Therefore, whilst not dispensing with the notion of simply reading as a woman or as a feminist, it needs to be recognised that those positions are always intersected by other elements.

Fuss' appropriation of Lacan's and Foucault's notion of subject positions is a useful way out of this theoretical impasse. Both of these theorists speak of the self less as a core than as a range of places or positions which individuals occupy. This occupation of subject positions need not necessarily be seen as a permanent choice or allocation – subject positions are part of a process of constant negotiation and change. Thus, rather than a simple either/or notion of the subject (I/Other; male/ female), there is rather 'a complicated field of multiple subjectivities and competing identities' (Fuss 1990: 33). We can see 'the reading process as a negotiation amongst discursive subject positions which the reader as social subject may or may not choose to fill' (Fuss 1990: 34). It is therefore possible to maintain the notion that the text constructs a dominant reading which the reader deciphers according to discourses which she has already encountered, and this dominant reading will construct gendered subject positions for the reader. However, it is clear from Fuss' analyses that the reader is not addressed in a unified way and that she has a range of options available to her: s/he is part of a negotiated process over the meanings of the text and about the range of subject positions which she will adopt or resist. It will be in the interest of readers to recognise some of the subject positions and reject them, whilst others will be adopted.

ANALYSIS OF A TEXT

In order to test out these ideas about gendered subject positions and reading, I decided to focus my analysis on a poem, entitled 'Blood' by Caroline Douglas.[7]

1   When the moon swings round
    And I bleed my woman's blood
    My belly swells and sings to me
    a low knowing chant
5   Then something dark, akin to witches,
    Heaves and turns, and I feel a strength
    An invincible power.
    I dream a foetus blooming on high blood tides,
    Possibility kicking my guts.
10 A baby shaped like shackles and chains
    Smiles sickly and selfish eyes.
    How sweet you moon-devil child,
    Waiting for my pale soul-sister to make you flesh.
    Leech! You would suck myself to dust.
15 I was not born for this!
    Though moon and blood conspire against
    my flat belly,
    I will deny this blatant fertility.

I chose this poem because it presented itself as feminist and it seemed to be indirectly addressing a female/feminist reader. Choosing a literary text rather than, say, an advertisement or a film calls upon certain literary competences which groups of readers may or may not have, as both Jonathan Culler and Pierre Bourdieu have shown (Culler 1982; Bourdieu 1984). It is for this reason that I chose university undergraduate students of English literature as a group of readers to analyse, since it seemed that they might have a similar level of access to these literary analytical skills. These students have also all had some access to feminist ideas, particularly concerning literary theory. I decided to construct a questionnaire (see p. 42) which would assess both the way that a text presents gendered subject positions to the reader, and the way that male and female readers respond to those subject positions.[8] The reason I decided to do this empirical work is that I found the poem to be a complex one and one for which there might be a range of possible readings. Furthermore, I wanted to move away from the notion that the text determines entirely the way that the reader responds *or* that the reader is free to make what s/he wishes of the text's meaning.

The questionnaire consisted of a mixture of multiple-choice questions which aimed to disambiguate certain key phrases and further questions which asked for support from within the text for the interpretation of those phrases; these questions were aimed to encourage the readers to focus on the language of the text and its meaning as a whole. There were also more open questions which asked the readers for their interpretation of the poem, that is whether they thought it was 'intended' for a particular audience, whether they classified it as a feminist poem and whether they enjoyed it.[9] I chose this rather restricted format, rather than leaving the responses of the participants open, in order to make the results collatable; this strategy will have had an effect on the responses of the interviewees, although there was a section at the end of the poem for further comments. I distributed 150 questionnaires to staff and students in a number of educational institutions to discover what the range of readings for the poem were; I received back 74: 25 from males and 49 from females. I labelled the forms according to sex, so that I could discover if there was a difference between men and women globally. I hoped that the questionnaire material would help me to trace certain elements in the reading process. Firstly, I was interested in examining the ways in which females and males read the subject matter of the poem, especially since there are a variety of different discourses circulating around aspects of experience described in the poem, namely, menstruation, pregnancy and witchcraft. These wider discourses fall into two groups; those conservative ideologies which construct menstruation and witchcraft in a negative way, and pregnancy as a celebratory event for women (for an analysis of these discourses see Laws 1990 and Treneman 1988) and radical feminist discourses which aim to celebrate menstruation and witchcraft and which question the necessity for women to have children (see Shuttle and Redgrove 1980; Tong 1989). I was interested in seeing whether readers could construct a dominant reading of the poem and whether they drew on linguistic cues within the text to formulate this position. Secondly, I wanted to see whether readers were able to locate a subject position which the poem seemed to be constructing, and whether they considered this to be addressing them. I was concerned to see whether readers felt that they could resist this positioning, that is that they could recognise a dominant reading and the position which was constructed for the 'ideal reader', but yet they distanced this from themselves. Finally, I wanted to see if it was possible to describe the limits of reading and the process of reading – the way that readers try out certain hypotheses about the meaning of the text, and test them against the cues in the text.

In order to test out some ideas on the way that feminist readers construct reading positions for themselves, I followed up this questionnaire with a session designed to ask some women who identify themselves as feminist how they read the poem in more detail than was allowed by the questionnaire. I presented the poem to members of the Loughborough University Feminist Research Group, a group of feminist staff and postgraduates mainly drawn from the English and Drama department. I asked the participants to comment in as much detail as possible on their reading of the poem. In this way I hoped to be able to make a distinction between those texts which position the reader as female and which are read by males and females as doing so, and those texts which position the reader as feminist; I wished to investigate the range of possible readings available to feminists with this latter category of text. In this way, Scholes' and Culler's assumptions about reading as a woman can be distinguished from reading as a feminist.

DOMINANT READING AND FEMINIST CODES/CUES

For many readers, a stereotypically feminist poem is one which describes periods or giving birth. The very mention of menstruation in this poem as 'woman's blood' and the questioning of the need for pregnancy seemed to constitute for the majority of female readers a 'code' that the poem was feminist and that it was directed at a female audience. For menstruation to be mentioned in a poem at all, the expectation of the majority of the respondents was that periods are discussed in a positive way, and these readers stated that they were cued by the reference to 'strength' and 'invincible power' in lines 6 and 7.[10] The majority of the readers were able to *recognise* this as a representation of a female character trying to come to terms with the potential of her body for menstruation or pregnancy.

SUBJECT POSITION AND MALE/FEMALE READER DIFFERENCES

Although it is not possible to make generalising statements on the basis of such a small survey, it would seem that there are certain differences between the males and females in this survey in the way that they approach this text. The majority of the readers were able to locate a subject position which the text was constructing. The majority of females stated that the ideal reader for the poem was a woman, although they differed as to what type of woman this might be, some of them positing 'any woman' and some of them being very specific, for example, 'a modern feminist who cannot decide whether to conceive'. Only 40 per cent of the male respondents stated that they thought the ideal reader was female; however, this may have been because they seemed to be interpreting the notion of an ideal reader in particular ways. Some of them stated that they did not think the address 'was limited to women – a shared sense of experience is not necessary for male comprehension' and others stated that they thought the poem *should* be read by everyone, a point which several of the female readers also made. This uneasiness about locating a female ideal reader may be partly due to the difficulty for them as readers to map a reading position for themselves as males.

Most readers, female and male, were able to recognise that certain information was presented as common sense; for example, that menstruation, the cycles of the moon and tidal movement are linked in some ways. In much early radical feminist writing this link is made explicit, so that women are seen to be biologically more in tune with nature and with the planets than men. There is an assumption that women's cycles follow the periodicity of the moon (Shuttle and Redgrove 1980). The majority of the readers could recognise that the poem was presenting this causal link, citing sentences such as line 2 where 'and' seems to be functioning in a causative way ('When the moon swings round/ And I bleed my woman's blood'); and line 3, where 'sing' links back through rhyme to 'swings' in line 1: ('the moon swings' and 'my belly . . . sings'). However, whilst *recognising* this information, few of the respondents felt that they had to agree with that supposition. Most stated quite clearly that the causality was a mythical or metaphorical one and went on to state that there was no factual connection. Thus, readers recognised indirect address, that is they could recognise that this information about menstruation was posed as being common sense, but did not adopt the knowledge which was proposed.

On the whole, males and females differed as to the reasons they gave for liking or disliking the poem: the majority of female respondents said that they liked the poem because they identified with the character: 'I like poems about my experience' or because they felt that the ideas expressed in the poem should be discussed more widely – a word which was frequently used was 'thought-provoking' – and one respondent said that she thought the poem 'said the unsayable'. This may be linked to a general recognition of the fact that menstruation is tabooed and that poems rarely discuss this aspect of experience. Most of the female respondents said that they enjoyed the poem for reasons ranging from that they thought it was 'honest and powerful and as a woman who menstruates I can identify with it' to 'I enjoy reading poems from a women's perspective', and 'I get a kick out of reading about my female power.' A small number of women questioned the views expressed by the poem and said that they wanted to have children, or had children and therefore did not enjoy the poem; thus they recognised a subject position that the poem was presenting, but they did not feel that it was a position which they wished to adopt. The majority of males said that they liked it because of the language or because of the challenging nature of the subject matter, for example 'I did enjoy the poem mainly because I had not read one that addressed such a theme.' Thus, the women readers recognised the subject position proffered by the text and either gained pleasure from identifying a closeness between that position and themselves, or they rejected the position. Male readers seemed in a more difficult position, where their pleasure in the poem was not related to their recognition of subject positions.

One area where there was a significant difference between males and females was on the question of whether the poem was feminist: the majority of the females (80 per cent) thought it was feminist. However, one very surprising result was the fact that all the male respondents answered in a similar way when asked if they would classify the poem as feminist or not. All but one of them stated that the poem was not feminist, ranging from statements such as 'I would prefer to classify it as a poem of independence' and 'No, why categorise the feelings of being trapped by one's body as feminist?' which seemed to be trying to universalise the poem to human experience, to statements such as 'Why should it be feminist? It speaks of what happens to all women, a common pain', and 'No, they seem perfectly legitimate thoughts for any woman to have irrespective of her views on society', which present the poem as articulating ideas common to all women. Many of the male respondents stated that they were uneasy about feminism, stating 'I would avoid the term' and 'I am unsure of the nature of feminism'. Thus, for many of the female respondents, recognition of the text as feminist seemed to be unproblematic whereas male readers worked hard to classify it in other ways. From this analysis, it can be assumed that the female and male readers have different interests at stake in reading the poem; for most female readers, the subject positions on offer and the classification of the text seemed fairly straightforward. For many of them, the text was 'speaking to them'; for the male readers this process of recognition of the dominant reading seemed to necessitate a resisting reading. Presumably, if this questionnaire had been sent to a wider range of people, some men would have responded that they saw the poem as feminist and would respond to the subject positions available to them in a more productive way.

THE PARAMETERS OF READING AND
PROCESS READING

From the questionnaire it is quite clear that the respondents did not stray far from a range of possible readings for the poem; although they disagreed as to whether the poem presented a positive, negative or ambivalent representation of witches, menstruation and pregnancy, the majority interpreted the poem in much the same way. Although this might be due to the questionnaire format, very few of them offered interpretations outside a limited range of possibilities. In order to try to analyse further this notion of other readings for the text, I asked a discussion group to comment on the poem. The members of this group have a wide range of political positions within feminism, yet they recognised the poem as presenting a particular view of menstruation, even though they might not agree with that position. These women were able to recognise the position of the poem as radical feminist rather than simply feminist in a much easier way than were the respondents in the questionnaire, because of their familiarity with different kinds of feminism.[11] I was interested to discover that these feminists were quite insistent on performing a 'resisting reading' to the supposed dominant reading in that most of the women dismissed the link between the moon and women's cycles, referring to 'radical feminist crap about blood' and 'disaffected Druids'. One person stated that she had tried to read the poem as a lesbian, stressing that no men were involved in this representation of fertilisation and interpreting 'pale soul-sister' as the desire to be impregnated by another woman. However, after toying with the idea for a while, she and the group decided that the poem did not really allow her to read in this way, and they explicitly stated that there were not enough linguistic cues in the text to justify her reading. Whilst it is clear that a range of readings are possible, this diversity can only be maintained with reference to the number of cues that can be found in the poem.

In terms of analysis of the process of reading, the group as a whole came to an agreement that the first time they had read the poem they had read it as a poem about a woman who was ambivalent about the prospect of being pregnant, but the second time they read it and whilst they were discussing in the group, they interpreted it in a much more sinister way by focusing on words such as 'leech', 'shackles' and 'selfish' to describe the foetus. This is important in terms of research on reading, because, as I noted earlier, most work focuses only on the supposed end product of the reading; but here, the respondents were keen to point out that they had changed their interpretation and that this process was ongoing in their subsequent readings of the text.

CONCLUSIONS

The conclusion that can be drawn from this analysis, complex though it is, is that a dominant reading of the poem has been recognised by most of the respondents. Most of the female readers responded in different ways from the male respondents with respect to recognition of the subject positions which the poem offers the reader. Many of the respondents considered the position which is mapped out for the reader as being a simple *position*: some of the male readers could recognise that it was not directed to them; the feminist group and many of the female respondents recognised that this poem was not speaking *to* them, either because they did not like the politics of the position, or because they viewed pregnancy in different ways. However, some of the female respondents interpreted the positioning as being one with which they had close personal links; they felt that the poem was about their experience and mentioned that they identified with the character. Thus, the focus on subject position rather than 'self' presented by a text enables an analysis which sees a range of choices about that subject position. Where I would differ from Fuss, however, is that she seems to view these choices as of the same order; there are clearly differences between texts which address the reader as feminist and those which address the reader as male or female.

Whilst there do seem to be some broad interpretative differences between females and males in this survey, it is also important to be aware of the differences within the groups of female and male respondents. Male respondents seemed to have much more difficulty with the feminism of the poem, to the point that they did not categorise the poem as feminist; the majority of the female respondents could recognise that it was feminist but did not feel that they necessarily had to agree with the position. There were a range of reasons for adopting a position of 'resisting reader' among the female respondents. Therefore, the notion of resisting readings needs to be expanded to allow for different positions from which to resist (there may be very reactionary resisting readings of this poem or very progressive ones).

This analysis has shown 'that investigating broad sex differences in reading can be productive in certain ways: it is clear that an approach to analysis which focuses on subject positions allows for the possibility that females will differ in their readings from each other, as will males. This mapping out of possible positions which can be adopted or resisted seems a more productive form of analysis than simply assuming that all females will read in particular ways. In this analysis, it was the interpretation of the poem as feminist which seemed to distinguish between males and females most clearly; whilst reading like a feminist is clearly something that anyone can do, there may be complex reasons why only certain sectors of the population do perform such readings.

APPENDIX: QUESTIONNAIRE

I am writing a chapter for a book on readership; could you answer the questions for me, as responses will form the basis of part of the chapter. I would stress that there are no 'right' answers to these questions. Thanks in advance for your help.

1. Is the poem about:
    (a) A woman who is happy not to be pregnant?
    (b) A woman who wants to be pregnant?
    (c) A woman who is ambivalent about pregnancy?
    (d) Other (specify)?
    What evidence have you drawn on to come to this reading?
2. How do you feel about the causality in lines 1–2? What is the connection between the moon and menstruation?
3. What does 'pale soul-sister' refer to?
4. How is menstruation represented here:
    (a) In a positive light?
    (b) In a negative light?
    (c) In a mixture of negative and positive light?
    (d) Other?
5. How is the woman's relation to her body portrayed?
6. 'Witches' is used in line 5:
    (a) Positively.
    (b) Negatively.
    (c) Ambivalently.
    Give reasons why you think this is so.
7. Who do you think is the ideal reader for this poem? Describe the type of person you think it is intended for.
8. Would you classify this poem as feminist? If so, or if not, on what grounds?
9. Is it the sort of poem that you enjoy reading or not? Give reasons.
10. Any other comments.

NOTES

1. I am using Roland Barthes' notion of a cultural code from *S/Z* (1975) in conjunction with some ideas which Colin McCabe put forward in his work on classic realist texts/films (1981).
2. In using the term *discourse* here in relation to ideology I am using two potentially conflicting terms of reference: those of Marxist theory and of discourse theory. Michel Foucault explicitly stated that he developed the term *discourse* in opposition to ideology (1981). However, both Diane MacDonnell's *Theories of Discourse* (1986) and Dorothy Smith's *Texts, Facts and Femininity* (1990) have attempted to move beyond this impasse towards a fusion of ideology and discourse theorising.
3. Some of the essays in Flynn and Schweickart's *Gender and Reading* (1986) mentioned above unfortunately fall into this trap, but as Boardman (this volume) argues, readings which are not based on empirical readings should not be discounted too easily; since empirical work has its own theoretical shortcomings, non-empirical analyses have an extremely important function.
4. Furthermore, even when we have identified a dominant reading within the text, it is not necessarily the case that we are aware, despite our critical training, of all of the ideological positionings which are taking place. We may also decide that, even having recognised the dominant reading, we will take pleasure as readers in elements which seem at first sight to be regressive.
5. Jennifer Coates' 1988 work on the way that participants in all-female discussion and friendship groups address each other is suggestive in this context; also consider Deborah Tannen's 1991 work on female–male conversation breakdown based on differing expectations. However, the problem with this work lies primarily in an assumption that all women will necessarily feel that their interests lie with other women and that other affiliations, such as class, race, politics, religion, may not dominate at certain moments.
6. There is no reason why men cannot read feminist texts sympathetically and for enjoyment; I do not feel that men as such can be feminists for reasons which are very specific to the history of the development of the Women's Movement in Britain and America (the importance of women-only spaces, etc.) but I do feel that they can be pro-feminist, meaning that they support many of the aims of feminists, but are very aware of their problematic status within the movement and within discussion groups, publication circles and so on.
7. This poem comes from an anthology edited by the Raving Beauties entitled *No Holds Barred* (1985), a collection of poetry which had been written by women from all over Britain.
8. I should note that the very fact that I was sending out the questionnaire will obviously have affected the responses; staff and students are aware of my feminism and may have felt that they were being asked to respond in particular ways.
9. The structure of this questionnaire may have skewed the readings in certain ways, since, as in most multiple-choice questionnaires, there were three choices; since, if the choice consists of a binary opposition and a third choice, the interviewee will assume that the third choice is the one which they are to choose, regardless of what they think is the right answer. The questionnaire was constructed so that the third choice was not always the 'right' answer.
10. There are certain elements of the text which are incoherent for me at least; for example, I cannot make sense of 'pale soul-sister' in line 13, and assume it may have a range of meanings. Most readers tolerate a remarkable amount of

incoherence in a text, and will simply pass over information which does not fit into their overall expectations of a coherent dominant reading. The respondents gave this phrase a variety of glosses but all within certain parameters: the moon, semen, the woman character's alter ego.

11. Reading a text in groups may also skew the results, since, especially in feminist groups, there is a tendency towards trying to reach a consensus.

REFERENCES

Althusser, L. (1984) *Essays in Ideology*, London: Verso.

Barthes, R. (1975) *S/Z*, London: Cape.

Betterton, R. (ed.) (1987) *Looking on: Images of femininity in the visual arts and media*, London: Pandora.

Bobo, J. (1988) 'The Color Purple: Black women as cultural readers', in Pribram (ed.) pp. 90–109.

Bourdieu, P. (1984) *Distinction: A social critique of the judgement of taste*, trans. R. Nice, London: Routledge & Kegan Paul.

Butler, J. (1990) *Gender Trouble: Feminism and the subversion of identity*, London: Routledge.

Cameron, D., McAlinden, F. and O'Leary, K. (1988) 'Lakoff in context: The social and linguistic functions of tag questions', in J. Coates and D. Cameron (eds) *Women in their Speech Communities*, Harlow: Longman, pp. 74–93.

Coates, J. (1988) 'Gossip revisited: Language in all-female groups', in J. Coates and D. Cameron (eds) *Women in their Speech Communities*, Harlow: Longman, pp. 94–122.

Crawford, M. and Chaffin, R. (1986) 'The reader's construction of meaning: Cognitive research on gender and comprehension', in Flynn and Schweickart (eds), pp. 3–30.

Culler, J. (1982) *On Deconstruction: Theory and criticism after structuralism*, Ithaca: Cornell University Press.

Davies, K., Dickey, J. and Stratford, T. (eds) (1987) *Out of Focus: Writings on women and the media*, London: Women's Press.

Fairclough, N. (1989) *Language and Power*, London: Longman.

Fetterley, J. (1978) *The Resisting Reader: A feminist approach to American fiction*, Bloomington: Indiana University Press.

Fetterley, J. (1986) 'Reading about reading', in Flynn and Schweickart (eds), pp. 147–64.

Flynn, E. and Schweickart, P. (eds) (1986) *Gender and Reading: Essays on readers, texts and contexts*, Baltimore and London: Johns Hopkins University Press.

Foucault, M. (1982) 'The subject and power', in H. Dreyfus and P. Rabinow, *Michel Foucault: Beyond structuralism and hermeneutics*, Hemel Hempstead: Harvester Wheatsheaf.

Fowler, B. (1991) *The Alienated Reader: Women and popular romantic literature in the twentieth century*, Hemel Hempstead: Harvester Wheatsheaf.

Fowler, R. (1991) *Language in the News*, London: Routledge.

Frith, G. (1991) 'Transforming features: Double vision and the female reader', *New Formations*, 15 (Winter): 67–81.

Fuss, D. (1989) *Essentially Speaking: Feminism, nature and difference*, London: Routledge.

Gamman, L. (1991) 'More Cagney and Lacey', Feminist Review, 37: 117–21.

Gamman, L. and Marshment, M. (eds) (1988) The Female Gaze: Women as viewers of popular culture, London: Women's Press.

Jardine, A. and Smith, P. (eds) (1987) Men in Feminism, London: Methuen.

Laws, S. (1990) Issues of Blood: The politics of menstruation, London: Macmillan.

McCabe, C. (1981) 'Realism and cinema: Notes on some Brechtian theses', in T. Bennett, S. Boyd Bowman, C. Mercer and J. Woollacott (eds) Popular TV and Film, London: Open University/British Film Institute, pp. 216–35.

MacDonnell, D. (1986) Theories of Discourse, Oxford: Blackwell.

Mills, S. (1990) 'Feministische close reading', trans. Martina Mitchell, T/extasy, Feministische Perspektiven in Grossbritannien: Feministische Studien, 8, 2: 70–87.

Mills, S. (1991) Discourses of Difference: Women's travel writing and colonialism, London: Routledge.

Mills, S. (1992) 'Knowing y/our place: Marxist feminist contextualised stylistics', in M. Toolan (ed.) Language, Text and Context: Essays in stylistics, London: Routledge, pp. 182–208.

Mills, S. (forthcoming) Feminist Stylistics, London: Routledge.

Modleski, T. (1986) 'Feminism and the power of interpretation: Some critical readings', in T. de Lauretis (ed.) Feminist Studies/Critical Studies, Bloomington: Indiana University Press, pp. 121–38.

Modleski, T. (1991) Feminism without Women: Culture and criticism in a 'post feminist' age, London: Routledge.

Montgomery, M. (1986) 'DJ talk', Media, Culture and Society, 8, 4 (October): 421–40.

Montgomery, M. (1989) 'Direct address and audience', Parlance: Journal of the Poetics and Linguistics Association, 1, 2 (Winter), pp. 35–55.

Mulvey, L. (1975) 'Visual pleasure and narrative cinema', Screen, 16, 3 (Autumn): 6–18.

Pearce, L. (1991) Woman/Image/Text: Readings in Pre-Raphaelite art and literature, Hemel Hempstead: Harvester Wheatsheaf.

Pearce, L. (1992) 'Feminism and dialogism', in H. Hinds, A. Phoenix and J. Stacey (eds) Working Out: New directions for women's studies, London: Falmer, pp. 184–93.

Pêcheux, M. (1982) Language, Semantics, and Ideology, London: Macmillan.

Pribram, D. (ed.) (1988) Female Spectators: Looking at film and television, London: Verso.

Radway, J. (1987) Reading the Romance: Women, patriarchy and popular literature, London: Verso (first published 1984).

Raving Beauties (eds) (1985) No Holds Barred: New poems by women, London: Women's Press.

Scholes, R. (1987) 'Reading like a man', in A. Jardine and P. Smith (eds) Men in Feminism, London: Methuen, pp. 204–18.

Shuttle, P. and Redgrove, P. (1980) The Wise Wound: Menstruation and everywoman, Harmondsworth: Penguin.

Smith, D. (1990) Texts, Facts and Femininity: Exploring the relations of ruling, London: Routledge.

Stacey, J. (1988) 'Desperately seeking difference', in Gamman and Marshment (eds), pp. 112–29.

Tannen, D. (1991) You just Don't Understand: Women and men in conversation, London: Virago.

Tong, R. (1989) Feminist Thought, London: Unwin/Hyman.

Treneman, A. (1988) 'Cashing in on the curse: Advertising and the menstrual taboo', in Gamman and Marshment (eds), pp. 153–65.

White, H. (1980) 'The value of narrativity in the presentation of reality', in W. Mitchell (ed.) *On Narrative*, Chicago: University of Chicago Press, pp. 1–23.

Williamson, J. (1978) *Decoding Advertisements: Ideology and meaning in advertising*, London: Marion Boyars.

Wittig, M. (1992) *The Straight Mind and other essays*, Hemel Hempstead: Harvester Wheatsheaf.

Chapter 2

Theories of Textual Determination and Audience Agency

An empirical contribution to the debate

Chris Christie

Lapsley and Westlake (1988) assert that after the work of Jacques Derrida there can be no question of specifying the effect which a text will have without taking into account the context of its reception. Referring specifically to the debates surrounding the political effectivity of film, their argument is that since 'the human subject has a degree of agency in the reading of a text . . . then the notion of dissemination renders any positioning by the text untenable'. Given this assumption that readings of texts can vary according to the contexts of those readings, the authors go on to specify why the hegemonic effect of a text can no longer be theorised as an automatic process which results from an engagement with the text. 'For if interpellation can only operate through an act of interpretation on the part of the reader then there is no guarantee that a text will always interpellate in the same way' (1988: 65).

While media analysis has begun to take as axiomatic the notion that texts can be differentially interpreted, the full implications of this notion are still relatively unrealised, particularly in those analyses where a degree of ideological determination by the text is assumed (see, for example, Mills, and Boardman, this volume). In this chapter I draw on a recent study of audience interpretation of a television programme to argue that although texts are generally perceived by analysts to be polysemic (i.e. capable of generating a range of meanings) the notions of audience 'agency' and 'interpretation' which are entailed by this axiom need to be retheorised.

The chapter has three sections. In the section which follows I trace the theoretical background of recent audience studies in order to consider the extent to which assumptions about audience activity are still perceived according to a problematic which, I would argue, is no longer relevant.

47

Specifically, I take issue with the implicit assumptions regarding the processes of textual determination which have led analysts to approach variation in audience interpretation primarily in terms of 'resistance' (see Mills, this volume). In the second section I go on to give details of a survey of audience interpretation, the results of which, in focusing on the level at which an audience's existing knowledge affects their engagement with a text, indicate that resistance is not an essential component of variation in interpretation. In the final section, I consider an alternative approach to audience studies, based on Sperber and Wilson's (1986) theory of relevance, which stresses that the 'meaning' of a text is not retrievable solely from the information linguistically encoded in that text and which allows a way of accounting for the audience's contribution to the interpretative process. The potential this theory has for making more explicit the relationship between the audience and the media text is then discussed.

AUDIENCE AGENCY AND INTERPRETATION

One of the directions which media analysis has taken as a result of a recognition that texts can have different meanings for different people is to move from textual analysis to a focus on how audiences respond to media texts (e.g. Morley 1980; Bobo 1988; Press 1991). An alternative direction is to focus on the often contradictory 'discourses' which constitute a media text (e.g. Doane 1988; Gledhill 1988). Both these directions have required that assumptions about the level and nature of activity involved in an audience's encounter with a text need to be retheorised. The latter direction, which focuses on textual analysis, will be considered briefly in the final section of this chapter in the light of the following discussion of media analyses which focus on the audience.

I begin by addressing the changing notions of audience activity implied by a series of developments in media analysis in order to show how recent studies of audience response are still drawing on notions of textual determination which have a counterproductive effect in terms of achieving their stated aims.

The current 'ethnographic moment' of audience studies, which focuses on the relationship between an audience's cultural background and their engagement with a media text, arises out of a specific genealogy (see Ang 1989; Tulloch 1990; Moores 1992). As such, the approach inherits assumptions which distinguish it from, for example, that of 'uses and gratifications' analysts, who focus primarily on how differences in audience response are related to differences in individual needs, and where audiences are described as 'free' or 'powerful' users of the media (Ang 1989: 100). In order to draw out the distinctive assumptions of the approach which Ang (1989) locates within the framework of 'critical cultural studies', I will briefly outline its theoretical background.

Shaun Moores (1992) takes audience research in current critical cultural studies to have originated with Morley's (1980) survey of the *Nationwide* audience, and he traces the theoretical background of this approach to accounts of the textual positioning of the subject developed in *Screen* in the 1970s. This view of the theoretical development of the paradigm is shared by Wren-Lewis (1983). However, while Moores stresses Morley's opposition to the assumptions of *Screen* theory (a brief account of which is given below), Wren-Lewis asserts that Morley's work is a development of the theory, and stresses the extent to which it shares many of its assumptions. I will consider the implications of Wren-Lewis' claim after the following outline of positioning theory.

Drawing on Lacanian psychoanalytical theory, Marxism and structuralist linguistics, the theories developed in *Screen* stressed the power of texts to reproduce the reader as a subject of ideology. This theoretical framework, which is summarised and critiqued in Morley (1980) and Moores (1992), offered a sophisticated account of how the dominant ideology of a society is reproduced through the subject positions inscribed within its media texts.

Briefly, the process can be described as follows: there is a single (ideological) position inscribed in a media text from which the text makes sense to an audience. In taking up this position, the audience recognises the text as addressed to her/himself, and is 'interpellated' by the text. In the act of interpellation the individual is constituted as a subject of the text's ideology.

This theory was extended to account for the effect of film, television and written texts. The focus of analyses within this framework was on the structure of the text and the inscription of the subject within that structure. The implied audience was perceived as passive in terms of the political effects of the text (see Willemen 1978: 49).

Criticism of *Screen* theory centred around the point that it failed to distinguish between, as Moores puts it, 'the reader implied by or inscribed in the text and the actual social subjects who interpret or decode texts' (1992: 142). In his account Moores goes on to cite Brunsdon's criticism:

> We can usefully analyse the 'you' or 'yous' that the text as discourse constructs but we cannot assume that any individual audience member will necessarily occupy

these positions. The relation of the audience to the text will not be determined solely by that text, but also by positionalities in relation to a whole range of other discourses . . . elaborated elsewhere, already in circulation and brought to the (text) by the viewer. (Brunsdon 1981: 32–7)

Although *Screen* theory was vigorously criticised from a number of perspectives, it is the response of the Media Group at the Centre for Contemporary Cultural Studies in Birmingham, found in the work of David Morley (1980) and Charlotte Brunsdon (1981), which is of particular interest in that they develop the notion of audience agency. Drawing on Hall's (1973) reworking of Parkin's (1973) theory of meaning production, their approach stressed the effect of an audience's socially constructed consciousness on the decoding activity required in an encounter with a media text.

Within this paradigm the text was perceived to be polysemic, but the meanings which could be taken from the text were constrained by their cultural context, theorised by Stuart Hall (1973) in terms of a code model of communication:

> Polysemy must not be confused with pluralism. Connotative codes are not equal among themselves. Any society/culture tends, with varying degrees of closure to impose its segmentations . . . its classifications of the . . . world upon its members. There remains a dominant cultural order, though it is neither univocal nor uncontested. (Hall 1973: 13, cited in Morley 1980: 12)

Although, because of the social nature of communication assumed here, the range of meanings a text holds is seen to be foreclosed, the fact that a selection of some sort has to be made means that the audience can no longer be perceived as passive. If interpretation is required, the audience must be assumed to have a degree of agency. The form of audience agency and interpretation which is assumed in analyses premised on this approach will be considered in the next section.

Active audiences

Perhaps the single most important development that arose out of the critical cultural studies response to *Screen* theory was Morley's (1980) introduction of real audiences into the debate. Although the theoretical assumptions of Morley's work have been extensively criticised, his study has also been extremely influential. Seiter *et al.* (1989: 1–15) for example, like Moores (1992), traces the current interest in ethnographic audience studies back to his survey, and it could certainly be argued that the terms in which many issues have been debated over the past decade were set by

Morley's work. One such issue which I shall focus on centres around the audience's recognition of a text's 'preferred reading'. The concept of a preferred reading is given by Morley as a crucial element of one of the premises on which his work is based:

> The message in social communication is always complex in structure and form. It always contains more than one potential 'reading'. Messages propose and prefer certain readings over others, but they can never become wholly closed around one reading. They remain polysemic. (1980: 10)

Given this premise of a text's potential for different readings in spite of its 'preferred' sense, Morley's project was to discover how television texts are actually read by audiences. He therefore conducted a series of interviews with different audiences of the television news programme *Nationwide* with the intention of investigating the relationship between (a) the demographic features of an audience, such as class and age; (b) the cultural frameworks they had access to, for example involvement in trade unions and further education; and (c) the different readings which these audiences produced of two episodes of the programme.

Although Morley's aim in the *Nationwide* survey is to focus on how the different social backgrounds of actual audiences affect their interpretation of a media text, the audiences' responses are addressed primarily in terms of their acceptance of, or resistance to, an inscribed ideological positioning by the text. This position, a product of the 'preferred reading' of the news items, had previously been outlined in Brunsdon and Morley's (1978) textual analysis of the *Nationwide* programme. The 1980 audience survey was therefore a development of these earlier findings.

The notion of a preferred reading has been questioned from various perspectives, and as Morley himself states, it is subject to a number of criticisms. In a later work Morley (1989: 18) asks whether the preferred reading of a text is best seen as (a) a property of the text, (b) a reading generated from the text by semiological analysis or (c) an analyst's statement or prediction of how most members of an audience will read the text.

This later criticism is not, it should be stressed, about the issue of textual semantics. Morley's respondents' acceptance or rejection of a preferred reading is not simply a matter of agreeing or disagreeing with what a text means, but is to do with succumbing to or resisting the ideological positioning of the text. In Morley's *Nationwide* survey, the 'preferred reading' is premised on a strongly deterministic theory of the text.

It is this which Wren-Lewis points out in his criticism of Morley's approach:

To emphasize the existence of the decoding subject is, of course, vital. *However, what is also crucial is this:* simply to point to a distinction between an inscribed subject (in relation to a 'preferred reading') and a real historical subject is not to deny the a priori *existence* of an inscribed positionality, merely to question its *effectivity*. (Wren-Lewis 1983: 184; emphasis in original text)

To this extent then, it could be argued that Morley is working within the paradigm he sets out to oppose in his critique of *Screen* theory's assumptions about audience activity (1980: 148). This is because in both Morley's work and later studies which are predicated on the same assumption of the social nature of meaning, there appears to be the implicit notion that variation in interpretation necessarily involves some level of engagement with and then rejection of the ideology inscribed in the text. Although the approach assumes a level of audience activity, it is still premised on a theory of textual determination, and this determination is, as I shall argue in the following section, based in turn on the assumption that the literal meaning of a text is uniformly apprehended across audiences.

Questions of agency and interpretation

Both *Screen* theory and the audience research which developed under the critical cultural studies paradigm share the assumption that media products work hegemonically and the aim of analysis is to uncover how that process works. Where audience studies differ from their antecedents is in the acknowledgement that texts are polysemic and therefore require interpretation (rather than a passive 'absorption') by an audience. As such, audiences are allowed a degree of 'agency' but this agency is perceived primarily in terms of the earlier problematic – that of textual effects.

Evidence of this can be seen in the fact that audience surveys within this paradigm which focus on variation in interpretation are almost inevitably approached in terms of an audience's active resistance to a dominant ideology. It is implicitly assumed that any respondents who produce a 'non-intended' decoding must be aware of the conflict between their own perception and the preferred meaning of the text. This is because within Hall's theoretical framework, which is often the basis of these audience studies, both the 'denotative' and the 'connotative' meaning of the text are seen to be uniformly decoded even by audiences who disagree with the truth or significance of the message apparently inscribed in the text (Hall 1980).

In his account of the encoding and decoding processes involved in the production and interpretation of a media message, Hall asserts that, according to their cultural background, an audience can 'accept', 'negotiate' or 'oppose' the preferred reading of a text. However, as the following extract from Hall's description of the 'oppositional' process indicates, in each case the audience initially apprehend this preferred meaning: 'Finally, it is possible for a viewer perfectly to understand both the literal and the connotative inflection given by a discourse but to decode the message in a *globally* contrary way' (1980: 137) (original emphasis).

Hall's theory has had a general influence on approaches to audience studies within a critical cultural studies paradigm. This can be seen in Morley's (1980) study, where his analysis focuses on and foregrounds the conscious resistance of his respondents to the apparent preferred reading of *Nationwide*. Hall's influence can also be seen in more recent examples of audience studies. For example, drawing on the theoretical framework described above, Jacqueline Bobo's (1988) study sets out to account for contradictory responses to the Steven Spielberg film of Alice Walker's novel *The Color Purple*.

Bobo explains differences in the interpretations of black male critics and black female audiences in terms of the latter's ability to 'read against the grain' of the film (Bobo 1988: 96). The black women Bobo interviewed are seen to have a 'pre-textual subjectivity', which provides them with a 'wary viewing standpoint'. The critical abilities of these women lead them to resist the dominant ideological positions inscribed in the film. However, by theorising their agency in terms of resistance, textual positioning is still a basic premise of the study. (See Christie 1993 for a more extensive account of Morley 1980 and Bobo 1988.)

What is at issue here is the fact that although audience 'agency' and 'interpretation' are invoked in these studies they are locked into a debate about the perpetuation of ideology. As a result, the focus is not on how interpretation occurs, but rather on how *resistance* occurs. While I would not dispute that ideology is a potent force, that it can be located in texts, or that a conscious resistance can occur, my argument is that by approaching audience studies solely from this perspective, only a very partial explanation of variation in interpretation can be hoped for. In order to explain any potential relationship between audience background and ideological effects, much more has to be discovered about the nature of interpretation itself, and this cannot be achieved within the narrow confines of the problematic inherited by audience studies from positioning theories.

The determining effect of this problematic is evident in the methodology of the studies I have focused on. What is implied by such an approach, although not always made explicit, is that texts are perceived as polysemic only to the extent that the dominant reading can be rejected, and an alternative imposed. The concepts of 'negotiation' and 'opposition' invoked in such studies entail this two-stage process. This assumption about the nature of variation has, in turn, an effect on the data which the studies set out to collect.

Because the aim of the studies is to explain the second stage of the process (the articulated resistance to the dominant reading) they do not question how and if the immediate understanding of a text can vary between audiences. The studies are designed primarily to provide data which will indicate any correlation between resistance and background. As a result, the process of interpretation itself is not an issue and there are no specific data offered which would give a clear indication of how the audience's interpretation of the text and their cultural background are connected. Therefore, while both Bobo and Morley offer interesting data and insightful explanations, without this further level of information, the connection between data and explanation must be considered more speculative than it need be.

This then raises the question of what methodology would provide a more specific indication of the relationship between cultural background and interpretation. In the section which follows I outline a study I carried out of audience interpretation of a television programme where I attempted to make these connections more explicit. I then go on to discuss what such an approach can add to media analysis and the analysis of interpretation in general.

AN EMPIRICAL INVESTIGATION OF AUDIENCE RESPONSE

My aim in this study, which is part of a larger work on linguistic processing (see Christie 1993) is to investigate how audience interpretations of a television programme can vary, and how this variation in interpretation relates to both the audience's cultural background and the text. I therefore selected a text which was not 'mainstream', in the sense that, from my own perception, it did not appear to refer to ideas and assumptions which are held by the majority of current audiences. My reasoning was that this would make more explicit the degree to which an audience's understanding of a text depends upon their existing knowledge. I therefore chose to focus on a feminist text and the responses of two female audiences.

The decision to focus on variation between female audiences was determined by the still prevalent assumption in much theorising (see Sara

Mills' comments in the Introduction to this volume) that women audiences constitute a homogeneous class. This study will therefore add to the growing body of work which is witness to women's heterogeneity.

The television programme

In early 1990 Channel 4 screened six half-hour programmes under the series title *Ordinary People*, which asked the question 'What makes ordinary people feminist?' Each of the weekly programmes focused on a specific issue such as art, work or education, and each programme comprised individual presentations by three women on their experience of this issue in connection with gender. The particular episode which I use in my case studies was entitled *The Politics of Experience*.

I outline below the content and format of the programme, but should stress that the outline is given here to indicate my own perception of the programme arising from repeated close viewings. Although this perception of the programme clearly affected my approach to the case studies, in that it determined the issues I focused on in the interviews, it is included primarily to make that process explicit and to facilitate discussion. As the data reported below will indicate, it is not necessarily a perception shared by an audience.

In the programme which I focus on, three women individually present their experiences of politics: Eugenia Piza Lopez, a South American woman whose work politicises the personal experience of women through consciousness-raising techniques including the use of film; a British MP Emma Nicholson, who talks about her career in the Conservative Party and the gender issues she works on in Parliament; and another British woman, Helen Steven, who talks about her spiritual beliefs and her experiences in campaigning for nuclear disarmament.

The format of the programme is somewhat fragmentary: each woman's presentation consists of a series of two- to three-minute slots which are interspersed with those of the other women, so although each presentation forms a relatively continuous narrative it is regularly interrupted by the other two presentations. Each presentation cuts between direct-to-camera speeches by the women and shots of action (such as Emma Nicholson walking past the Palace of Westminster) with a voice-over continuing their speech. To this extent the presentations are perceptibly edited.

Because my aim in the case studies was specifically to draw out variation in the interpretation of the issues raised by the programme, I focused primarily on the presentation by Eugenia Piza Lopez, as I perceived this to contain the least 'mainstream' set of assumptions. I will give a brief summary of her presentation in order to contextualise the responses I set out to elicit and which I quote below.

Lopez's presentation opens with a statement of her background: she was the daughter of intellectuals, whose questioning of society was wide but did not extend to issues of gender. She gives as an example of this limitation her mother's dedication to the preservation of her daughter's virginity. This obsession with virginity led Lopez to begin to question the assumptions about gender she encountered, which in turn led to her perceiving gender as a political issue. Eventually Lopez began working with women in an (unspecified) area of rural South America, where she made a film of the endless working day of these women, with the expressed intention of raising their awareness of the value of their work.

In order to illustrate the implications of textual polysemy, I shall at this point try to make explicit how my reading of Lopez's presentation was constructed. The précis I have given above is the result of a series of inferences, that is logical connections, I have made based on my own asssumptions about gender politics and the text of Lopez's speech. For example, I am assuming a series of causal connections which are only implied in the text. I will try to draw out what is at issue here by using as an example this quotation, which follows Lopez's description of her mother's obsession with the former's virginity.

> And it really alienated my understanding of my own body and my sexuality because it made me feel that there was something wrong with it. There's something wrong with being the owner of your own body. Your body is not yours. It is for somebody else who will eventually indulge it when you get married. And it got to a point where I felt as a woman and not exclusively as a human being, but as a woman, there are a number of things I want to say. There are a number of things I want to struggle for.

In my own understanding of her message Lopez is here referring to her emergence into gender politics, and moreover I am assuming that she is stating that this development was at least in part caused by the attitude to virginity which she came up against. In order to make these inferences, however, I have had to resolve certain ambiguities in the text. It is the presence of these ambiguities which gives the text the potential for different interpretations. I want here to indicate just one ambiguity which I am conscious of having resolved.

Where Lopez states in the above quotation 'And it got to a point where I felt as a woman' the conjunction 'and' has a number of possible functions. For example it could be there (a) simply to list a series of distinct phenomena; (b) to imply a temporal connection between two phenomena

– in which case it could be alternatively stated as 'and then'; or (c) it could imply a causal connection which could be alternatively stated as 'and therefore'. My own understanding of the text assumes the latter function – that a causal connection is being made.

The point I am making here is that what the text 'says' is open to interpretation, and that it is my own existing assumptions which lead to my (not necessarily conscious) selection of one rather than another interpretation. I am also claiming that the way in which I resolve the ambiguities of this text is significantly related to the way that I read the overall message. The particular assumptions which lead to the process of disambiguation I describe above are, of course, feminist. As a working definition of the term, I will use Ang's (1989: 109) description of a feminist approach as one which 'locates gender relations as a site of struggle'.

While it would be problematic to talk of feminist assumptions as though they formed a coherent perspective from which a complete television programme is viewed, I would argue that at certain points in the text it is possible to make explicit how these assumptions have informed my own interpretation (see also Mills, this volume). In the above case, for example, it is because I take the emphasis given to female virginity to be an effect of gendered power relations that I then go on to infer that there is a causal relationship between Lopez's experience of her mother's obsession and the things she later wants to 'struggle for'.

The significance of these issues will be discussed more fully after the following description of the respondents and their interpretations.

The respondents

In order to explore the potential variation in interpretation which the television programme could engender, I carried out a survey using two groups of women with distinct differences in experience. The first group consisted of four women who were aged between 25 and 35 and had all left school at the age of sixteen. They were all married with young children, one was a housewife and the rest were in paid employment, as a fork-lift truck driver, a bar worker and a catering production worker. They were a friendship group who all lived on the same estate and who regularly met at one another's houses.

The second group were three women who knew each other as a result of meeting on a taught postgraduate course, and who went on to mix socially. They were all students at the time of the interview and were aged between 25 and 40. Two of the women had children, and two were married.

My decision to work with groups rather than individuals was motivated by two considerations. Firstly, I felt that a one-to-one interview might be somewhat intimidating and believed that a group setting at the home of one of the respondents seemed the best way of avoiding this. I also felt that this form of interview would lead to discussion between the respondents which would draw out fine points of interpretation within each group's terms of reference.

Although the respondents were selected partly because of the similarity of the existing level of education within the groups and the difference in education between the groups, it should be stressed that the two groups should not be perceived as approximating to a homogeneity of viewpoint, nor as representative samples of a population. Moreover, in advance of the data, it should be stressed that the difference in education may not be the most pertinent distinguishing feature of the groups. As Jordin and Brunt (1988: 24)) point out, it is what groups do rather than what they represent which makes this type of interview potentially so interesting.

I interviewed the two groups separately. In each case the group met at the home of one of the women in their set, where I played a video recording of the television programme. I then asked the women a series of questions about the programme, replaying the relevant section to refresh their memories where necessary. I give details below of some of the responses.

The responses

I use just three transcription codes in what follows in order to facilitate understanding of my respondents' speech:

'/' denotes an interruption by the following speaker.
'. . .' denotes a pause.
'–' denotes a 'false start'.

This latter code is included because, while it is relatively easy to make sense of spoken utterances containing false starts, in that they are signalled by the speaker using a range of vocal effects such as increased volume or speed, in the form of a transcribed text such utterances are less easily understood.

After the initial showing of the programme I asked each group what they thought the title The Politics of Experience might mean. The first group, who had left school at sixteen, answered as follows:

J: Well if someone said to me – if someone said you're going to see a programme about the politics of experience I would expect it to be/

K: I'd expect to see someone like Ted Heath/
J: Yeah – or not necessarily – Margaret Thatcher – I'd expect it to be about
someone who knows who's well into politics
K: Or an older person who's been in politics a long time describing about their
life . . . who's experienced.

The second group (i.e. those who had gone on to further education) replied
as follows:

L: Well I would think it was relating a bit to this idea of um the personal being
political and that you don't need to think of politics only as party politics but just
how you live your life and what your – what you do in your day-to-day decisions
is actually sort of political things as well . . . so they're concentrating on these
women – women's experience and calling it a political experience but not a party-
political experience
E: Yeah I'd agree with that yeah . . . it comes from your own experiences it's
sort of grown out of your own experience as opposed to the – accepting a dogma
that's handed down.

For group 1 the referents of the terms 'political' and 'experience' are quite
distinct from that of group 2. For group 1 'experience' in this context is a
form of 'practical knowledge' arising out of having taken part in
government. Their invocation of Margaret Thatcher and Ted Heath
indicates that 'government' is also the referent which this group provides
for what constitutes 'politics'. For group 2 'politics' has a much wider field
of reference, potentially covering their referent for 'experience' in the
sense of 'how you live your life'.

Later in the interview I asked the groups how they saw Lopez's remarks
about her mother's concern for her virginity to be connected with her later
comment:

And it got to a point where I felt as a woman and not exclusively as a human
being, but as a woman, there are a number of things I want to say. There are a
number of things I want to struggle for.

Group 1's response was:

J: I think she's just basically – just I think she's trying to give you an idea of how
– what they think like in that country – well her family are more concerned about
that she doesn't sleep with anyone before she gets married instead of being
concerned how she's spending the rest of her life in the sense of work or whatever
if you know what I mean that's their first priority
M: Losing her virginity
J: Yeah like don't lose your virginity sort of thing
K: And stick to one man
L: She wanted to be able to do her own/
J: I don't think she was saying that she wanted to sleep around or anything I
think she was just trying to say that's what they thought sort of thing – how bad
she thinks their priorities were.

Group 2 responded:

> L: Yeah I think she was just sort of really meaning that her awareness that she wasn't the owner of her own body was something that went along with her awareness of those other things that she was concerned about as well – it was part of her wider struggle for it.
>
> E: Yeah I mean for me it's er the connection is that she was saying that the preoccupation for her wasn't just to do with you know being a virgin, but there were other things in life that mattered um that beyond that – that she wanted to be able to talk about and argue about and challenge – that was beyond that preoccupation.

The responses indicated that members of both groups understood Lopez's statements as implying that she, in contrast with her mother, did not think her virginity was a particularly important issue, and that she was more concerned with other issues. The groups vary, however, in terms of their perception of the relevance of the issue of virginity: why Lopez should talk about it at all. J, in group 1, sees the issue of virginity as providing general background information to the life Lopez is describing, emphasising a cultural difference: 'what they think like in that country'. L, in group 2, although not very specific about what the connection might be, saw Lopez's remarks about virginity to be related to her other concerns: 'it was part of her wider struggle.'

As a final example of the variation in interpretation shown by the groups, I asked them whether they thought the things Lopez was interested in were political. Group 1's response was:

> General: No
> K: To me it's her attitude to their way of life
> [Interviewer: So you don't think their way of life has got anything to do with our way of life over here?]
> General: No
> J: No it's not as over the top as what it is over there
> [The discussion then ranged for some time on the attitude of men to their wives working in paid employment in various cultures and ended with:]
> K: But that's got nothing to do – to – that's got nothing to do with politics
> J: It's not politics as we know it as in the Cabinet and all that
> K: That's what I associate with politics
> J: I mean that's not what they talk about in the Cabinet is it? 'Oh shall we let the wives go out to work?'
> [General laughter]

Group 2 responded:

> G: In the sense that they involve people – politics is about people – political with a small p
> E: I'm not even sure that I understood exactly what she was involved in . . . I mean she seemed to talk about a sort of vague notion of women's groups and things but I don't really feel that I understood what she actually was doing or what her goal was or . . .

L: I sort of felt she was sort of something to do with making films to raise people's consciousness about the position of women . . . and if that is what she was doing – I would say that was political

E: Yeah politics to me is about power – I think/

L: I suppose politics/

E: or structures of power usually but they can also – politics with a small p can also include informal power relations and I think because she seemed to be working with women it would probably be more sort of in terms of the informal structures of power

L: Yeah I think that it's um – there is this notion in feminism that the personal is political – it's something that we talk about – so from that perspective it is political – if you agree that – but if you only accept politics as being sort of to do with classical or even wider things of power – like they would say it's political to buy Ecover washing up liquid as opposed to something else because you are, you know, you're putting your money in a sort of – along the lines of saying I'm buying this because it was supposedly ecological – that would be political. But other people might not see that as being political – that decision.

My purpose in including this last set of responses was that I felt they indicated the different frameworks in which the two groups understood the issues of the programme. For group 1 the issues raised by Lopez were specifically related to the presenter's own experience and culture rather than something which was directly connected to the everyday life of the respondents. This also extended the notion of 'politics' which they expressed as having little to do with issues which directly involved them as women. Group 2, although coming away from their own viewing of the programme with no clear idea of what Lopez was actually involved in, did make a series of connections which linked Lopez's work with an everyday act of their own such as buying washing-up liquid, and they could term them both 'political'.

To summarise, there is a difference between each group's understanding of the issues raised by the programme. For group 1 the connection between what Lopez says about her mother's attitude to virginity and the other things she talks about is in terms of providing a picture of how women live in a culture foreign to their own. The group make distinctions between their own experience and those which Lopez describes, and the link between their own everyday experience and what constitutes 'politics' for them is explicitly repudiated.

The concept of 'politics' which I took to be implied by the programme title, and which was brought up by me in the interview is not accommodated in group 1's perception of what the programme was about. In contrast, group 2 saw the issue about virginity to be connected with a 'wider struggle' related to issues of power. 'Politics' for this group encapsulates all of these issues.

DISCUSSION

The data I give above indicate the extent to which the sense an audience makes of a text is dependent upon their existing knowledge. Although it could be argued that Lopez is addressing the audience as feminist, the power of her address is circumscribed by the knowledge the audience has prior to their encounter with the text. Textual address alone is not effective. Only the audience who indicate that they have already had access to the assumptions about politics which Lopez is calling on (i.e. the personal is political) infer that they are being addressed on issues that directly concern themselves. The audience with a more mainstream notion of what constitutes politics (Parliament, the Cabinet) see themselves as being addressed in terms of what might be described as 'cultural differences': how the experiences Lopez recounts contrast with their own lives.

As I have argued above, this notion of an *a priori* audience position has been addressed by media analysis in the past and one way of approaching it has been to analyse the assumed ideological effects of the text and then look at how a pre-existing audience position allows these effects to be resisted. One of the many criticisms to which this approach is subject is that it assumes an anterior process which is rarely problematised: in order for resistance to take place, the audience first has to understand the media text. To the extent that there is no empirical evidence to indicate that a unitary understanding of a broadcast communication actually occurs, it would be difficult to sustain a general claim about the generated effects of the text once this process of interpretation is foregrounded. Moreover, in aiming primarily to provide data which explain resistance, the way in which the audience actually makes sense of the programme is missed.

I want here to open up the terms of the debate about variation in interpretation by focusing on what audiences actually do. I would argue that what is needed at this point in audience studies is a more formalised theory of interpretation, and that recent developments in the field of linguistics might offer a framework for such a theory.

Audience interpretation within critical cultural studies has generally been understood in terms of a code model of communication. A code assumes a pre-agreed association between signal and message, an assumption which leaves the model open to questions about how such an argeement occurs and what monolithic notion of culture must be implied by such an agreement. This is particularly problematic in terms of the complex decoding activities and associations which are assumed in semiotic analyses, a critique of which can be found in Pateman (1983).

There have been various attempts to work round the rigid structure of signal/message association which the code model assumes by bringing in notions such as 'aberrant decodings' (Eco 1979) and 'oppositional' and 'negotiated' decodings (Hall 1973, 1980) in order to allow scope for variation in interpretation to be addressed. However, these concepts have been used in analyses which focus on how the results of the interpretation correlate with its assumed cause (i.e. the assertions of Bobo's 'wary' female viewers that the film of *The Color Purple* offers positive images of black women; the assertions of Morley's trades-union respondents that a feature on the *Nationwide* programme is right wing) and do not offer an adequate account of the process itself which would explain how these variations actually occur. This is caused in part by a lack of data in these studies which would provide evidence of the source of specific interpretations.

The inadequacies of the code model in providing a feasible description of what happens during the communication process are outlined by Sperber and Wilson (1986: 2–21), who go on to theorise an alternative, inferential model of communication. The significant feature of this model for audience studies is that it is premised on the assumption that communication is not explicable in terms of a meaning which inheres in a text, and as a result it leads to a focus on the process of interpretation rather than on textual meaning.

Briefly, the model of communication which Sperber and Wilson posit assumes that the features of a text are just one piece of evidence amongst many that an audience uses in producing an interpretation. Other pieces of evidence employed in the process include the audience's existing knowledge and assumptions the audience make about the intentions of the speaker. In interpreting a text the audience makes inferences (i.e. a series of logical deductions) based on a selection from the available evidence. The organising principle behind the selection is the 'relevance' of the evidence. (The concept of relevance is explored in Joanna Thornborrow's chapter on advertisements in this volume, and explained in depth in Sperber and Wilson (1986: Chapter 3).)

It is axiomatic to Sperber and Wilson's thesis that communication inevitably involves risk, and this becomes particularly apparent in the case of broadcast communication, where the evidence the audience draws on cannot provide verifiable proof that their interpretation is that which the speaker intends. This hazardous enterprise is exacerbated by the processes of mediation such as programme editing which make audience assumptions about 'intention' even more contingent. To speak of audience reception in general terms within this paradigm is therefore somewhat problematic. This is not to say that there are no constraints on what a text can mean at a given historical moment. Sperber and Wilson's theory is based on the assumption that the grammatical and semantic elements of a language are encoded in that they constitute a formally learned association between signal and message. However, the particular significance of their approach lies in their argument that these encoded features are used by an audience primarily as evidence, and are subservient to the inferencing process which all communication requires. Therefore, for example, the word *and* has an agreed (encoded) and finite range of meanings at a specific moment. However, the process which leads to the choice of which meaning will actually be taken by an audience is not a decoding action but an inferential one. It is at the level of this, usually non-conscious, choice that difference in evidence will lead to a difference in interpretation.

For example, in inferring the relevance of Lopez's remarks on virginity, the two groups in my study use distinct sets of assumptions as evidence. The evidence potentially available to the interviewees was made explicit in their responses to questions which focused on the groups' understanding of the term 'politics'. Their responses to the first and last question show that the members of Group 1 did not have, as part of their existing knowledge, the assumption articulated in varying ways by members of Group 2 that 'the personal is political'. Because of this, the two groups activate different sets of assumptions when asked to explain the relationships between Lopez's remarks on virginity and her remark that 'there are a number of things I want to struggle for'. L in Group 2 draws on her previously articulated assumptions about politics to infer that Lopez's growing awareness about the issue of virginity was 'part of a wider struggle'. In contrast, J in Group 1 infers that Lopez is indicating a difference in culture, intending to show 'what they think like in that country'. To produce this inference J draws on a separate set of assumptions, which in this instance appear to be based on the evidence of Lopez's nationality.

By drawing on relevance theory, it is possible to show how variation between interpretations of a media text can be traced to the existing assumptions held by the audience. Unlike audience studies which are primarily concerned to show how different social groups 'resist' or succumb to ideology, where this process is generally theorised without supporting evidence, a methodology based on Sperber and Wilson's inferential model of communication can make explicit the source of variation in interpretation.

By providing a systematised framework for exploring how a text can generate different meanings, the model makes it possible to unpack the relationship between the audience as a social entity and their understanding of a text in a way that the code model precludes. The data and methodology I describe above, which draw on the tenets of relevance theory, are an indication of how this relationship might be made explicit. Although space precludes a more detailed discussion, I hope that this account also indicates how ostensibly distinguishing demographic features such as education, gender or race, which are often used in audience studies, may be too broad a categorisation to draw out the most relevant distinctions between audience members. Clearly the restrictions of space also have required that the complexity of issues involved in my study have not been fully addressed here. However, my aim has been to show how, in allowing a focus on the audience's interpretative processes, not in terms of texual determination but rather in terms of the assumptions an audience makes, it is possible to begin to isolate what evidence an audience uses in the processes of understanding a text and to trace the source of this evidence in terms of the audience's cultural background.

How these audience assumptions are then theorised is a question which still has to be considered. One concept which may lend itself to this approach is that of 'discourse' in the sense of structured meaning. While this notion is often invoked in texual analyses as a way of accounting for the different meanings a text can contain, it has in the past made assumptions about audience behaviour which might, with an orientation towards audience studies, be explained more fully.

Christine Gledhill (1988) for example, in her analysis of how the conflicting discourses in the film Coma allow a feminist reading, cites a series of arguments which oppose empirical audience studies, stating that 'concern with the pleasure and identifications of actual audiences seem to ignore the long-term task of overthrowing dominant structures' (Gledhill 1988: 71). However, it could be argued that without access to data which would indicate whether actual audiences understand the film in the terms which discursive analysis proposes, the discovery of texual features is of limited value in terms of the achievement of this aim.

REFERENCES

Ang, I. (1989) 'Wanted: Audiences', in Seiter et al. (eds), pp. 96–115.
Bobo, J. (1988) 'The Color Purple: Black women as cultural readers', in Pribram (ed.), pp. 90–109.
Brunsdon, C. (1981) 'Crossroads: notes on a soap opera', Screen 22, 4: 32–7.
Brunsdon, C. and Morley, D. (1978) Everyday Television: Nationwide, London: British Film Institute.

Christie, C. (1993) 'Relevance theory and the analysis of audience response', PhD thesis, Strathclyde University.

Doane, M. A. (1988) The Desire to Desire: The woman's film in the 1940s, London: Macmillan.

Eco, U. (1979) The Role of the Reader: Explorations in the semiotics of text, Bloomington: Indiana University Press.

Gledhill, C. (1988) 'Pleasureable negotiations', in Pribram (ed.), pp. 65–89.

Hall, S. (1973) 'Encoding and decoding the TV message', CCCS pamphlet, University of Birmingham.

Hall, S. (1980) 'Encoding/decoding', in S. Hall, D. Hobson, A. Lowe, and P. Willis (eds) Culture, Media, Language, London: Hutchinson, pp. 128–38.

Jordin, M. and Brunt, R. (1988) 'Constituting the television audience: A problem of method', in P. Drummond and R. Patterson (eds) Television and its Audiences, London: British Film Institute, pp. 231–49.

Lapsley, R. and Westlake, M. (1988) Film Theory: An introduction, Manchester: Manchester University Press.

Moores, S. (1992) 'Texts, readers and contexts of readings', in P. Scannell, P. Schlesinger and C. Sparks (eds) Culture and Power: A media, culture and society reader, London: Sage, pp. 127–57.

Morley, D. (1980) The 'Nationwide' Audience: Structure and decoding, London: British Film Institute.

Morley, D. (1986) Family Television: Cultural power and domestic leisure, London: Comedia.

Morley, D. (1989) 'Changing paradigms in audience studies', in Seiter et al. (eds), pp. 16–42.

Parkin, F. (1973) Class Inequality and Political Order, London: Paladin.

Pateman, T. (1983) 'How is understanding an advertisement possible?', in H. Davis and P. Walton (eds) Language, Image, Media, Oxford: Blackwell, pp. 187–204.

Press, A. (1991) Women Watching Television: Gender, class and generation in the American television experience, Philadelphia: University of Pennsylvania Press.

Pribram, D. (ed.) (1988) Female Spectators: Looking at film and television, London: Verso.

Seiter, E., Borchers, H., Kreutzner, G. and Warth, E. M. (eds) (1989) Remote Control: Television, audiences and cultural power, London and New York: Routledge.

Sperber, D. and Wilson, D. (1986) Relevance: Communication and cogition, Cambridge MA: Harvard University Press and Oxford: Blackwell.

Tulloch, J. (1990) Television Drama: Agency, audience and myth, London: Routledge.

Willemen, P. (1978) 'Notes on subjectivity', Screen, 19, 1: 41–69.

Wren-Lewis, J. (1983) 'The encoding/decoding model: Criticisms and redevelopments for research on decoding', Media, Culture and Society, 5: 179–97.

Chapter 3

Freedom, Feeling and Dancing
Madonna's songs traverse girls' talk

Barbara Bradby

TALKING ABOUT TEXTS

In recent years there has been some convergence between literary criticism, with the trend known as 'the return of the reader' (Freund 1987), and communication studies, with the shift towards 'qualitative audience research' (Jensen and Jankowski 1991). Textual analysis, on the one hand, has moved towards a theory of meaning not as resident in the text, but as realised in the act of reading (Iser 1978). However, in developing theories of 'the implied reader' of a text, reader-response theory has always insisted on the separation of this implied reader from any real reader (Iser 1978: 36). The resulting paradox for those still committed to deducing the act of reading from a purely textual analysis has often been pointed out (Allen 1987), and has led to some imaginative attempts to operationalise reader-response theory by studying how actual readers come to understand a poem as a process through time (Benton *et al.* 1988).

Communication research, on the other hand, has long been concerned with actual readers, and centrally with the viewers of television. Dissatisfaction with the positivism of previous studies, whose attempts to measure the television audience as the aggregate of individual viewers had disregarded altogether the 'texts' of television, led to Morley's innovative, qualitative work, which used group discussion to explore the meanings taken by actual viewers from a BBC news magazine programme (1980). But despite the fact that his study followed the publication of a textual

This chapter is based on an article that appeared in *OneTwoThreeFour*, no. 10, Autumn 1990 (Los Angeles). The present version is substantially rewritten in order to accommodate a study of the popular music audience to the concerns of the present volume about 'readership'.

analysis of the same programme by Brunsdon and Morley (1978), there is curiously little connection to the conclusions of that analysis, which had emphasised the programme's appeal to its audience through the ideologies of family and domesticity. Some subsequent studies of television and its audience have integrated textual analysis more closely with audience analysis, notably Buckingham in his study of the BBC soap opera, *Eastenders* (1985), and Hodge and Tripp in their work on a children's cartoon (1986). In reviewing the new model of 'reception analysis', Jensen proposes a methodology that involves the 'comparative analysis of media discourses and audience discourses, whose results are interpreted with emphatic reference to context' (1991: 139; see also Christie, this volume).

In both areas, gender has emerged as a major factor in the study of readership. Feminist textual analysis has shown the neutrality of 'the reader' of reader-response criticism to be an illusory construct, obscuring masculine forms of address and posing difficulties for a reader who recognises herself as female (Fetterley 1978). And qualitative research with actual readers and viewers has been used to show how the meanings for women of popular forms such as romance and soap opera differ from their stereotyped trivialisation in mainstream criticism (Hobson 1982; Radway 1987). Other studies have compared the actual responses of women and men to short stories (Howard and Allen 1990) and poems (Mills 1992a and Ch. 1, this volume); or the different uses and meanings made of television (Morley 1986) and video (Gray 1987) by women and men.

The present study shares the concern of this recent work to investigate the relationship between the text and actual, gendered readers, in this case that between Madonna and the audience of pre-teen girls who brought her to fame in the mid-1980s. Earlier work on the 'implied' audience for rock music used the psychoanalytic model of film theory (Mulvey 1975, 1981) to show that rock positions the audience as male (Taylor and Laing 1979; Bradby and Torode 1984). Though some female groups have succeeded in implying a female audience through creating an internal audience within the vocal group and singing to each other about a male 'him', most female singers have continued to address an implied male audience by singing to a male 'you' (Bradby 1990). Textual analysis of Madonna's song, 'Material Girl', shows how she breaks with this tradition by positioning the male audience under her control as 'boys', and by implication, performing for other girls/women (Bradby 1992). Madonna's appeal to a female audience, then, must be set within this context of the predominant 'masculinisation' of the rock audience.

This contexualisation of Madonna's gendered address of the audience arises in part out of her own use of intertextual references to other forms of gendered address, such as Marilyn Monroe's appeal to the male gaze. However, it is not clear to me that Jensen's 'emphatic reference to context' is the way to proceed with respect to the social identities of actual audiences. Morley's television audience research has been criticised for reducing the understanding of groups interviewed to their social-class background (Jordin and Brunt 1988). This is to make an assumption which has by now been widely questioned, that language reflects social identity in a straightforward way. It is to assume that talk emanates from a preconstituted social subject (e.g. from a subject who *is* working class, middle class, male or female, black or white) rather than allowing the possibility that subjectivity is itself constituted in interaction.[1]

In a recent critique of such research, Buckingham (1991) shows how subjectivity, in relation to both race and gender, is *negotiated*, rather than pre-given or fixed, in interviews about television watching that he conducted with 8- to 11-year-old school children. He further argues that his own participation in the interviews must form part of the analysis: his presence, together with the school setting of the interviews, encouraged the children to produce 'adult' responses. For instance, they talked of the bad effects of television violence on (younger) children, produced sophisticated reasons for not believing television advertisements and criticised sexism in cartoons and racism in sitcom casting. These points can be applied to the study presented in this chapter, which can be seen as a *negotiation* between different feminine subjectivities within a group of 11-year-old girls; similarly, the role of the adult interviewer, and an assessment of what is being 'done' socially in the interview/conversation, form part of the analysis.

In approaching the issue of gender and readership through audience research into the meanings that pre-teen girls take from Madonna, this chapter argues that the social meanings of Madonna must be discovered in what her fans *do* with her work. It finds that, while the most visible resources being taken from Madonna are clothes styles, her song texts also enter into the talk of her fans and provide resources in a discourse that challenges the dominant view of female sexuality. It is this talk that actualises the meaning of the song texts in the social world, and it is in this sense that the fans can be said to be 'reading' Madonna.[2] However, Madonna herself is a complex 'text', very much in dialogue with the dominant view both of female sexuality and of herself. Her ambiguous appropriation of the image of the 'whore' at the visual level, lays her and her followers open to recuperation by the dominant discourse, in a reading that ignores the verbal text of the songs. This discourse of 'the tart' is used by some of the girls in the study to try to undermine both Madonna, and, at times, their *own* playful practices with Madonna's image.

Cowie and Lees (1981) were the first to point to the *discursive* character of the control exerted over female teenagers' behaviour, which centred in their London study around the notion of 'the slag'. This ubiquitous term was used in a quite irrational way by boys and girls, and while girls recognised its unfair application in particular cases, they did nothing in their talk to challenge the meaning of the term itself. It formed part of a discourse in which the opposite term was 'drag', the two terms being capable of labelling all female behaviour apart from safe subservience to a boyfriend or husband. The depressing nature of the analysis in Cowie and Lees, later expanded in a book by Lees (1986) entitled *Losing Out*, left no scope for change, with women being unwitting victims of a discourse they were helping to reproduce. The temptation was to reduce the 'slag/drag' discourse to a seemingly eternal structure of virgin and whore, instead of seeing how this structure is reproduced through local practices, which can themselves change.

The present study draws on Dorothy Smith (1988) in seeing the work that women do on their bodies as a crucial part of the construction of a discourse of femininity. This work is taken for granted in the texts (fashion magazines, pop songs, etc.), which mediate these local practices for women and in turn structure women's lives through working on the gap between image and desire. Presumably, then, making this work visible should also show possibilities for creative change at a local level. Smith herself argues that while the discourse of femininity 'co-ordinates' female consumers for the fashion industry, the fashion market cannot itself control the discourse. Hence the examples of discontinuities in fashion – 'Afro' hairstyles or punk's anti-fashion – appear as resistances to the dominant discourse of femininity, formed out of the local practices of women and mediated through texts (Smith 1988: 53).

What Smith does not explain is when a discontinuity with the dominant discourse becomes a different discourse, and from what standpoint something is to be judged as a 'resistance' or 'opposition' to 'femininity' (Mills 1992b). These are quite real questions that arise in looking at Madonna's ambiguous appropriations of dominant imagery. I would suggest that Smith's notion of women's 'work on the body' needs extending to encompass *talk*, which in practice is the main way in which such work is made social. The place to investigate the work women do in relation to texts of femininity, then, is in the local, social organisation of talk. It is here that we can expect to find a social 'reading' of Madonna, and can see how actual readers interpret the ambiguities of her texts through their everyday practices. However, before turning to such a study of pre-teen girls' talk about Madonna, I will look at some of the claims that have been made in feminist writing on Madonna.

MADONNA: THE IMAGE AND THE TEXT

Feminist criticism has had an awkward relationship with Madonna. Most feminists have been highly appeciative of her work, but it is also true that many of them write from a perspective that assumes that the reader (or even the author herself) needs some convincing. 'How I learned to stop worrying and love Madonna', ran the title of an article by Sheryl Garratt in 1986. Certainly, Suzanne Moore implies that British feminists have by now stopped worrying when she writes scathingly of 'a lifestyle feminism that involves little more than liking Madonna and reading the odd Virago novel' (*The Independent*, 26 March 1992). But even in 1991, the front-page flier for an American fan's piece in the British *Independent on Sunday* (21 July 1991) read 'Camille Paglia defends Madonna against the feminists'. The flier is misleading, since Paglia presents a recognisably feminist analysis of Madonna's videos, but the claim is not entirely without substance, since in the process, she attempts to distinguish herself from 'the old-guard establishment feminists who still loathe Madonna'.

Academic writing on Madonna has seen her as innovative largely in her use of *images*, and has concentrated overwhelmingly on her video work. A frequent argument has been that her novelty lies in the way she combines contradictory images: 'Madonna embodies and offers a solution to all the contradictions that bombard young women: a whore who's still a virgin, a wise woman who's still a naive little girl, an innocent who can bite forbidden fruit and remain untainted' (Garratt 1986: 13). Ann Kaplan (1987), in her analysis of the video for *Material Girl*, argues that Madonna highlights the contradiction between the narratives of the 'good girl' and the 'bad girl' of Hollywood construction. It is this process of self-conscious highlighting of the constructedness of female images by the male gaze that makes the video so radically ambiguous and 'postmodern'. Brown and Fiske (1987) argue more straightforwardly about the same video that Madonna is 'in control' of the images in a way that Monroe was not, and call it a feminist video.

Yet Kaplan rightly points out that this play with the showbiz images of virgin and whore does not step outside the framework of the patriarchal 'gaze'. Hence she is dubious as to whether *Material Girl* is a 'feminist' video, preferring to include Madonna in the catergory of a 'co-opted postmodernism' (Kaplan 1988). I have argued elsewhere that to analyse Madonna's videos simply as four-minute films is to miss the fundamental point that these images are themselves accompaniments to songs (Bradby 1992). The ubiquitous critical commentary that Madonna is a woman who is 'in control' is better substantiated by an analysis of the *song-text* of *Material Girl* which shows her using *maternal* language to control men/boys. On the career-breaking album on which this song was the first track, *Like a Virgin*, this 'maternal' discourse is combined with a strong 'virginal' discourse of sexual unavailability. It is this combination of the 'virgin mother' at the level of discourse that produces the 'strength' of Madonna, rather than an elaboration of some eternal strength of 'the whore', as Paglia claims to find in her reading of the videos.[3]

Earlier writing was more interested in Madonna's audience – the teenage and pre-teen girls who brought her to global fame in the mid-1980s. Both Williamson (1985) and Garratt (1986), for instance, insisted that to write off Madonna as just another 'sex symbol' is to fail to understand her massive appeal to young *girls*, which must start from the fact that Madonna is 'never a victim, never passive' (Williamson 1985: 47). As Garratt put it: 'girls knew that Madonna was in control. She always got what she wanted' (1986: 13). Beyond this, Williamson argued that what is special about Madonna is that 'she does in public what most girls do in private' (1985: 47). This is appealing in two ways: firstly, her performance embodies the relationship of her fans to herself as star, since 'she dances on stage as everyone has at some time danced in their own room, fantasising being on stage'; and secondly, 'her conscious, ebullient confidence in her sexual image, utterly unembarrassed . . . is the exact opposite of the sense of shame that poisons young girls' enjoyment of their own bodies from the moment they open a teenage magazine' (Williamson 1985: 47).

These authors were also confident that Madonna's image was attainable for young girls. It was 'easy to copy' because 'what Madonna gave was an attitude that could be bought off the peg at your local Top Shop' (Garratt 1986: 13). As Williamson put it, 'lipstick and lacy tights are available to us all' (1985: 47), claiming also that 'part of the style is the implication that hard work has gone into it'. Madonna's 'special something':

> is not her voice, her talent, her experience – but her energy, her will-power, her sexual confidence. At a time when there are pitifully few ways for anyone, especially a woman, to 'make it', these are qualities that every woman does or can have. (Williamson 1985: 47)

Some of these claims for Madonna as feminist role-model are borne out by the only study which does include some material from the fans themselves

(Fiske 1989). Drawing on comments from diverse sources (a discussion with two teenagers, fans' letters, an MTV documentary, a student essay), Fiske documents the feelings of self-assertion and independence that teenage girls get from Madonna, expressed often in terms of sexuality. For instance, Fiske quotes fans from an article in *Time* magazine (27 May 1985: 47): 'She's sexy, but she doesn't need men', and 'She gives us ideas. It's really women's lib, not being afraid of what guys think.' But he also documents the linguistic struggle that teenage girls experience in defending Madonna's independent sexuality against the patriarchal norms that define overt female sexuality as 'tarty'. He quotes 'Lucy, a 14-year-old fan', talking about a Madonna poster in 1985: 'She's tarty and seductive . . . but it looks alright when she does it, you know, what I mean, if anyone else did it it would look right tarty, a right tart you know, but with her it's OK, it's acceptable' (Fiske 1989: 98). Fiske comments here that 'Lucy can only find patriarchal words to describe Madonna's sexuality – "tarty" and "seductive" – but she struggles against the patriarchy inscribed in them' (1989: 98). He argues that Lucy's talk displays the tension experienced by adolescent girls between a positive view of their sexuality and the patriarchal view, 'that appears to be the only one offered by the available linguistic and symbolic systems' (1989: 98). Yet Lucy's talk contains no alternative to the dichotomy of 'tarty' and 'acceptable'. A fan's letter to a teenage magazine, which defends Madonna against the accusation that she is 'a slut and a tart', does, however, provide some small basis for an alternative discourse in arguing that 'she has a lot of courage just to be herself' (Fiske 1989: 99).

The next section will look specifically at whether Madonna was easy to copy for a group of pre-teen girls, who told stories of 'dressing-up as' Madonna at the age of ten. How they negotiated the dominant discourse of 'acceptable' femininity, both in their own practice, and in their feelings about Madonna, is an important part of their talk. But, while all the authors reviewed here emphasise Madonna's clothes and *appearance* as what is copied,[4] is this all that the 'star text' consists of? Or, we can ask, does the acquisition of Madonna's confidence imply using also the *verbal* resources that she provides, notably the texts of her songs? In the group interviewed, one girl does find positive language for Madonna which appears to escape the dominant discourse of 'the tart'. In the following section I go on to argue that this language is closely related to Madonna's own song texts.

'DRESS YOU UP IN MY LOVE': 10-YEAR-OLDS ENACT MADONNA

The study is based on an interview in Dublin in 1986 with five girls, then aged eleven years, conducted and transcribed by Mary O'Connell as part of an undergraduate research project in sociology (O'Connell 1987).[5] Since the interview took place in a home setting and the interviewer was the mother of one of the girls (though her daughter said little in the interview), the atmosphere is informal, and much of the time the girls appear to be talking to each other rather than to the interviewer. However, they are generally also talking *for* the interviewer, as adult audience, and it is easy for her to step in and redirect the conversation to herself. My own observation is that this happens when the girls' talk takes them over the boundary of girlhood into adulthood, and the interviewer is shocked/ amused by the display of 'adult' discourse by these girls she knows in everyday life. The interviewer's reactions are often along the lines of 'Did I hear you right?', but the effect of the interruption is to attempt, not always successfully, to re-impose the definition of them *as* 'girls' in relation to her.

There are several examples of this kind of interchange below – Helen's wearing of suspenders, Rhoda's use of her mother's hair dye, the painting on of 'beauty spots', Rhoda's wearing of her mother's jogging bra – but perhaps the most pervasive reaction that comes through is the interviewer's surprise that several of the girls are willing to call both Madonna and their own imitations of her 'tarty'. The interviewer's interest in this use of the 'tart' discourse by the girls has the effect (in retrospect unfortunate) of making it more difficult for the girl who opposes this view to gain her attention and hence that of the group. On one level, her reaction is that of any adult hearing pre-teen girls using language with adult, or at least adolescent, sexual connotations; on another level, it is more specific to the context, which is one of 11-year-olds talking about what they did when they were ten. For them, describing the way they looked *then* as 'tarty' is one way of showing to the adult and each other than they have 'grown up' in the intervening year. But it seems that for the mother who remembers how much they enjoyed dressing up as Madonna, the negative assessment of what was perceived as pleasurable fun at the time is in itself surprising.

In order to understand this better, it is necessary to see how the girls understood Madonna herself to have changed in the intervening year. The contentious point here was the release of the video for the single, 'Open Your Heart', from the *True Blue* album, in which Madonna first appeared in the black corset with conical bra cups which was still shocking adult viewers in 1991. The video plays with images of prostitution and sexual fantasy and the gap between innocence and experience, symbolised by the little boy at the peep-show, with whom Madonna runs away at the end. For the film critics, the video provides another twist to Madonna's play with the male 'gaze', so explicit in her early videos (Kaplan 1987: 157; Born 1992). But there is no doubt that the girls felt betrayed. For some, such as Sinead in the following extract, Madonna's appearance as a 'tart' in the 'Open Your Heart' video proved that she had been one all along, and invalidated previous fandom. Others find ingenious ways of preserving 'their' star in the face of this evidence, most interestingly by defining the video as *separate* from the song, the video being for the boys, while the song remained the girls' possession. In the process, Rhoda, Helen and Sinead all show in different ways that the experience of listening to the song is a separate one from that of viewing the video (Mary is the interviewer)[6]:

5807	RHODA:	doesn't care about her lady fans, because she's only showing off her body for the boys.
5808	MARY:	Cos this was done for the boys? 'Open Your Heart' was done for the boys?
5809	RHODA:	Yeah. Yeah. It wasn't done for the girls.
5810	SINEAD:	The so- the song's very good//but she just wrecks it//I think.
5811	RHODA:	/The song – the song's like is for the boys *and* girls/ /really horrible/
5812	HELEN:	But nobody likes the song any more since she done that video. Everybody, like in the *True Blue* video like 'Open Your Heart' was out *after* the *True Blue* tape, right, And on the *True Blue* tape everybody *loved* the song 'n all, but then when they found out the *video* they thought it was (.) stupid.

Rhoda here sees girls as *excluded* from the video (5809), which was directed at the male gaze, while the song *includes* the girls in its audience (5811). Sinead (5810) makes the separation in the rather extreme form of seeing the 'song' as an object quite separate from Madonna. Helen, with her chronological account (5812), shows how getting to know a song on the tape is a separate experience from watching the video, although the latter has the potential to affect the former. If these ideas on the separate existence of song and video have been slightly forced by the 'Open Your Heart' issue for these girls, they are nevertheless interesting as accounts of viewing and listening by fans of popular music.

The whole interview, then, is in some senses a flashback, a re-assessment of previous practices and desires in the light of the unfolding of the 'star text'. This unfolding interacts with the unfolding of the girls' own lives, and with the childhood social practice which involves 'doing' being your age by showing that you are different from your younger self. The interviewer is more interested in what it feels like to be a fan, and has to learn in the interchange with the girls that this experience is not eternal, but changes with the context both of the girls' own lives and that of their 'star'. The choice by some of the girls of the 'tart' discourse in order to distance themselves from Madonna and fandom last year seems to throw the interviewer off balance, perhaps in part because it involves an *adult* discourse of (anti-)female sexuality.

It is the girls themselves who, in the opening exchanges of the interview, structure the conversation as an argument about whether Madonna is 'tarty' or not. Sinead makes her first claim that Madonna is 'tarty' in response to the interviewer's opening question, which refers to a poster that she had pinned up on the wall for the purpose:

0101 MARY: Can you tell me first of all what you think generally of that poster?
0102 RHODA: She's sort of (.)
0103 SINEAD: I think tarty.
0104 HELEN: Yeah, I, eh, it's yeah, but that's the way she used to be you know, it's OK I mean it's good you feel . . .

Sinead tries to substantiate this claim many times in the interview, aided by the interviewer's interest in exploring this assessment of Madonna. Sinead is not entirely successful, however, until much farther on in the interview, when she succeeds in shifting the topic onto the video of 'Open Your Heart', which, we have seen, is condemned by all the group.

Helen, on the other hand, in the above sequence, with her disclaimer 'but' (0104), makes it clear that she is disagreeing with Sinead's condemnation, and, perhaps knowing that Sinead is prejudiced by Madonna's present (i.e. the 'Open Your Heart') image, invites her to look at 'the way she used to be'. She then gathers strength to say, 'It's OK, I mean it's good', while her final, unfinished, 'you feel . . .' demonstrates her identification with Madonna.

Throughout the interview, Sinead and Helen are the clearest exponents of these two positions, Sinead repeatedly accusing Madonna of being 'tarty', and Helen coming up with a variety of defences against the accusation. Two other participants, Rhoda and Dara, support sometimes one and sometimes the other, until Helen is finally isolated over the 'Open Your Heart' issue. The fifth girl, Ciara, is largely silent. A striking feature of the form taken by the conversation is the extent to which girls *collaborate* in building answers to questions, as do Rhoda and Sinead in the extract above, and in telling stories, as do Helen and Dara in the extract below (where their conversational collaboration mirrors their collaboration in the dressing-up incident being recalled). But this collaborative form clearly cannot be simply equated with a consensus view of relations within the female group.

It is after considerable discussion of whether Madonna's image is 'tarty' or not, that the interviewer asks the children whether any of them have ever dressed up as Madonna. Sinead immediately answers 'No', but the others all answer 'I did', and Helen gains the floor. She tells how she got Dara to help her dress up when they were on an Irish-language summer camp together:

2517	MARY:	What did you ever wear Helen? When you dressed up like her.
2601	HELEN:	I wore eh pink belly top with 'healthy' on it and I wore the her green mini skirt and eh pair of sparkly tights, you had, the green one//
2602	DARA:	/Oh yeah, and buckets of jewellery/
2603	HELEN:	An eh, and *a pair* and a pair of suspenders and oh it was awful, right? I was walking around you know like I had to walk around em and here's her: 'You can't see the suspenders', and here's me: 'What?'
2604	MARY:	What was she saying? 'You can't see the suspenders?'
2605	DARA:	'Cos you're supposed to be able to see the suspenders.
2606	HELEN:	The I had to go like this.
((laughter))		
2607	MARY:	What did you do? You pulled up the skirt?
2608	HELEN:	I put me hands in the pockets and went like *that*.
2609	MARY:	You pulled up your skirt//to show the suspenders? Oh. OK.
2610	HELEN:	/Yeah/

Despite her earlier defence of Madonna and her image, Helen clearly signals her own embarrassment during this dressing-up incident, with the words, 'it was awful, right' (2603). The precise reason for the embarrassment, though, is far from clear. 'I had to walk around' (2603) seems to indicate that Helen felt some compulsion to be on display, which was embarrassing in itself (i.e. the presence of strangers on the summer camp makes this scenario 'public' by comparison with the privacy of the home, even though we understand the setting as *interior*). But the continuation of her story indicates that embarrassment derived also from her failure to understand the point of what Dara was saying to her ('and here's me: "What?"' (2603)). The point seems to be, as O'Connell puts it, that the 'incorrect' placing of the suspenders meant that 'the extraordinary was about to collapse into the ordinary' (O'Connell 1987: B15), that is for a correct Madonna look, the suspenders needed to be in the extraordinary position on top of the skirt, not in the ordinary position under it. A third source of embarrassment is then revealed as Helen re-enacts her pulling up of her mini-skirt in order to show the suspenders underneath (2606–10).

Helen has made her point and gained the attention of the group, but at the expense of proving the *opposite* of her claim at the opening of the interview that 'it's good you feel . . .' (0104). We should note also that Helen has gained the group's attention by gaining the adult interviewer's attention. She shifts from addressing Dara as 'you' to referring to her as 'her', and so implicitly addressing the adult interviewer, who takes over a more teacher-like role, eliciting clearer explanations from the child, and reformulating her point at 2609.

In the sequence of conversation that follows, O'Connell's analysis shows how Sinead re-asserts her claim to dominance in the group, from which she had been excluded by her negative answer in response to the dressing-up question. She effectively 'tops' Helen's story by telling one that is even more 'extraordinary', first because the setting is a 'disco', rather than the childish one of a summer-camp, and second because it is about a *boy* who dressed up as Madonna (O'Connell 1987: B16). Her conclusion that 'he looked ridiculous' however, while confirming her disdain for the image and for attempts to imitate it, is interesting in that she does not use the word 'tarty' in referring to the dressed-up boy. This is like Helen's later opposition of the word 'stupid' to the other's assessment of Madonna as 'tarty' in the 'Open Your Heart' video. 'Ridiculous' and 'stupid' are negative assessments, but they do not work through a negative *sexual* assessment, as does 'tarty'.

Soon after this, Sinead finds a means of re-entering the group of dressers-up from which she had earlier excluded herself. Helen has introduced the topic of Madonna's beauty spot, and after a few exchanges, the interviewer links this back to the topic of dressing-up:

```
2714  MARY:    Did you put on a beauty spot when you dressed up as her?
2801  SINEAD:  Yeah.
2802  RHODA:   We all do when we dress up like//
2803  MARY:    /You all put on the beauty spot/
```

While Sinead can be interpreted as replying on Dara's behalf here, she clearly abandons her distance from the topic of dressing-up, and Rhoda's inclusive 'we all do' (2802) gives Sinead permission to come back into the group (O'Connell 1987: B17). This is confirmed in the subsequent exchange:

```
2805  MARY:    And what's your first reaction when you look in the mirror?
2806  SINEAD:  Oh my God!
2807  DARA:    Oh my God, tar-ty.
2808  SINEAD:  Oh my God.
2809  CIARA:   Oh I'm not goin out like this.
2810  RHODA:   Oh no the hair's not right//
2811  SINEAD:  I'm puttin on a coat.
```

Sinead's three turns here, in conjunction with the collaborations by Dara
and Ciara, show how her re-entry to the group of dressers-up is quickly put
to work on behalf of her opening claim that Madonna is 'tarty'. The
contributions of these three girls here clearly show the public/private
dichotomy acting as a spatial constraint on their behaviour. The
collaborative meaning conveyed is that to go outside looking like this
would be to look 'tarty'. It is as if the girl's look in the mirror merges into
that of the disapproving society outside. Her positioning in front of the
mirror forces her to enter as *subject* into the dominant discourse of female
sexuality, and there is no way she can see herself as *object* as anything but
'tarty'.

Rhoda's contribution, on the other hand ('Oh no the hair's not right'
(2810)), introduces a different explanation for not liking the image in the
mirror, and is in fact the preface for her own story. She launches into this
directly after the above exchanges, only to be checked by the astonished
disapproval of the interviewer (2813):

2812   RHODA: A bit more blondy so you run into the bathroom rob your mam's
                blond dye and you go WRRR and put it all over your head.
                Then you go out. Good. Now I look like her.
2813   MARY: Have you done that?
2814   RHODA: No I haven't done it//
2815   SINEAD: /People would/
2816   RHODA: I would yeah, but if I was goin to a fancy dress.

Here the interviewer's role as adult and mother intrudes into Rhoda's
evocation of the girls' world ('rob your mam's blond dye'), as she expresses
her shock at the idea of a young girl using hair dye. Rhoda is pulled up
short by this as she realises she is in fact in the adult world, which exercises
power over the girls' one, and she immediately retracts her statement
(2814). Sinead's slightly patronising intervention ('People would') is an
adult-type remark which succeeds in supporting Rhoda while allowing the
speaker to distance herself from such childish behaviour. It is this that
allows Rhoda to face up to the interviewer's disapproval and contradict her
retraction (2816), first by repeating Sinead's 'would', and introducing the
hypothetical situation of a 'fancy dress', and then, affirming 'I *did*',
continuing with the real story:

2901   RHODA: I, I *did* for em for for goin to to the Guides and dressed up. I *did*
                blond me hair and I *got* I got it all out//cos it was only the *fake*
                one, y'know.
2902   MARY: /Did you? OK/
2903   RHODA: And I went up to the Brigins[7] and I got a big bow round me
                hair as well and I got me brother's *blazer* on black blazer and
                then made this belly top outa me mam's ((laugh)) bra, for
                running ye know that// ((laugh))

2904	MARY:	Outa your mam's what?

2905 RHODA: Ye know the the em the kind they're they're these like they're the *image* of belly tops now and they're for runnin a race if the ladies//

2906 MARY: Ah right like a jogging bra.

2907 RHODA: Yeah and I worn them and I wrote 'healthy' all over them ((laugh)). She killed me.[8] And then I got these pair of tights on and this real really short skirt. Well it was well like this but it was up like that ((hoists skirt)) all the way up ((laugh)) and then I got me mam's tights on and I cut all holes in them and then I stuck *ouva* I stuck ouva pocket a big cross that I got for me communion ye see and then and then I was just padded the skirt and I put this belt around it and it was me brother's Pisces belt right? And it had a big huge Pisces sign on it and I just put it around me and I was walking up to the Brigins (.) horrible, Guides I mean, and I was walkin up the road and creak creak, creak creak, creak creak and all the noise it was really *horrible*.

2908 MARY: How did you feel when you looked in the mirror though before you went out in the outfit?

2909 RHODA: Well you see I was lookin in the mirror and I felt really awful cos I didn't want to get on me brother's bike cos I didn't want to go on me brother's bike so I was just walking up the road or in the mirror an I was just lookin at myself and saying 'Right Rhoda now you've to go up to the Guides right, walk like this', so I had to walk out all//

2910 MARY: /Did you feel you looked like her, Rhoda?/

2911 RHODA: Well (.) I (.) felt I did just around here ((gestures from the shoulder down)) but the hair, no way, no way. It was too short.

Rhoda's final turn here (2911) sums up the story as 'proving' her initial claim that 'the hair's not right' (2810), despite all the intervening work in the bathroom with Mam's blond dye which had warranted saying 'Good. Now I look like her' (2812). Once again, as in Helen's story, we can analyse Rhoda's embarrassment ('it was really *horrible*' (2907), 'I felt really awful' (2909)) into different components. Firstly, there is a simple point about going out like this *in public*, found in the twice-mentioned 'walking up' ('to the Brigins'/'the road') juxtaposed with the exclamation 'horrible' (2907). But secondly, there is the worsening of the experience through not looking right, which in this case centres on the hair. Paradoxically, Rhoda is happy to say her hair looked 'like her' in the (private) bathroom (2812), but not when generalising about the whole (public) experience (2911). And thirdly, we find the identical phrase used by Helen to indicate a social compulsion ('I had to walk' (2909)), which in Rhoda's case is very interestingly developed as a contradiction within her self, a compulsion imposed, as it were, by the 'other' in the mirror on herself, 'Rhoda'.

Of course to dwell solely on these negative aspects is to miss out on a lot of the fun of the story, which is definitely present in the cumulative elaboration of additional elements of the look. But, as in the instance of the hair, which forms the preface and conclusion to the story, the intervening fun and pleasure of working to get the look right all take place in the *home*. As soon as Rhoda starts to anticipate the *street* walk up to the Guides, her only feeling is of embarrassment. We should add that, despite the embarrassment and the disapproval of her mother, Rhoda *did* follow through with the act in public, and hence can experience the pleasure of being the most successful story-teller in the group.

Following Rhoda's long story, Helen picks up on the point about the hair and explains how she does hers. But she still does not feel she can ever really look like Madonna:

> 3104   HELEN: I feel like kind of that me *hair* is like her but me face you know me *face* isn't but then the rest of me *is* kind of y'know. I just feel in me me face cos you can never get your *face* the same as hers.

Helen seems happy to accept the interviewer's gloss on this feeling as one of being 'disappointed', but Dara rejects this in favour of the labels 'stupid' (3107) and 'tarty' (3110):

> 3105   MARY: And do you be disappointed?
> 3106   HELEN: Yeah sometimes.
> 3107   DARA: I always used to be trying to dress up as being like y'know not even at d- not even at discos or fancy dress 'n lookin back on it y'know I was dead stupid y'know. But em,
> 3108   MARY: Why was it dead stupid?
> 3109   SINEAD: Your own image.
> 3110   DARA: Well I dunno. You're just trying to be something you're *not*. You're trying to be something you're *not*. An lookin back on it now when I wo- I wore lipstick and everything I just looked tarty y'know.

Dara is here supported by Sinead in collaborative talk, and herself supports Sinead's proponence of the 'tarty' assessment, whereas previously she had collaborated with Helen.

After this, Helen intervenes with another dressing-up story about going to school dressed up and incurring a male teacher's wrath ('Mr B. gave *out stink*' (3111)), but the interviewer returns the topic to Dara's last statement for clarification, expressing disbelief of Dara's claim that she thought she looked 'tarty' at the time. The interviewer's intervention does have the effect of isolating and so perhaps exaggerating the importance of the 'tarty' discourse in Dara's talk, and in that of the group as a whole:

> 3204   MARY: When you dres- when you *used* to wear make-up and dress up like her and looked in the mirror. What was your *first* thing? Was your *first* thing tarty?
> 3205   DARA: Well not *then*. I used to think 'Oh that's OK'. But then I used to think, 'Oh that's a pretty poor imitation of Madonna' and *then//*

3206 MARY: /Why would you think it's a pretty poor imitation of her?/
3207 DARA: Because I wasn't able to do it properly. I didn't have the clothes.
                  Y'know cos you'd need money to go out and buy the lace and
                  everything.

Here, Dara admits that thinking she looked 'tarty' is only a retrospective assessment of her attempts at dressing up, and was not felt at the time. By describing what she in fact felt 'then', she may think that she will still be able to maintain her use of the 'tart' discourse in the present, as a more sophisticated explanation of why she felt 'stupid' at the time. But the interviewer effectively blocks this option, by giving credence only to her explanation as of last year. The effect of the interviewer's intervention, then, has been to put Dara back into the category of 'girl', and to disqualify her from the adult/adolescent age category that she has tried to enter with the 'tart' discourse. Dara, of course, then cleverly turns this back on the adult, by detailing her lack of money and clothes.

In commenting on these stories, O'Connell notes her own surprise at the vulnerability to social disapproval shown by the girls. Her reading follows Cowie and Lees (1981) in showing how the fear of being called a 'tart' or of 'looking tarty' acts as a form of social control over the girls. Such disapproval can come from outsiders (parents, teachers) or from insiders in the group (O'Connell 1987: B26).

While broadly agreeing with this interpretation, I would argue that it does overlook differences and contradictions within the group, both those between individual girls, and differences in opinion that have developed over time. The clearest conflict is that between Sinead and Helen, as outlined above. But the clarity of these two girls' arguments when talking abstractly about Madonna's 'image' is blurred when they get to talk about their own experiences of imitating it. Helen's general opposition to the view that Madonna is 'tarty' is on the surface contradicted by her own embarrassment when she dressed up, although one can argue that the embarrassment derives mainly from the 'incorrect' wearing of the garments. And Sinead's anxiety to prove that Madonna is 'tarty' is almost undermined when she admits that she has tried to imitate her in the past. Dara admits that 'at the time' she thought she looked 'OK' dressed as Madonna, and that it is only looking back that she sees the image as 'stupid' or 'tarty'. Rhoda's elaborate account of her own experience appears to move from a simple dislike of appearing *in public* looking like Madonna, to a more complex dislike based on the feeling that she had not got the look quite 'right'. Her account of her instructions to herself in the mirror indicates an awareness of *self*-contradiction around the experience too.

It should also be said that the very telling of the stories represents an act of defiance against the social disapproval that the girls are so clearly cognisant of, and that this defiance is a source of pleasure and of prestige within the group. But at the end of the day, the girls' stories do demonstrate that Madonna is not as 'easy to copy' as Williamson and Garratt imply. Madonna may look 'utterly unembarrassed', but this is hardly the way her fans feel. There is clearly 'something missing', which means that in dressing up as Madonna, the girls are open to construction by the currently dominant discourses of female sexuality. I would suggest that part of the problem the girls encounter is that in 'dressing up' as Madonna, they are materially imitating only one part of her act: what is missing is the language and music of her songs. In Madonna's own performances, it is these *lyrics* that make her image a powerful one (Bradby 1992). Given that direct musical imitation, or verbal quotation of lyrics is not generally an appropriate resource in conversation, we must look for indirect ways in which knowledge of lyrics may be displayed, and their 'power' demonstrated through appropriation.[9] The next section therefore looks for any evidence in the girls' talk that such appropriation does take place.

FREEING THE IMAGE: WHEN SONGS BECOME TALK

In returning to the interview, it is worth observing that since the conversation is rather dominated by the voice of Sinead arguing that Madonna is 'tarty', it follows that what positive meanings the girls are able to find in Madonna are constructed as defences against this attack. Sinead's conservatism is a fairly secure position within the group, not least because of the way in which it attracts the interviewer's attention, and it is Helen who shows far more ingenuity in inventing defences for Madonna. To show how Helen elaborates her alternative, we turn back to the opening minutes of the interview, where both Sinead and Helen attempt to prove their claims, which were as follows:

0101 MARY: Can you tell me first of all what you think generally of that poster?
0102 RHODA: She's sort of . . .
0103 SINEAD: I think tarty.
0104 HELEN: Yeah, I, eh, it's yeah, but that's the way she used to be you know, it's OK I mean it's good you feel . . .

In the argument that follows these opening shots, Sinead attempts to prove her claim by saying that Madonna is 'posing' for the poster, but the others collaborate in arguing back that the poster shows Madonna 'just dancing', in concert during the tour to promote her second album, *Like a Virgin*.

After a few minutes, these positions are entrenched (0312–13) and Helen succeeds in shifting the topic onto Madonna's clothes (0403):

0312 HELEN: She looks like she's just dancin.
0313 SINEAD: I just think she's just posin there em cos there's no lights behind her//and there usually is in a big concert.
0314 RHODA: /Yeah cos, yeah cos/
0315 MARY: Well do you *like* the poster anyway?
0401 S H D R: Yeah.
0402 DARA: She's good.
0403 HELEN: I think the clothes she's wearin are nice.
0404 MARY: Tell us about her clothes so Helen. What do you think about her clothes? What do you like about them?
0405 HELEN: Em – I like the way – they just kind of you know eh it's as if that you know she wasn't planning, I know she *was* planning to put those clothes on but you know, it's as if that she just mixed them all up and you know just decided to put on anything you know and then that *feels* nice you know and can dance around in them and feel kind of real not tight up you like you know something like a tight skirt or something you know.

Here (0405) Helen cleverly concedes her awareness that Madonna's unplanned look is in fact planned, while defending her against the charge of 'posing' by counterposing the values of 'feeling nice' and 'dancing'. The merging of her identity with that of Madonna is shown clearly as she moves from using the subject 'she' ('decided'), through the impersonal 'that' ('feels nice') to the subjectless 'can dance' whose continuation '(can) feel' is then related subjectively to 'you'.

Soon after this, the interviewer asks about Madonna's use of lace, and Helen speaks in a neutral way about Madonna's 'showing off' her body. Gradually this builds up into a *defence* of the idea of 'showing off' one's body, against the predominant view that this indicates 'tarty' behaviour:

0811 HELEN: I think it looks lovely on her//the white lace.
0812 RHODA: /Ordinary people/
0813 HELEN: I don't think the black looks very nice now but the white does.
0814 RHODA: Ordinary people who are getting married they they don't use lace at all they just use it on their hands for gloves or somethin but she uses it//she's usin it for everything.
0901 SINEAD: /She uses it on her *legs*/
0902 HELEN: She's usin' it to show off her legs or somethin//
0903 MARY: /Why is she so interested in showing off her body and her legs and that?/
0904 DARA: Cos she used to be a page three girl.
0905 SINEAD: Cos mainly it's an image like like so so that she'll get a lot of boys likin' her//and not mainly for her music but for her . . .
0906 HELEN: /Yeah I'd say that it feels nice y'know it feels good you know/

However Helen's use of 'nice' and 'good' is here interrupted by a challenge from Sinead, who takes her as meaning 'comfortable':

0907	SINEAD:	Yeah but it'd hurt ye it'd be all itchy.
0908	CIARA:	It scrapes your skin it does.
0909	HELEN:	Like I mean when the bellytops or somethin' you know it'd be nice y'know
0910	SINEAD:	or sort of
0911	HELEN:	like it makes her feel kind of real kind of *free* or somethin you know.

Helen's two replies to Sinead and Ciara here are very interesting. Her first reply (0909) backtracks from talking about lace to talking about 'bellytops', which would be a more obvious candidate for feeling 'nice', in the challengers' sense of 'comfortable'. But then in her second attempt (0911), and after two uses of 'kind of', Helen emphatically reaches the word 'free', as if she had been groping for it for a while. If this is then compared with Helen's first statement on Madonna's clothes (see above, 0405), it will be seen that this word 'free' represents the completion of a phrase that was there incomplete. In that first statement, 'and feel kind of real (0405)' was abandoned as a positive evaluation of what the clothes feel like, in favour of a negative one telling us what it is *not* ('not tight up you'). But here (0911) Helen completes this as 'it makes her feel kind of real kind of *free*.'[10]

Where the words 'feel nice' and 'feel good' had failed to clinch the argument, Helen's triumphant 'feel . . . *free*' seems to have an authority that shakes off the opposition, and the topic is closed. Now, as applied to clothes, 'nice', 'good', and 'free' could all be aspects of the comfort of a feel. But Helen does not talk just about 'it' (i.e. the *clothes*) feeling 'free' here, but about 'it' making 'her' feel free. And as applied to a *girl*, 'nice', 'good' and 'free' have very different implications. Specifically, for a girl to be 'nice' and 'good' makes her into a 'drag', the conventional antithesis of her being a 'bad girl', 'whore', or in these girls' discourse, 'tarty'. Helen here finds a word with positive connotations, part of whose meaning here seems to be that Madonna is 'free' from these conventional sexual evaluations. But if we ask where this word comes from, it is striking that Helen has here completed not just her own utterance, but also the first line of the chorus of Madonna's best-selling song 'Into the Groove': 'Only when I'm dancin' do I feel this free'. Helen's 'defence' built up in these opening minutes of this interview/conversation can indeed be seen to be very closely based on the three key words of this line: dancing, feel(s), and free. What she is doing, it seems, in the argument with her friends, is to put these words to work in order to demonstrate Madonna's 'freedom' from their social control via the label 'tarty'.

The song itself gives a rather specific meaning to the word 'free', as freedom from a spectator's gaze ('Tonight I lock the door where no-one else can see'), merging into an idea of being free from inhibitions. It seems to exclude any idea of feeling 'free' as connoting *passive* sexual availability. In fact, the song constructs dancing as a form of sexual pursuit for the girl, whereby she can make the boy hers:

> Live out your fantasy here with me
> Just let the music set you free
> Touch my body, we can move in time
> Now I know you're mine.

The singer is clearly in control of who sees into her room, and when anyone enters, they do so because she wants them to, and on her terms. The boy is ordered, in the opening lines, which form a principal, repeated refrain throughout the song: 'Get into the groove boy, you've gotta prove your love to me'.

The sense of 'freedom' articulated in this song from the singer's point of view, therefore, is a very positive one. It starts out from a base position of independence, not as a futile 'defiance', but as a position from which the singer is literally 'in command' of her own body, and her own sexual choices. From the feminist point of view, the notions of dancing, feeling and freedom in this song seem to have liberatory potential, particularly when put against the predominant pessimism about pop lyrics orientated towards a female audience (Goddard *et al.* 1977; Frith and McRobbie 1979). And Helen's use of these notions as resources in this conversation can be seen more generally as confirmation that the meanings circulated in the song are being taken up by listeners and put to work to change relationships in their own worlds.[11]

A second incident where Helen appears to use Madonna's lyrics in constructing a defence for her occurs when Sinead and Rhoda together accuse Madonna of being jealous of other women. This is in response to a request from the interviewer to decide whether Madonna is 'a nice person or a good person or a bad person':

3802   SINEAD: *I've heard that* I've heard that she she's very jealous if like like like if they're getting more (.)//attention than her.
3803   MARY: /What would you decide overall?/
3804   SINEAD: I'd I'd say she's a nice person but I wouldn't like to live with her for too long//like live in a flat with her.
3805   RHODA: /No/
3806   RHODA: Say she *has* a friend and sh- they go off for this boy and she thinks he's really *generous* and macho and is very kind an all that she'd get really jealous of her friend//and she wouldn't talk to her friend.
3807   HELEN: No what she'd do is she'd get the fella to go after *her* and not// she, she wouldn't.
3808   MARY: /Would girls do that?/

Rhoda's hypothetical 'story' at 3806 elaborates Sinead's claim of jealousy (3802) along stereotypical lines. However, we should note that the desirable qualities attributed to the boy, particularly the emphasis on generosity, seem to come from the girls' own culture, so that Rhoda's story may well be illustrating a problem within the girls' world. Helen's interruption of Rhoda at 3807 with an alternative ending for her 'story' is therefore very striking, as it uses this hypothetical 'Madonna' to provide a different solution to this everyday problem of rivalry: rather than being silenced by petty jealousy, Madonna would 'get the fella to go after *her*'. But in providing this alternative ending, Helen is following very closely the words of the last two lines of the song 'Material Girl', which there also give the 'story' a different ending (see Bradby 1992):

> Experience has made me rich
> And now they're after me.

Once again we find Helen struggling to formulate an alternative against the predominant consensus. She does not, for instance, gain the floor here, but is interrupted by the interviewer at 3808, who returns it to Rhoda.[12] And once again, we find that her formulation is close to the letter as well as the spirit of a best-selling Madonna song.

On a third occasion, Helen also uses an idea from these same two lines, this time to re-interpret Madonna's relationship with her father. This is during an explicit discussion of the song 'Material Girl', which, predictably, Sinead has interpreted as making Madonna into a 'prostitute', very much along the lines of the analyses by Garratt (1986) and Kaplan (1987):

> 4808 SINEAD: In that song (?) type of like making out that she's a prostitute. That she wants the money. Not love like.

Helen has tried various lines of defence, and eventually comes up with the idea that Madonna is 'just making fun outa money' in this song (5304, 5306). Rhoda elaborates on this theme (5307), and brings in Madonna's father (5401):

> 5307 RHODA: In the Virgin Tour when she's just singin 'I'm a material girl'. Now at the end she says 'Do you think I'm a material girl? Well I'm not!'
> 5308 SINEAD: 'Well you are wrong!'
> 5309 HELEN: An she starts takin off her pearls and her//lace gloves.
> 5310 SINEAD: /She doesn't throw them into the audience though/
> 5401 RHODA: An her dad, her dad pretends, her *pretend* dad comes out//
> 5402 ?: /No that's her *real* dad/
> 5403 RHODA: Oh is it? Well, whoever it is, he, he says 'you come in here *now* Madonna'. An she says// 'But Daddy, I'm having a good *time*'.
> 5404 ?: /'But Daddy, I'm having a good *time*'/
> 5405 MARY: What do you think that's saying?

5406 DARA: I'm having a great time doing a strip.
5407 SINEAD: That, that, that her father thinks she's a bold girl for doin it
               and then like she's bein real innocent like.
5408 ?:   But her dad
5409 HELEN: But her father must be real *proud* of her like. For making, for
               being rich like that. Her father must be real proud of her.

Helen makes her re-interpretation at 5409 *against* the conventional
accusations that Madonna is both a 'bad girl' and that she 'plays the
innocent' (5406, 5407). She has prepared the ground for it by getting the
others to acknowledge that Madonna both *is* rich and is carefree about
riches. But the sense of Helen's intervention in the argument at this
stage is to reverse the power relation of father over daughter. He can
no longer just be seen as someone with the authority to stop her doing
what she is doing, since he must also acknowledge her success and
her wealth. And the precise words used by Helen seem to refer us
back to the lines from 'Material Girl' quoted above, since she stops
short of saying 'for making (money)' and instead says 'for being rich like
that', where 'like that' seems to refer to the scene in 'Material Girl' that
was being discussed.

In these three instances, Helen has apparently used Madonna's verbal
discourse in working out a defence for her against the conventional
accusation that she is 'tarty' or 'a prostitute'. In this way, it is possible
to see the *text* of the songs as a resource that can *empower* girls in the
hard linguistic struggle against the social control of their sexuality. We
could say that Madonna's songs 'traverse' Helen's talk, in the sense that
the lyrics both enter into it and cross her speech, enabling a crucial
rewriting of the script of sexual identity. As mentioned above, research
on girls' perceptions of the sexual labelling process ('slags or drags') has
tended to see girls as *silenced* by the labels.[13] Helen's talk shows that
Madonna's own determination to keep singing and acting in the face of
criticism and censorship is not just an individual stand. Her imitators not
only dress up in her clothing, with all the contradictions that ensue
for them, but are able to use her language as a much more versatile
resource. Clearly these pre-teen girls have not 'solved the contradiction
between the virgin and the whore' for all time. But there are ways in
which they seem to be freeing themselves from this dichotomy, and in
this process, talk is crucial. Without the talk, the images can be interpreted
along the same old lines. And if Madonna's lyrics help shape that talk
at crucial points, then it is also important that they can no longer be
ignored in favour of a concentration on her more obviously 'exciting' visual
images.

TEXTS, TALK AND SEXUAL/SOCIAL CHANGE

So if we return to Dorothy Smith's notion of a discourse as linking people socially who do not know each other, mediating their relationship via texts, then popular music does appear to work like this. There is much to link the talk of these pre-adolescent girls in Ireland, for instance, with that of the teenagers quoted by Fiske, not least the attempts in both to articulate publicly an opposition to the discourse of the 'tart'. The two sets of interviews also contain remarkably similar opinions about Madonna's marriage to Sean Penn, and about the 'real meaning' of 'Material Girl' as put about by Madonna herself. Both of these were topics featured in teenage magazines at the time, but the way in which the children work with the texts is in relation to their own preoccupations about whether boys should control girls, etc. It is in this sense that their talk is 'mediated' by texts.

Helen's addition of the discourse of 'dancing' and 'feeling free' from 'Into the Groove' gives substance to the discourse of sexual confidence in relation to men evident in the teenage fans quoted in Fiske (1989: 98ff.) As a *women's* discourse, the notions of dancing, freedom and social/sexual change have of course been linked in the past: but Isadora Duncan and Irene Castle are remote and obscure antecedents for young girls.[14] In the era of 'rock music' from the 1950s to the 1970s, dancing, freedom and the rhetoric of social/sexual change had arguably been appropriated by men (in forms which vary from the narcissistic to the chauvinistic) and women's dancing had been constrained by the framework of the 'male gaze'. Undoubtedly, the television serial *Fame* and the film *Flashdance* put female narcissism on the map in the early 1980s, and were important antecedents for Madonna, girls in the 1980s relating to this newly emerging cult of the female body (McRobbie 1984). But this narcissism allowed to girls was legitimated only through the puritanical cult of hard work with which it was always combined, in sharp contrast to the dissolute hedonism of male rock narcissism.

In the interview analysed here, this discourse of freedom and dancing is recognisably a female one, mediated in Helen's talk by Madonna's song texts. As a discourse of 'anti-feminine self-reliance' (Mills 1992b), it must struggle against the very entrenched position of the dominant discourse of acceptable femininity bounded by the notion of the 'tart'. One could argue that both these discourses are 'texually mediated', the discourse of 'the tart' presumably being more widespread textually, but in relation to *Madonna*, being noticeably more present as a reflexive point of reference in her videos than in her songs. To ignore the song texts then, does seem to lead to a potentially more conservative position, then, or to one that is simply voluntaristic, as in Paglia's claim that acting the whore gives women strength.

The point here is not to be textually 'true to' Madonna, but to show what resources need to be used in explaining how today's teenage girls, or some of them at any rate, have moved on from the ideology of romance that seemed so eternal to commentators in the 1970s. Having lived through the 1980s as the mother of a teenage girl, I was aware at the time of the use being made of Madonna lyrics in the anti-school culture (e.g. walking past a teacher singing, 'Like a virgin, touched for the very first time', with the word 'fucked' being quietly substituted for 'touched'), and at the same time, the quite serious talk of 'using boys' that came into the conversations of these girls, as a way of exploring their sexuality outside of the ideology of love and romance. My own feeling, as some sort of participant observer of that 1980s teenage experience, is that Madonna has been an important source of empowerment for that discourse of independent sexuality. Of course the discourse of 'tarts' and 'whores' is all around waiting to pounce. But there is more awareness of its irrationality, more rage at its injustice, than seems to be evident in the earlier studies on the topic.

Despite the dominance of Sinead's discourse of 'the tart' in the interview analysed here, there is abundant evidence of the confidence these young girls derived from Madonna, both in their practices of 'dressing up' and in the later recounting of the stories. I have tried to show the rather complex way in which the girls' desire to gain the interviewer's attention by appearing 'grown up' interacts with her need to reject them as equals in sexual knowledge and re-affirm their status as 'girls' in the interview situation. It is this interaction that serves to highlight the 'tart' discourse, with its corollary of 'acceptable femininity', and to obscure Helen's more original and feminist discourse. While interested in the 'tart' discourse, the interviewer does not herself seem convinced that it is consistent with the pleasure and excitement that the girls derived 'at the time' from dressing up as Madonna.

The study confirms the usefulness of seeing the reading of a text as inscribed in local, social practices, and particularly in talk. The text itself is not arbitrary or irrelevant to this reading, but turns out to have a close relationship with the talk which defends and identifies with Madonna. The difficulty with Madonna is that her own 'texts' work on different levels, the visual level often being in apparent conflict with the verbal/ musical level. And at the visual level, her ambiguous collusion with, or appropriation of, dominant patriarchal imagery opens the possibility for a reading such as Sinead's, which follows many media texts in trying to recuperate Madonna for the patriarchal discourse of the 'tart'. But the study also shows clearly that there is no one female readership position. Both feminine and anti-feminine positions are available to and are used by the girls. The difficulty involved in sustaining the view of Madonna as 'tart' in relation to the girls' own stories of dressing-up, however, results in shifts and contradictions in the girls' speech.

What emerges as important from this study of the reading of a star text by her fans is not just the existence of 'contradictions' within and between the girls' discourses, but the way in which local practices and local talk feed into a global 'text' like Madonna, so forming a new 'cat's cradle' (Smith 1988) of social/textual relationships, a new discourse of female sexual independence. That this new discourse exists in competition with the old ones of 'acceptable' femininity and romance is a commonplace of much 'textual' analysis of what Madonna has done with the verbal and visual representation of women. To see that competition being worked out in the everyday practices and talk of pre-teen girls, however, is to see discursive change from a different angle, a different textuality that shows both the possibilities and the difficulties in social/sexual change.

NOTES

1. Here Althusser's theory of 'interpellation' is useful, but does not go far enough (1971). His theory indeed implies that language precedes the subject, rather than the subject being constituted prior to language. But it does not of itself allow us to move on to a recognition that subjectivity is itself more of a 'process' than a fixed 'position', that process being part of the process of social interaction: we recognise ourselves in relation to other selves, not just in relation to ideologies (see also Mills, this volume).

2. At this point the present article parts company with much of the work on 'fandom' in the recent collection edited by Lewis (1992), which concentrates on fandom as fantasy and abandons any notion of making meaning of particular texts. Even Jenkins' article on *Star Trek* fans (1992) is only about 'readings' of that text in the sense of creating stories and songs which go far beyond the original, particularly where female fans invent emotional lives for the characters, etc. In the present case the relationship between text and its 'reading' is both less self-conscious and more direct.

3. Paglia writes, 'I am radically pro-pornography and pro-prostitution. Hence I perceive Madonna's strutting sexual exhibitionism not as cheapness or triviality but as the full, florid expression of the whore's ancient rule over men' (*Independent on Sunday*, 27 January 1991: 4).

4. This is in line with recent academic work on the relationship of women fans to women film stars of the 1930s, 1940s, and 1950s, which also stresses clothing as

the material practice through which women emulate a visual image. See especially Herzog and Gaines (1991), but also Stacey (1991).

5. O'Connell gave me a copy of the transcript and permission to do further work on it and publish my own analysis. She declined my offer of working together on the transcript and should not be held responsible for any of the errors or shortcomings of the present paper.

6. In the extracts from O'Connell's transcript (1987A) quoted in this paper, '(.)' indicates a pause, '//' indicates an interruption of the current turn by the following one, '/words/' indicates that these words interrupt the previous turn, '((words))' indicates that the enclosed words describe gestures etc. of the speakers, and '(?)' indicates that the material in parentheses cannot be transcribed. Conversational turns are numbered as *abxy*, where *ab* indicates the transcript page number, and *xy* indicates the number of the turn in the order in which they are transcribed.

7. The Brigins is the younger version of the Girl Guides in Ireland, the equivalent of the Brownies in Britain. Given the way age categories emerge as important in the dynamics of this interview, it is interesting that Rhoda's talk displays confusion as to whether she is in the pre-teen or the teenage category of this state-run youth service.

8. The use of the verb 'kill' in this sense is common in working-class Hiberno-English, perhaps more usually as the parent–child threat, 'I'll *kill* you (if you do that).'

9. See Simon Frith's (1988) article, 'Why do songs have words?', for a review of the literature on pop/rock lyrics, including the issue of whether audiences listen to them or not. The rather literal research of the 1960s in the United States, which declared lyrics irrelevant to enjoyment of rock music on the grounds that memory recall of particular lyrics was bad, has given way in the 1980s to approaches to meaning in popular song influenced by semiotics and psychoanalysis, in which textual/musical analysis has been important (Taylor and Laing 1979; Bradby and Torode 1984; Bradby 1990).

10. Looking further back, to the opening exchanges of the interview, we see that Helen's first attempt at a defence (0104) also ended with an incomplete 'you feel . . .'. This 'you feel . . .' is actually repeated again at 0106, but Sinead has by then diverted the topic, and Helen is drawn into discussion about the details of the poster again. The present 'feel . . . free' can then be seen also as a completion of these incomplete opening statements about how Helen herself ('you') feels.

11. We could also note that Williamson's opinion that Madonna 'dances on stage as everyone has at some time danced in their own room, fantasising being on stage' seems closely related to the lyrics of this song (1985: 47).

12. Once again, we can note how the interviewer ignores Helen's more feminist intervention, and at 3808 addresses *Rhoda* again, expressing disbelief that 'girls' would get 'jealous'. The effect is to challenge Rhoda and Sinead's right to use the adult, sexual discourse of 'jealousy', and so try to re-impose the boundary between 'girls' and adults again, but in doing so she herself draws attention to the less than feminist discourse of these girls, and leaves Helen's more feminist ending unvalorised.

13. Girls, too, seem to see themselves as silenced by boys' labels. This is poignantly illustrated in the following quotation from an Irish study:

> They're all dirty fucks the fellas here. I'd like to be able to talk to them, have jokes and all but you can't. . . . You feel like roaring crying to yourself sometimes. . . . They have all kinds of names for us, brazzers and whores and rides and prostitutes. But we've no names for them. (Sweetman 1979: 21–2)

However, we can note that the girl quoted does in fact name the 'fellas' as 'dirty fucks', so belying her claim to linguistic impotence.

14. Susan Cook's work on the dancer Irene Castle (1991), popular in the United States in the first two decades of this century, shows how then, too, the promotion of dancing as a social activity for women was linked to the promotion of less restrictive fashions in clothing and hairstyles, and how Irene herself came to symbolise a series of 'modern' sexual freedoms for women.

REFERENCES

Allen, R. C. (1989) 'Reader-oriented criticism and television', in R. C. Allen, *Channels of Discourse*, London: Routledge, pp. 74–113.

Althusser, L. (1971) 'Ideology and ideological state apparatuses', in *Lenin and Philosophy*, London: New Left Books, pp. 121–73.

Benton, M., Teasey, J., Bell, R. and Hurst, K. (1988). *Young Readers Responding to Poems*, London: Routledge.

Born, G. (1992) 'Women, music, politics, difference: Susan McClary's *Feminine Endings: Music, gender and sexuality*', *Women: A cultural review*, 3, 1: 79–86.

Bradby, B. (1990) 'Do-talk and don't-talk: The division of the subject in girl-group music', in S. Frith and A. Goodwin (eds), *On Record: A rock and pop reader*, New York: Pantheon; London: Routledge, pp. 341–68.

Bradby, B. (1992) 'Like a virgin-mother: Materialism and maternalism in the songs of Madonna', *Cultural Studies*, 6, 1: 73–96.

Bradby, B. and Torode, B. (1984) 'Pity Peggy Sue', *Popular Music*, 4: 183–206.

Brown, M. E. and Fiske, J. (1987) 'Romancing the rock: Romance and representation in popular music videos', *OneTwoThreeFour*, 5: 61–73.

Brunsdon, C. and Morley, D. (1978) *Everyday Television: Nationwide*, London: British Film Institute.

Buckingham, D. (1985) *Public Secrets: Eastenders and its audience*, London: British Film Institute.

Buckingham, D. (1991) 'What are words worth: Interpreting children's talk about television', *Cultural Studies*, 5, 2: 228–45.

Cook, S. (1991) 'The career and times of Irene Castle: Revolutions in music and manners', *World Beat: An International Journal of Popular Music*, 1:34–44.

Cowie, C. and Lees, S. (1981) 'Slags or drags', *Feminist Review*, 9 (Autumn): 17–31.

Fetterley, J. (1978) *The Resisting Reader: A feminist approach to American fiction*, Bloomington: Indiana University Press.

Fiske, J. (1989) *Reading the Popular*, London: Unwin Hyman.

Freund, E. (1987) *The Return of the Reader: Reader-response criticism*, London: Methuen.

Frith, S. (1988) 'Why do songs have words?', in S. Frith (ed.) *Music For Pleasure: Essays in the sociology of pop*, Oxford: Polity, pp. 105–28.

Frith, S. and McRobbie, A. (1979) 'Rock and sexuality', *Screen Education*, 29: 3–19.

Garratt, S. (1986) 'How I learned to stop worrying and love Madonna', *Women's Review*, 5 (March): 12–13.

Goddard, T., Pollock, J. and Fudger, M. (1977) 'Popular music', in J. King and M. Stott (eds) *Is This Your Life? Images of women in the media*, London: Virago, pp. 143–59.

Gray, A. (1987) 'Behind closed doors: Video recorders in the home', in H. Baehr and

G. Dyer (eds) Boxed in: Women and television, London: Pandora, pp. 38–54.

Herzog, C. C. and Gaines, J. M. (1991) '"Puffed sleeves before tea-time": Joan Crawford, Adrian and women audiences', in C. Gledhill (ed.) Stardom: Industry of desire, London: Routledge, pp. 74–96.

Hobson, D. (1982) Crossroads: The drama of a soap opera, London: Methuen.

Hodge, B. and Tripp, D. (1986) Children and Television: A semiotic approach, Cambridge: Polity.

Howard, J. and Allen, C. (1990) 'The gendered context of reading', Gender and Society, 4, 4: 534–52.

Iser, W. (1978) The Act of Reading, London: Routledge & Kegan Paul.

Jenkins, H. (1992) '"Strangers no more, we sing": Filking and the social construction of the science fiction fan community', in L. A. Lewis (ed.) The Adoring Audience: Fan culture and popular media, London: Routledge, pp. 208–36.

Jensen, K. B. (1991) 'Reception analysis: Mass communication as the social production of meaning', in K. B. Jensen and N. Jankowski (eds) A Handbook of Qualitative Methodologies for Mass Communication Research, London: Routledge, pp. 135–48.

Jensen, K. B. and Jankowski, N. (1991) A Handbook of Qualitative Methodolgies for Mass Communication Research, London: Routledge.

Jordin, M. and Brunt, R. (1988) 'Constituting the television audience: A problem of method', in P. Drummond and R. Patterson (eds) Television and its Audiences, London: British Film Institute, pp. 231–49.

Kaplan, E. A. (1987) Rocking around the Clock: Music, television, postmodernism and consumer culture, London: Methuen.

Kaplan, E. A. (1988) 'Feminism/Oedipus/postmodernism: The case of MTV', in E. A. Kaplan (ed.) Postmodernism and its Discontents, London: Verso, pp. 30–44.

Lees, S. (1986) Losing Out: Sexuality and adolescent girls, London: Hutchinson.

Lewis, L. A. (ed.) (1992) The Adoring Audience: Fan culture and popular media, London: Routledge.

McRobbie, A. (1984) 'Dance and social fantasy', in A. McRobbie and M. Nava, Gender and Generation, London: Macmillan, pp. 130–61.

Mills, S. (1992a) 'Knowing y/our place: Marxist feminist contextualized stylistics analysis', in M. Toolan (ed.) Language, Text and Context: Essays in stylistics, London: Routledge, pp. 182–208.

Mills, S. (1992b) 'Negotiating discourses of femininity', Journal of Gender Studies, 3, 3: 271–85.

Morley, D. (1980) The 'Nationwide' Audience: Structure and decoding, London: British Film Institute.

Morley, D. (1986) Family Television: Cultural power and domestic leisure, London: Comedia.

Mulvey, L. (1975) 'Visual pleasure and narrative cinema', Screen, 16, 3: 6–18.

Mulvey, L. (1981) 'Afterthoughts on "visual pleasure and narrative cinema"', Framework, 15–16: 12–15.

O'Connell, M. (1987) 'Ordinary girls unpack Madonna's extraordinary gloss', (A = interview transcript, B = analysis), unpublished project, Department of Sociology, Trinity College, Dublin.

Radway, J. (1987) Reading the Romance: Women, patriarchy and popular literature, London: Verso (first published 1984).

Smith, D. (1988) 'Femininity as discourse', in L. Roman, E. Christian-Smith and K. Ellsworth (eds) Becoming Feminine: The politics of popular culture, London and New York: Falmer, pp. 37–59.

Stacey, J. (1991) 'Feminine fascinations: Forms of identification in star–audience relations', in C. Gledhill (ed.) *Stardom: Industry of desire*, London: Routledge, pp. 141–63.

Sweetman, R. (1979) *On Our Backs*, London: Pan.

Taylor, J. and Laing, D. (1979) 'Disco–pleasure–discourse', *Screen Education*, 31 (Summer): 43–8.

Williamson, J. (1985) 'The making of a material girl', *New Socialist*, (October): 46–7.

Part II

Linguistic Readings

Chapter 4

Motherhood and the Surrogate Reader
Race, gender and interpretation

Zoe Wicomb

Africa is Woman. This cry of the early colonial poets galloping through the land echoes warmly in the chants of the poets of the New South Africa as they sing their praise songs to Mama Afrika. Woman as Mama remains a metonym for Africa; protean woman, who once also served the colonial project, has been refashioned to serve the national liberation movement. For the imagined community of the nation (see Anderson 1983) with its reliance on 'tradition', woman as mother, whose reproductive and nurturing powers are foregrounded, is a revered symbol of survival. It is her body that is written as a map: its rivers and plains and peaks, source of life and sustenance, landmarks and boundaries of the early colonial struggle, are also discursively drawn in the struggle over reproductive control.

It will come as no surprise that advertising, taking its cue from both high and popular culture, should promote the feminisation of Africa and the role of black woman as mother. A current full page advertisement for maize (a traditional staple supplanted by western processed food) found in a number of newspapers and magazines, has the following bold print:

I am woman.
I am the nation.
I am the maize generation.

Reference to motherhood, the reproduction of the maize generation and women's role in maintaining tradition, are inferences promoted through the parallel structure of the sentences. The false equivalence can of course be seen in the absence of an article in the first sentence, where woman is a self-declared abstraction, a notion as imaginary as that of nation. The accompanying updated image of motherhood is that of a sleek young

99

woman with processed hair rather than the 'traditional' turbaned Mama. For all its reference to tradition, the advertisement cannot succeed without reshaping the image of motherhood, itself a tradition in need of constant re-invention.

In one issue of *True Love*, a popular black South African magazine, eleven advertisements for food products address the reader directly as a mother who is responsible for the physical well-being of husband and children. With such reliance on the reproductive function of woman, the advertising of contraception or birth control would seem to pose a problem. The following study of a family planning advertisement in *True Love* focuses on the contradictions inherent in the magazine's construction of womanhood and on the ways in which the reader/viewer is directed towards drawing these contradictions into a particular ideological reading.

To argue that an advertisement for family planning genders the reader and directs her/him towards a specific position in the text is perhaps a tautological claim. But my analysis aims to show how the text, produced and consumed in the specific political context of South Africa, strategically inscribes a gendered subject. The contradiction inherent in the concept of revered Mama/subordinate woman, demands a flexible negotiation of her position in the text. Whilst the advertisement positions woman as mother, it must at the same time discourage her from being a mother; whilst it addresses woman as subject of the text, she is simultaneously subjected to a hidden male addressee. The text does not construct a fixed subject position for the reader; instead, conflicting interests demand that a male reader be stealthily inscribed in a text ostensibly addressed to a female, thus reproducing male control over reproduction and maintaining the unequal gender relations that prevail in society. In a culture where references to sexual relations often invoke 'traditional' differences, advertising must be careful not to offend patriarchy in its re-invention of womanhood.

Criticism of advertising, typified by Judith Williamson's influential *Decoding Advertisements*, generally focuses on the ways in which they produce and reproduce the dominant values of capitalism and shape our behaviour in accordance with a consumer society. I do not depart from such criticism, but in order to uncover the complex negotiation between contradictory positions of real and surrogate readers, I rely on the following analytical approaches:

1. A pragmatic analysis that explores the role of inferencing in the production of meaning.
2. A foregrounding of the relationship between image and text, and an exploration of linguistic categories as a model for analysing the image.

3. An acknowledgement that the particular medium of the magazine provides a local context for the generation of meaning.

The advertisement in question addresses itself to a female reader who is apparently able to make decisions about her own reproduction. My analysis, however, hopes to show how the gendered reader constructed by the text is necessarily unstable. Such a reader is crucially aware of another reading over her shoulder: she sees herself and her understanding of the text in relation to and dependent upon another's understanding, a male to whom the text is not directly addressed but whose role as surrogate reader is crucial to the female's production of meaning. These unstable positions intersect in a variety of discourses, most notably the common discourses of race, nation and tradition. My analysis will uncover the inscription of race in the text and show how at the intersection of race and gender a particular reading is generated. White magazines do not carry advertisements for family planning; studying the textual strategy of gendering alone would therefore be inadequate since the target group is not only women but specifically black women. Where population development advertisements do occur in white newspapers, women are addressed as responsible members of a new democratic nation whose duty it is to educate the less fortunate about family planning. Significantly this advertisement dispenses with imagery and relies for its visual impact on upper-case typography alone. Its slogan, 'Helping Women to Help Themselves', culled from feminist discourse, neatly outlines the difference between the racially coded categories of those who have too many children and those who can offer advice to their poor, ignorant and fecund sisters.

PRAGMATIC ANALYSIS

Pragmatics is concerned with language in use and so studies meaning from a functional perspective. The following exchange:

A: It's the phone.
B: I'm in the bath.
A: OK.

is a textbook example of how the meaningfulness of a text does not always rely on its grammatical structure. A reader, drawing from her knowledge of the world, must contextualise the situation in order to make sense of the exchange. Aspects of meaning that are not grammatically encoded and which semantics cannot account for are thus dealt with pragmatically through the process of inferencing (see Thornborrow, and Christie, this volume).

Speech-act theory, developed by Austin and Searle (Levinson 1983: Ch.5), a pragmatic area of enquiry that considers language as a form of action since it constitutes performatives such as declaring, promising, asserting, etc., offers a useful theoretical tool. It allows for a distinction between sentence meaning and utterance meaning which may diverge precisely because an utterance takes place within a particular context which in turn influences its particular illocutionary force.[1] Thus the sentence, *I am cold*, could in a certain context have the perlocutionary effect[2] of a window being shut by the addressee.

Advertising which has the unambiguous intention of selling a product and thus affecting the behaviour of the reader readily lends itself to a pragmatic reading in which the relationship between meaning and context is foregrounded. Such a reading is concerned with the implicatures[3] and presuppositions drawn from cultural knowledge; an utterance will be connected to its context by a bridging assumption.[4] But, as Fairclough notes in his critique of mainstream pragmatics, the application of speech-act theory or Gricean implicature often results in a 'Utopian image of verbal interaction which is in stark contrast with the image of critical language study of a sociolinguistic order moulded in social struggles and riven with inequalities of power' (Fairclough 1989: 10).

In this chapter I try to extend the application of pragmatics from its usual single utterances or short exchanges to include extended discourse and its participation in ideology. Pragmatic or context-based analysis of an advertising text is thus used to show how revised images of race and gender relations, promoted in popular magazines like *True Love*, remain uncommitted to radical change. Unequal social relations are produced through discursive formations which I investigate using Michel Pêcheux's theory of the grammatical inscription of ideology (Pêcheux 1982). My analysis relies on Pêcheux's notion of 'interdiscourse' by which a subject's multiplicity of relations (which destabilises the very concept of gendering the reader) can be seen to be determined by the complex of existing discourses. Through a linguistic analysis I hope to uncover the interdiscourse by which flexible subject positions are inscribed for readers. A scripto-visual analysis ought to show how the contradiction in the notion of womanhood is also visually constructed and how the relationship between image and text generates further meanings that reproduce the conflicting interests of male and female.

SCRIPTO-VISUAL ANALYSIS: MEANING AT THE INTERSECTION OF IMAGE AND TEXT

Although linguistic analysis of advertisements is a much needed departure from semiotic or content analysis, such replacement of focus would amount to a denial of the material reality of advertisements – the fact that they constitute both image and text. Saussure's suggestion that language could be used as a paradigm for the study of all sign systems has led to the widespread use of terms such as 'photo-grammar' or 'visual syntax'. However, critics neglect to explain what precisely such terms might mean. Gillian Dyer's *Advertising as Communication* (1982) simply lists twenty or more rhetorical figures with examples of advertisements explaining the difficult Greek names. How this taxonomy could help us towards the meaning of an advertisement is left unexplained.

Image–text readings generally rely on Roland Barthes' influential 'Rhetoric of the image', in which he gives a semiotic account of scripto-visual relations in a Panzani advertisement (Barthes 1977). The analysis focuses on the distinction between denotation and connotation or literal and ideological meaning. The text, according to Barthes, performs the function of anchoring the image which is polysemous, that is, it fixes 'the floating chain of signifiers in such a way as to counter the terror of uncertain signs' (Barthes 1977: 39). Barthes' account of the production of meaning is thus a one-sided operation of text on image, with no cross-readings that allow for an image to influence the reading of a text. Nor are relations of contradiction between the two, as found in many advertisements, discussed.

Judith Williamson draws from structuralist and post-structuralist theory to explain ideological meanings in advertisements. The role of the reader in the production of meaning is foregrounded; the 'referent system' ensures that things already mean to us 'and we give this meaning to the product, on the basis of an irrational mental leap invited by the form of the advertisement' (Williamson 1978: 43). The reader is positioned in such a way that a cognitive leap is the only means of making sense of an advertisement. The example used – the unidentified face of Catherine Deneuve behind bottles of perfume – demands that we as readers make the link between the two units: that to be beautiful we must use Chanel perfume. In the process we are constituted as female subjects. But Williamson does not reflect on the cognitive process by which women are constituted as subjects, nor does she take into account the context in which such advertisements are read. No information is therefore given on where the advertisements were found. That the process of inferencing is not considered crucial is evident from the way she refers to the cognitive activity as irrational.

A pragmatic reading of advertisements is outlined by Trevor Pateman, who uses an example of a fine-art image transposed to the context of advertising (Pateman 1983). He cites a still-life depicting apples, wine bottle, pheasant, cheese, etc. reproduced as an advertising image with the word 'Stilton' added outside the frame and so shows that meaning is contextual rather than structural. In other words, the meaning of the fine-art image changes when the topic/comment structure, or the relationship between the elements of the image (cheese and the rest of the still-life), changes. Denotation, Pateman claims, is therefore not simply given or obvious; it is accessible only through considering the context: 'In other words, the changes in context effect a structural reorganisation of the operative meaning (the operative semantics) of what is (in some sense) 'the same image'. . . The determinations of meaning are here contextual (pragmatic) rather than structural' (Pateman 1983: 195).

Pateman does not go on to explain what kind of comment is being made on the topic, nor does he take into account that the advertisement could be read by someone who has no recourse to meaning through altered context. He also disregards the ideological implications of producing meaning. A pragmatic reading is surely also available to those who know nothing of still-life as a painting genre. A process of inferencing would nevertheless be triggered off by seeing the cheese in the category of attractively arranged comestibles, whether in terms of a painterly quality or a still-life photograph. The aestheticisation of the objects need not be assigned to a prior genre. Relevance of the other objects will be assumed on the basis of a hyponymic relationship with the cheese, read as a component of the beauty and wholesomeness of the group. Those who know nothing of classy food will infer that Stilton goes with apples, wine, pheasant, etc. and absorb such information about the 'correct' accompaniments to consuming it as prescribed by the dominant culture. The reader's cognitive activity is thus a prerequisite for the ideological function: such advertisements can be read as recipes where the foregrounded product is only the chief ingredient, the rest of the items being essential to achieving the beauty of the dish. This didactic nature of advertising offered as cultural information is usually overlooked by those who argue for its function of providing information about available goods.

Pateman's argument against Barthes' denotation/connotation distinction is a welcome departure from the semiotic approach which dominates analysis of advertisements. Whilst the argument against denotation is not convincing, his critique of connotation for relying on what he calls the 'Dictionary Fallacy' (Pateman 1983: 204) is suggestive. This 'dictionary' assumes the pre-existence of connotations so that all meaning is seen to lie *in* the text or image. Such a view, he points out, cannot accommodate new connotations; nor does it recognise the activity of inferring meaning or the cognitive activity of working out the kind of connotation which is appropriate in a particular context. Pateman accepts that connotations may be valid in semantically conventionalised examples as in roses connoting romance, but even then the conventionalisation 'shortens the inferential circuit but does not eliminate it' (Pateman 1983: 204). Instead, he argues that the theory of relevance (Sperber and Wilson 1986), which assumes an intention to communicate and therefore guarantees relevance, will allow the viewer to work out the relevance of the topic to the comment (see Christie, this volume).

Whilst relevance is useful, a single way of reading images is not feasible; images cannot always be read in terms of topic and comment. Many sophisticated advertisements make no reference to the topic; instead they refer self-reflexively to previous images used in the campaign. The topic is deliberately suppressed in order to insist on a negotiation of meaning between the visual and linguistic information.

Victor Burgin uses the term 'scripto-visual' in his discussion of a photograph which he says is 'invaded by language in the very moment it is looked at', so that it 'prompts a complex of exchanges between the visual and verbal registers' (Burgin 1983: 232). His analysis foregrounds ideological meanings that exploit the 'popular pre-conscious' and the 'pre-text',[5] concepts not unrelated to presupposition. But Burgin's reliance on semiology in his discussion of specific advertisements, does not allow for the role of pragmatic inferencing in the construction of meaning. Whilst the 'pre-text' does refer to that which already exists as common cultural knowledge, such knowledge is simply a given entity which the manifest text is somehow tacked on to in the 'pre-conscious'. This process takes place in the act of looking, which is where Burgin locates the production of meaning.

What seems to be neglected is an examination of the nature of exchanges between the visual and verbal information. Cross-readings or pragmatic negotiation between image and text – as is also required in the reading of image–text artworks – involve secondary inferential processes which are unavoidable when making sense of contradictory meanings generated by the two media (see Pearce, this volume). Each provides a context for the other from which inferences can be made. The various accounts of the image as a visual *language* remain metaphorical and offer little help in understanding it. It is the case that many viewers, unconsoled by the fact that they themselves construct meaning in the act of looking, remain baffled by most contemporary images and prefer to avert their eyes. What follows is an attempt to explore the metaphor and develop a pragmatic way of reading an image.

Pragmatics of the image

A semiotic reading of the image, based on the code model[6] of communication, has limitations precisely because, as in the case of language, not all aspects of the image are in fact coded (see Christie, this volume). Since I hope to argue a case for the pragmatics of an image, it is useful first of all to determine which of its aspects are stable and coded like a grammar.

A distinction between meaning and syntax, as in Noam Chomsky's example of *Colourless green ideas sleep furiously*, could be applied to a photograph in which the following system of rules exists independently of its meaning:

1. The imposition of a frame on spatial continuity provides its basic form, just as a syntagmatic arrangement of words forms the sentence.
2. Three-dimensionality is encoded in the two-dimensional presentation of a photograph.

The reproduced example by the Dutch photographer, Jan Dibbets (Figure 4.1), can on one level be seen as an analogue to Chomsky's sentence. In terms of the above elements, we read it as a well-formed image but the structural qualities do not help us to make sense of it; instead, the reader is spatially disorientated. In terms of denotation there is no correspondence between the image and something in the world. We see part of a room with a square on the wall that does not make sense. In order to understand the image I will test the use of pragmatic categories like inferential procedures and speech-act theory.

The art-photograph, just as a commercial image, exists within a context, and as such can be studied from a functional perspective. An image viewed as goal-orientated behaviour will generate meaning which we can infer from a context, and in that context a viewer interacts with the image. In advertising, the image sets out to persuade the reader to buy a product; in the context of an art gallery the Dibbets image demands that the reader makes sense of it by visualising an original rhomboid shape drawn on the

Figure 4.1 Jan Dibbets' photograph, 1987

wall by the artist to compensate for perspectival distortion that would produce a square in the photograph. The linguistic distinction between sentence meaning and utterance meaning could be applied. The image on the wall without a viewer is one of spatial distortion (natural meaning), but interaction with it demands the application of certain maxims orientated towards behaviour (Gricean non-natural meaning).[7]

All photographs need the participation of a reader who must scale up or reduce in scale an image according to her knowledge of the world. Similarly, tonality in black-and-white photographs must be translated into colour by a reader; colour photographs, too, are only approximations of colour in the world. The composition of an image is also dependent on focus (total, middle-distance, near, etc.) from which the reader infers relative importance of the elements. Thus pragmatic methods for deriving meaning from an image will be used where the viewer contextualises the scene of the image.

In terms of Gricean implicatures (Levinson 1983: Ch. 3) we can speak of Dibbets' flouting of the maxim of quality since the space is falsely represented. But a bridging assumption, that in fulfilling its function as art the image questions the primary function of the photograph to represent from a single point of view, restores a co-operative principle (see notes 3 and 4). We are able to work out how the distortion occurred. More economically, Sperber and Wilson's relevance theory, which assumes an intention to communicate and therefore a guarantee of relevance, suggests that the art viewer will calculate how the image has been distorted and infer the relevance of such spatial disorientation. Similarly, Austin's speech-act theory can usefully be applied to determine how an image attempts to modify our behaviour. Instead of accepting the point of view which Dibbets offers, we recognise its separation of two different sorts of illusion: three-dimensional space of the room and two-dimensional space of the square. We are directed to imagine the shape that has been drawn on the wall but since this proves impossible from the viewing position offered by the photograph, another cognitive response to the 'illocutionary force' is mobilised. We attempt to step into the (illusory) three-dimensional space to assume a new point of view which will accommodate the shape as square.

Such pragmatic analysis of the art-photograph could be applied to an advertising image where the wider context of the total advertisement as persuasive device is clear. As I later show in my reading of the family planning advertisement, the text constitutes an immediate context for the image and *vice versa*. Our interpretation of an image will thus intersect with that of the text to allow for a proliferation of meaning beyond the potential of any one of the media.

MAGAZINE AS CONTEXT

Meaning is also produced by a reader who participates in the wider context in which the advertisement is consumed – the magazine in which it is found. Kathy Myers in 'Understanding advertisers' comments on the way in which magazines promote advertising messages: 'A quantifiable benefit to advertisers is that magazines provide a hospitable environment for the digestion and assimilation of advertised information' (Myers 1983: 205). Such environments are created by articles and features that provide an inferential pool from which readers draw presuppositions to make sense of an advertising text.

Collusion between magazines and advertisers occurs in a number of ways. In the issue of *True Love* which carries the text for analysis, the following examples can be seen to support the message of the advertisement. Articles on successful businesswomen listed in the contents page as 'People in Focus' or the feature in this edition 'on the first black woman nursery owner' listed under Gardening, activate the suppressed message in the family planning advertisement: that fewer children mean economic success, which is the first requirement of the New Bourgeois Black who is regularly promoted in the magazine. Another example is an article on a new morning-after pill, developed in France, that comes out strongly in condemnation of abortion, a view arrived at via a survey. Interviews with 'responsible' women who are also public figures explain why such a pill is unsuitable for the black community. Whilst pointing out the hazards of a new drug, the majority favour state-controlled contraception as opposed to the lack of responsibility amongst individuals which the pill is said to promote. In terms of women as nation, the foregrounding of France as a foreign country is significant: South African women, with their national culture of collective action, stand opposed to foreign practices and products that target the individual.

That the cover of this issue of *True Love* offers '16 pages of Mother Love' whilst at the same time advertising family planning, is, of course, not contradictory. What is of interest is the discursive formation of the entire magazine by which its subtitle, *For the woman who loves life*, and the very notion of motherhood as used in the advertisement as well as in supportive articles, becomes defined in economic terms. What remains suppressed in this incubation of meanings is the role of the state in determining such meanings or the function of such meanings in resisting social change.

Supportive readings also rely on other advertisements which demonstrate how marketing practices address certain target groups. Advertisements for food products in this issue of *True Love* as well as in other popular magazines like *Pace* and *Tribute* offer an example. Food is routinely presented as the concern of mothers. African women, interpellated in the text as Mama, are urged to prepare or serve the product, more often for their husbands and male offspring. It is suggested that the product, with its emphasis on health and growth, ensures the maintenance and reproduction of the species. But far from contradicting the advertisement for family planning, such emphasis on female responsibility for nurturing and reproducing is crucial for the presuppositions on which population control is founded. My analysis of the family planning advertisement will consider in detail the contradiction offered by a lengthy feature in the same issue of *True Love* on forced contraception in the workplace.

A further context on which inferences rely is the wider one of power relations in South Africa. The very growth of black magazines, funded by white financiers at the time of the demise of apartheid, demands scrutiny. A look at the magazines of the month – *Pace*, *True Love*, *Drum* and especially the glossy *Tribute* – shows only too clearly their function in the construction of a new South Africa: to foster and co-opt a black middle class whose interests do not always overlap with those of the mass democratic movement. Given a stake in the economy, the New Bourgeois Black during the period of transition becomes invaluable in helping to determine the direction of the economy. And such direction is in turn determined by a revised construction of nation in which reproduction, controlled within the institution of the family, has a crucial role to play.

Meaning and community

In such a context of conflicting interests the unitary notion of a gendered reader becomes untenable. To ensure that the reader reads 'correctly', that is, as a woman who is persuaded that having fewer children is desirable, as a man who is persuaded that reproduction remains within his jurisdiction, and as a black person who sees that a small family makes economic sense, the advertiser must accommodate a range of meanings. Stanley Fish's account of 'interpretive communities', in which meaning is selected from a range of possible interpretations, could be seen to address the problem:

> communication occurs within situations and . . . to be in a situation is already to be in possession of a structure of assumptions, of practices understood to be relevant in relation to purposes and goals that are already in place . . . meanings come already calculated, not because of norms embedded in the language but because language is always perceived, from the very first, within a structure of norms. (Fish 1980: 318)

Such an approach, while marking out constraints on the reader's production of meaning as well as accounting for pockets of consensus about the meaning of a text, rejects normative readings determined by an author. But the limitation of interpretive communities, as Mary Louise Pratt points out, is that they are 'not seen in their relations to and interaction with each other' (Pratt 1987: 57), an enduring problem when dealing with texts produced in a divided South African society. My analysis also hopes to follow Edward Said's injunction that 'we must go a great deal further in showing what situation, what historical and social configuration, what political interests are concretely entailed by the very existence of interpretive communities' (Said 1983: 26).

Not only must the text accommodate different interpretive communities, but 'the purposes and goals that are already in place' should be considered in terms of being legitimated by a particular community. The text must take cognisance of the fact that readers themselves are not unified subjects and that they participate in any number of interpretive communities. For instance, where the dominant trend in the South African liberation movement is to see gender issues as a distraction from national liberation, race and gender become contending spaces in which to locate yourself as a reader. The family planning advertisement is also meaningful in the specific political context where a structure of dominant white minority norms concerned with demographic survival interacts with black norms related to economic survival. Such interaction is conflictual, just as gendered readings of a text which advocates 'responsible' reproduction will conflict. In my analysis I hope to show how the battles between interpretive communities are accommodated within the image–text of the advertisement.

CONTRADICTION BETWEEN ARTICLES AND ADVERTISEMENTS

Where we believe the discourse of advertising, which is clearly signalled, to be separate from that of the magazine, we may fail to appreciate the power of the latter in promoting consumerism. Not only do the contents of magazines reveal overt collusion with advertisers, they could also offer support by apparently contradicting advertisements. Black magazines can be read in Pêcheuxian terms as discursive formations in which their entire contents constitute a discursive–ideological process that sets up dependency relationships between articles and advertisements; each becomes meaningful for the New Bourgeois Black in relation to the other. This relation may appear to be contradictory, as I will later show in the analysis of the family planning advertisement, but Pêcheux's definition is helpful in making sense of the contradiction:

> I shall call discursive formation that which in a given ideological formation, i.e. from a given position in a given conjuncture determined by the state of the class struggle, determines 'what can and should be said' . . . words, expressions, propositions which are different literally can, in a given discursive formation, 'have the same meaning', which if you follow me, is in fact the condition for each element (word, expression or proposition) having a meaning at all. (Pêcheux 1982: 111–12)

Coherence, or inferable relationships of meaningfulness between different parts of the discourse, can, for instance, be found in the magazine *True Love* (April 1989), where an article on forced contraception, page 56, comfortably co-exists with a family planning advertisement on page 36. The article exposes factory employers' insistence on a three-month Depo Provera injection as a condition of employment for all women to ensure maximum industrial production. A black doctor employed by the factory explains the Depo-related complaints suffered by women and points out that the expense of medical fees for the treatment of such complaints does not make economic sense. The report focuses on Madadeni, a town in the so-called independent Kwazulu Homeland, where birth control in the workplace was introduced by the Department of Health. Factories have their own nursing teams who administer Depo Provera and the report's humanist emphasis is on the scandalous reason for contraception – not administered because of a crisis baby boom, but to increase industrial production.

With the help of Pêcheux's theory of the grammatical inscription of ideology, the contradiction, generated by the widely known fact that Depo Provera is routinely used by government-sponsored family planning which is advertised in the same magazine, can be understood. His theory is applicable to a pragmatic analysis since he claims that we call up a body of ideas, or interdiscourse, from the dominant ideology from which to make bridging inferences. What appear to be metonymic relations between propositions are in fact an adding of inferences.

Michel Pêcheux's model of discourse

Pêcheux cites the 'impossible' sentence, *He who saved the world by dying on the cross never existed*, as evidence for the functioning of language as discourse. The existence of conflicting domains of thought from the discourses of atheism and Christianity within the same sentence becomes possible through what he calls preconstruction, by which an external or independent construction thought before or elsewhere, that is, someone saved the world by dying on the cross, opposes the global assertion of the sentence, that is, no-one saved the world by dying on the cross. It is syntactic embedding or the relative clause which accommodates the preconstructed in discourse. Thus the sentence, *Black women, who love children, will not have any of their own*, contains the following propositions:

1. Black women love children (from the discourse of tradition).
3. Black women will not have children of their own (from the discourse of the New Bourgeois Black).

But we can insert the following sentence between 1 and 3, a preconstruction which arises as a bridging assumption between them:

2. Love of children precludes having any of your own.

Sentence 2 intervenes as support for a thought contained in 1 to form a 'sustaining effect', an implicature that allows for 'articulation' between 1 and 3. Sentence 3 falsely assumes a causal relationship with 1:

3. (Therefore) black women will not have children of their own.

The explicative or non-restrictive clause is thus shown to generate relations of cause and effect (articulation) between the preconstructed and the main clause.

Pêcheux's division of discourse into intradiscourse, interdiscourse and transverse discourse provides a framework for the investigation of discursive formations. By intradiscourse he means 'the thread of the discourse', how what is said now relates to what has been said before and what will be said afterwards. Such cohesion is a product of various relations of substitutability which are achieved through markers such as co-reference, lexical replacement, reiteration, synonymy, hyponymy, paraphrase, etc.

Interdiscourse refers to the preconstructions from which inferences are drawn or connections between elements (words, propositions, expressions) of discourse are made. It determines the range of possible substitutions or bridging assumptions available in any society: 'the embedding effect of the preconstructed and the effect I have called articulation – initially considered as psycho-logical laws of thought – are in reality materially determined in the very structure of inter-discourse' (Pêcheux 1982: 113). Ideology operates within discursive formations precisely because interdiscourse remains disguised or rather is absorbed/forgotten in intradiscourse. The process of this absorption, the crossing point where interdiscourse simulates intradiscourse, is called transverse discourse. Thus what appear to be innocent markers of cohesion, or merely a function of grammar, are in fact a set of bridging inferences based on metonymy (relationships of part to whole, cause to effect and symptom to what it designates).

Pêcheux uses the following example of substitution to illustrate the operation of transverse discourse: *We observe the passage of an electric current. The deflection of the galvanometer . . .* (Sx). The replacement suggests that the two terms are synonymous but it is, of course, not the case since one is caused by the other. He argues in spatial terms that the sequence Sx appears to be crossed by another sequence, Sy, the transverse discourse which links together or syntagmatises the substitutables: *The passage of an electric current causes the deflection of the galvanometer.* This syntagmatisation within the thread of the discourse and in the form of a non-restrictive relative clause produces an 'articulation' effect. Thus the process yields a supplementary construction such as: *We observe a deflection of the galvanometer, which indicates the passage of an electric current,* in which causality is embedded.

Advertisement and article as discursive formation

Pêcheux's example could be developed to encompass the two extended texts in *True Love*, which I label (Ty), as a discursive formation within the magazine (Tx). More specifically, the key information outlined in the Forced Contraception feature (a) invokes a series of opposites to the family planning advertisement (b) which makes for textual cohesion. For key factors in the article which are considered undesirable, the advertisement substitutes positive features as follows:

1. Factory workers as affected versus the professional woman as agent or subject of the discourse.
2. Callous production control versus considered reproduction as reason for contraception.
3. Local factory nursing teams versus national institution for administering contraception.
4. The Kwazulu Homeland as exemplary site of political exclusion versus Pretoria, administrative capital, suggesting political inclusion.
5. Compulsory mass contraception versus thoughtful individual choice.
6. Ill-health and repression versus health and well-being.

The sequence Tx is perpendicularly crossed by another sequence so that our reading of the apparently contradictory texts ((a) that Depo Provera in the workplace is bad (b) that Depo Provera dispensed by family planning is good) establishes an interconnection which becomes what Pêcheux calls the transverse discourse (Ty) of the magazine. Through the antonymies listed above, (a) and (b) become syntagmatised in a relationship of cause to effect, thus generating an accessory statement or 'sustaining effect' along the lines of: the exposure of forced contraception at work indicates the necessity of individual choice as offered by family planning.

The linear axis of (a) to (b) forms an intradiscourse by which textual cohesion – mainly through lexical reiteration, collocation and substitution since both texts deal with the relation of female reproduction to the socio-economic system – can be endophorically[8] established between the two magazine texts. A logical distortion occurs: far from (a) producing an unfavourable reading of (b) by which readers are put off the advertisement for family planning, the interdiscourse or preconstructed elements provide an inferential base for a supportive reading of (b).

That Depo Provera is routinely used by the Family Planning Association is therefore a contradiction suppressed in the transverse discourse of the magazine by which we come to see it as desirable when properly and nationally dispensed to an upwardly mobile middle class who freely acknowledge its value.[9] Birth control is by no means the only contradictory element in *True Love*. Surrounded by advertisements for hair straighteners, facial creams and other aids to normative western standards, we find the regular feature 'Punchline' upbraiding the very black middle class for abandoning its indigenous culture in favour of the alien west. As an afterword on the last page, the article offers final reassurance to its upwardly mobile readers: all is well, and traditional values can comfortably be kept smouldering beneath the capitulation to reformist capitalism; the two are not incompatible. In the analysis below, the contradictions which operate in South African society can be seen to be held within the image–text of the family planning advertisement (Figure 4.2).

ANALYSIS OF THE FAMILY PLANNING IMAGE

The visually prominent text 'I love children far too much to have one before I'm ready', is marked in a number of ways to propose an equivalence between viewing and reading. Firstly, it is lifted out of the context of the speech situation that makes up the main part of the text, that is, direct address of the reader (see Mills, this volume). Secondly, it extends the

Figure 4.2 Advertisement from *True Love* magazine, April 1989, South Africa

context in the sense that we can imagine the teacher at work through the visual synecdoche of the blackboard. Careful design allows this black rectangle with white print to 'lift out' physically with the help of its visible blue shadow. This typographic projection finds an analogue in the image above: the woman who participates in a scene/event with the children appears to occupy a central position, yet, like the text-board, is lifted out of that scene in the manner of televisual address where interaction is momentarily interrupted so that the commentator can speak to the camera, or participate in another speech event with the audience. We infer from their dress that the children are her pupils, and their preoccupation or obliviousness to the other scene in which their teacher momentarily participates (directly addressing the reader through her gaze) testifies to her success as a teacher.

A discussion of the relations between participants in the photograph reveals the image to contradict or undermine the authoritative text. In this intimate scene, the deictic centre is unstable and, like the text's insertion of a male addressee which I later show in my analysis of the linguistic information, shifts between the older boy and the teacher. The group forms a circle, reinforced by the way in which the teacher is touched by the senior boy and girl. Their hands are prominent and respective curvature suggests a visual chiasmus with the body of the teacher as connecting space. Deixis (here graphically represented by the boy's index finger) points to the spatial context delimited by the circle, but the visual salience of the boy's finger also puts him in a position of centrality. The children are engaged in something related to the papers held by the teacher; the sight-lines between the children reveal the topic to be an exchange between the boys; the older girl looks to the older boy for his response whilst the younger girls focus on the younger boy. The teacher is almost redundant in this scene. Although the papers are held and probably produced by her, this source of the discussion is obscured. Her responsibility or agency in the production of knowledge is removed as she participates in quite another scene, that of direct engagement with the viewer. The male children are portrayed as being in control; the older boy's left hand rests proprietorially on the shoulder of the teacher. Her youth questions her authority and suggests an equivalence with the older boy: her shirt is of the same cut as the school uniform; her meek, pretty smile bridges the gap between professional and private, teacher and mother, thus allowing her to be lifted out of the teaching scene to utter the main text.

Image as indirect speech act

It is, nevertheless, her position as school teacher through which we read the black/white rectangle: we view it as a blackboard upon which the authority figure has written the didactic words, converted into a slogan by quotation marks. The blackboard text demands to be viewed and read; like children learning to read, which is learning to recognise orthographic representation, we look-and-say, repeating her words. Teaching convention thus permits the deixis to float. Every one of us can voice the slogan and, if we are responsible black people, can become the subject of the text, uttering the words as our very own. In other words, we are not interpellated by the image-as-text; instead we produce our own subjectivity, as responsible mothers-of-the-nation.

Careful design of the text area, reminiscent of a label that wraps around a can, insists on reader participation. A consideration of the relationship of rectangles and their potential for spatial transformation, makes for persuasive graphics which could be argued in terms of an illocutionary act, or an attempt to accomplish some communicative purpose within a given context. The felicity conditions for the directive to send away for further details include both the authority of the teacher to direct the reader and the reader being a responsible person who responds to such a directive.

The blackboard rectangle on the left (white writing on black) lifts out pictorially, that is, asserts through its blue shadow, a separate material reality which encourages the reader to consider the separate material reality of the analogous rectangle on the right (black on white). The blackboard shape lifted out of the yellow 'label' carries illocutionary force inciting the viewer to material action: act upon the conventionalised dotted line, cut out the coupon on the right, and send away for more information. The curious affirmative, 'Yes, I would like to receive . . . Family Planning', on the coupon text underlines perlocutionary take-up as a response to the speech act. An absent rectangle on the yellow strip, the perlocutionary consequence of cutting on the dotted line, is literally foreshadowed on the left hand by the blue out of which the slogan has been lifted. Thus graphic design can be viewed as an indirect speech act which works on a shared assumption that visual information, just as in speech, has the intention of accomplishing purposeful communication in a particular context.

Analysis of family planning text

Conflict, played out in the public amenities of South Africa, shows how government reform has alerted the white population to a crucial fact which segregation had concealed: the extent to which they are outnumbered. Public amenities, now 'swamped' by blacks, present town councils, although sensible to the economic need for change, with problems. White consternation at the number of blacks who have materialised on the beaches on public holidays, for instance, makes one wonder in whose interest family planning is being advertised in black magazines.

The family planning advertisement is a good example of how ideological contradictions are concealed in advertising. In the following pragmatic reading, which takes into account the political context, I hope to uncover the conflicting interests of male and female, black and white, urban middle class and traditional rural blacks. This conflict is also expressed in the contradictory relations between image and text; however, by applying speech-act theory to the graphic lay-out, the total visual presentation can be shown to offer forceful support for the advertising message.

Personal deixis establishes a speech situation in which a schoolteacher (I) addresses the reader (you) directly. The text is her testimony, spoken in the first person by a professional woman who is also surrogate mother. The advertisement thus cleverly transfers the values of a traditional culture, where many children represent wealth and fertility, to a new context, a professional one, which accommodates many children as well as a maternal figure. The professional woman is simultaneously stripped of her negative connotations. This balancing act is maintained throughout: love of children and the undesirability of having any.

The opening sentence, 'I'm a school teacher and I really love my job and all my pupils', ensures that we do not assume loving all the pupils to be an entailment of loving the job. The premodifier 'all' makes possible a scaling down to loving her job and *some* of her pupils, a condition that this teacher is not guilty of. 'Really' loving her job emphasises her professional status; nevertheless the transference of love via the co-ordinating conjunction, allows the job to embrace the pupils, but as new information, specific to her. The speaker is therefore no ordinary 'unnatural' professional woman; her profession includes love of children, 'all' her children, just as a mother would not discriminate between her offspring. Sentence 2 reinforces the link between teacher and mother – 'even though they try my patience some days', neither would wish away the children. She has chosen the correct career, even when their behaviour is trying, so negating any causal relationship between their behaviour and her love for them: loving children is simply natural.

The next stage of the argument exploits the traditional culture's attitude to children which extends beyond caring for the biological offspring – 'I already look after 32 children.' To abandon thirty-two children for one of her own would make numerical nonsense and amount to a betrayal of her pupils. The sentiment draws from the discourse of nationhood: a mother-of-many is easily substituted by mother-of-the-nation, whilst at the same time reconstructing the traditional mother in terms of a career.

In this paragraph we have a report of the speaker's conversation with friends in which marriage as a prerequisite for reproduction crops up as a preconstruction in the relative clause, 'since I got married'. The conventional implicature is that she would not be expected to have children before being married. And to have a child is expressed in the fixed syntagm – 'start a family' – thereby anchoring reproduction within the institutions of marriage and the nuclear family. For all its reliance on tradition, the grammatically inscribed values clash with traditional social organisation where the birth of a child can never be seen to *start* an extended family. Nor do these values coincide with the social reality of urban life, where many women have children within a matrifocal household without male support.

'In fact, since I got married a lot of my friends have been saying that because I'm so good with children I should start a family' is the only complex sentence in which the hierarchical nature of the propositions is not reflected in the order of the clauses. Instead, the order is temporally determined: something cannot happen unless something else has already happened; the ideological world is shaped through the use of aspect. The verb 'got married' is followed by the progressive 'have been saying' of the main sentence which precedes the future 'should start'. And the time conjunction 'since' reinforces the embedded notion that reproduction cannot take place before marriage. 'In fact', which fronts the first subordinate sentence, 'since I got married', functions pragmatically as a cataphoric reference to caring for her pupils. Not only does it allow the reproduction–marriage relationship to slip in as a preconstruction, but also presents the text as a speech situation.

Between paragraphs 2 and 3, as in the cinematic process of 'suture' (Kuhn 1982: 53), the presence of an addressee is pragmatically sewn into the text. The privileged position of the reader as confidante can be inferred from the semantic distinction between 'I always laugh and say . . .' and 'But what I really *mean*', to which the addressee is given access. Where the first is a rhetorical response for friends, the second, a revelation of the reason underlying the first, is reserved for those more intimate than friends – a nameless category to which the reader, by dint of the very speech act, has been admitted.

The saying–meaning distinction also signals a decentring of the speaking subject to include the thoughts of a husband who concurs in the reasons for delaying reproduction. The addressee is destabilised: men too are addressed, if indirectly, and readers have the choice of reading as either female or male; there is in any case no difference in perspective, or so the text asserts. Deixis accordingly shifts from I/my to we/he/our.[10] Men, as surrogate addressees, are thus assured that women are not taking matters in their own hands and the husband's response is presented as knowledge which implies discussion prior to this explanation or speech act: 'My husband knows how important my career is to me. But he also knows that we will have a family some day.' The almost parallel structure of these sentences appears to establish, through the husband's knowledge, an equivalence between career and family. But there is an important difference between him *knowing how* and *knowing that*; both are arguments of the verb, but the first presupposes the second. That her career is important is a presupposition which needs no reassurances, so that the job in fact takes precedence over having a child, a necessary weighting for the ideological definition of the family which follows.

More than a mere biological unit, the family as ideological construct becomes the base from which the advertising message operates. The lexical item 'family' in paragraph 3 is presented as part of a prepositional phrase which, as postmodifier, is subordinate to 'commitments' in the noun phrase, 'commitments of a family'. And these commitments are economic, so that buying a house before having a child is the key constituent and by implication those who do not follow this order are irresponsible, that is, not sensible to the commitments which the concept of family is subordinate to. The obvious result of the woman having a career is not mentioned; we are left to infer that more money will contribute to achieving a family. This promotion of middle-class values, the material welfare in order that 'our children will enjoy all the advantages of being planned', reveals family planning as a euphemism for not having children. Home ownership in the townships is severely restricted; it follows from the advertisement that only the tiny middle class ought to reproduce themselves.

In the final paragraph the reader is addressed directly as 'you'. The speaker reminds us that she loves children and offers herself as a yardstick for the caring woman. Her position as teacher is doubly exploited; she has the authority not only to be the model but also to utter the final homiletic slogan: 'If you love children as much as I do, planning them is the best thing you can do.' This declarative sentence can be read as an implicit performative, urging the reader to follow the teacher's example. The advertisement achieves much of its persuasiveness from presenting itself as a speech situation. Typically, informal language, conversational

contractions like *I'm*, *we'll*, *they'll*, avoidance of advertising imperatives
and simple sentence structure favouring co-ordination rather than
subordination contribute to its authenticity. But the force of the last
sentence turns it into a speech event, 'or culturally recognised social
activity in which language plays a specific . . . role like teaching in a
classroom' (Levinson 1983: 279).

CONCLUSION

We do of course have the power to resist the illocutionary force of sending
away for Sister Mildred's free information on how not to reproduce
ourselves, just as we do not have to accept the advertisement's construction
of parenthood. But the question of succumbing or resisting is not the whole
story. Kate Linker points out that 'representation, hardly neutral, acts to
regulate and define the subjects it addresses, positioning them by class or
by sex, in active or passive relations to meaning. Over time these fixed
positions acquire the status of identities and, in their broadest reach, of
categories. Hence the forms of discourse are at once forms of definition,
means of limitation, modes of power' (Linker 1984: 392). Whilst a reader
is unlikely to define herself in terms of a position offered by a single
advertisement, it seems equally unlikely that she would remain immune
to positions constantly mapped out in discursive formations of which such
advertisements form part. However, the very existence of the above
statement shows that ideological meanings can be resisted and if we
consider meaning to be negotiated between reader and text, then the
variation in the effect of ideological messages could be located in both
reading practices and a particular reader's interests.

Pêcheux provides a useful method for examining the cultural assumptions which enable us to make sense of a text, but his ideological
determinism does not allow for a level of political awareness that rejects
the interdiscourse into which we are interpellated. Willed resistance is
patently possible but dependent first of all on prior understanding of the
ideological message; understanding in turn relies on close reading and a
reader's knowledge of language. As Sara Mills points out in the
Introduction to this volume, an advertisement, unlike a poem, does not
invite close reading. However, the oppositional close/slack reading
may itself be in need of deconstruction, as may be the distinction between
'real' and professional readers (see Mills, this volume). A continuum
between casual and professional reading can surely be assumed where

people read slackly if the product is of no interest to them and carefully when it is.

This chapter, whilst uncovering the flexible gendering of the reader, also raises the problem of tracing the reader's position in terms of gender alone. For all its simplicity, the family planning advertisement succeeds in holding together some of the contradictions that operate within society. These are revealed through pragmatic analysis which uses the context of South African politics as a pool from which to draw inferences. The unstable positions offered to a reader can be seen to be determined by the complex of existing discourses within the specific contexts of national liberation and apartheid's reform. The discourse of nation and tradition, long drawn upon to boost the black liberation movement (see Wicomb 1991) is also used to maintain male domination. Caught between the discourses of apartheid's reform and that of its overthrow, feminist concerns have been branded as a distraction from the more urgent task of national liberation. Whilst reconstruction recognises the respectability of enshrining women's rights in the constitution – both the Afrikaner Nationalist Party and the ANC have inserted the necessary clauses – women are no less vulnerable. Gangs of jackrollers, youths who rape young girls with the avowed purpose of impregnating them and disrupting their education (*Weekly Mail*, 25 October 1991), roam the townships with impunity; in the overcrowded black university hostels, female students are routinely harrassed and 'disciplined' (*Sunday Times*, 27 October 1991) in the name of tradition. Such invented tradition does not only serve to justify sexual abuse, it also intersects with the discourse of race, thus allowing the perpetrators to argue that those who tackle the question are guilty of racism and cultural imperialism.

Given this context, black women students are likely to read population-control advertisements with some care and anxiety. A text which takes this context into account, does not position its reader achromatically; she is gendered either as a black woman or as a white woman whose different interests, recognised by advertising that cannot afford the ideological conflation of the two, are differently addressed. Thus the notion of a monolithic 'real reader', whose identity is determined in opposition to the literary analyst, seems less than useful in studying textual strategies and their ideological effects.

An important question raised by close reading is what the purpose of extracting an even lengthier text from an advertisement might be (see Thornborrow, this volume). Criticism, which borrows much of its terminology from the language of politics, often sees the exposure of ideological meanings as a political end in itself. It is unnecessary to dwell on the difference between writing textual glosses on advertisements and being sexually abused in shanty townships, but it is important to explore possible connections. I would suggest that close reading, put to pedagogical use, has an important interventionist function to fulfil and that attempts to change slack reading habits are more useful than the documentation of such practice. Knowledge of language and its ideological function and an awareness of how advertisements exploit the existing discourses could lead to material changes in people's lives; the resisting reader (see Mills, and Boardman, this volume) could be moved to resist more actively. Slow as they might be, women's initiatives for fighting sexual abuse on black campuses spring from precisely such knowledge and a resulting outrage at modes of representation and exploitative modes of address such as 'Mama' which, under the guise of reverence, position us as passive receivers of abuse.

This chapter hopes to have shown how language-in-use could be a paradigm for looking at images. An enduring problem, however, is that whilst asserting the importance of developing ways of reading images, a study which uses the medium of language necessarily privileges the linguistic. Advertisements have traditionally been analysed in schools and media-studies courses as if they were literary texts, with a focus on identifying rhetorical figures and lamenting their ideological meanings. Widening the scope to include the study of imagery is of course essential, but there are still unresolved problems around the question of how and why we teach advertising and what students should expect to get out of it.

Learning about how we are manipulated by persuasive linguistic and visual techniques are worthy aims but the criticism that media studies focuses on analysis and neglects production is difficult to meet. Many teachers would be reluctant to promote advertising by encouraging students to design advertisements, so that they are left with the pessimistic message that being vigilant is all that they can do in a world artfully manipulated by advertising. A way out of this one-sidedness of academic practice would be to turn the study of advertisements into an empowering activity where techniques are uncovered in order that they can be used for alternative purposes. Image–text art by women like Barbara Kruger, Maude Sulter, Carrie Mae Weems or Martha Rosler which addresses issues of gender, race and class could be studied to show how the techniques of advertising can be used to produce works that question the dominant culture rather than conserve its values. These scripto-visual works do not advertise anything; instead they intervene in the culture by compelling the reader/viewer to question not only the representation of gender or race, but the medium itself. Rather than producing passive recipients who are charmed by the aesthetic impact of advertisements, the education system could harness such fascination to produce works that use the techniques of advertising to challenge cultural assumptions.

NOTES

1. Performing a speech act involves performing a locutionary act, which is to produce a grammatical utterance. Austin uses the extraordinary example of *Shoot her!* to explain how such an utterance could have the illocutionary force of ordering, advising or urging an addressee to perform the act of shooting.
2. The perlocutionary effect of the utterance *Shoot her!* is to force, persuade or frighten the addressee into shooting the person. Such an effect could, however, only take place if certain conditions of appropriateness, or felicity conditions, hold. For instance, the utterance can have the required perlocutionary effect only if the addressee is holding a gun.
3. Grice's theory of implicatures is about how people use language. He identifies maxims such as clarity, relevance and sincerity which encompass a general co-operative principle to ensure efficent conversation. If we fail to understand an utterance according to one of the maxims, we make inferences or implicatures that restore a co-operative principle at a deeper level.
4. Implicatures involve an addressee in bridging the gap between the actual utterance and what she might have expected, so that a bridging assumption is added in order to make sense of the utterance.
5. Burgin describes the popular pre-conscious as containing 'the ever-shifting contents which we might reasonably suppose can be called to mind by the majority of individuals in a given society at a particular moment in its history; that which is common knowledge'. Such common knowledge or ideas are transmitted through various cultural media and become inscribed in the popular pre-conscious to serve as an advertisement's pre-text. Thus an advertisement's actual verbal text interacts with its pre-text, the preconstituted fragments in a field of discourse.
6. According to the code model, communication is achieved by encoding and decoding messages so that the linguistic message at source is equivalent to that at destination. However, the existence of a gap between semantic representations of sentences and the thoughts of a speaker renders such a model invalid since it is a process of inference rather than further decoding that fills the gap.
7. Grice discusses the discrepancies between what a speaker means by an utterance and the meaning of the sentence. In the case of ironic utterances, what the speaker means, or meaning-nn (non-natural meaning), will be in conflict with the natural or sentence meaning. We process meaning-nn as an inference which is openly intended to be communicated as opposed to the incidental transfer of information (Levinson 1983, p. 16).
8. Textual cohesion (according to Halliday and Hasan 1976, p. 33) depends on relationships within and between sentences. Endophoric relations in a text show how the meaning of pronominal expressions like *it* can be recovered within a text by referring (a) back to a previous sentence or earlier part of a sentence, or (b) forward to find the referent later in the sentence or text. Endophora is

distinguished from exophora where interpretation lies outside the text, in the context of situation.

9. The Population Development Programme, incorporated by the Department of National Health, has since 1989 taken over most of the advertising for limiting reproduction. These messages unambiguously present development as a reduction in population. Advertising dispenses with the image, occupies a full newspage in upper case and directly addresses people to take responsibility for educating others. One of the advertisements, 'Helping Women to Help Themselves', appeals to white middle-class women to get involved in the self-help programmes for black women. Others target farmers to encourage their workforce to limit reproduction.

10. In a patriarchal society, where manhood is invested in the number of offspring, advertising must be careful not to exclude or alienate men. *Drum* magazine of the same date as *True Love* carries an advertisement of an overdressed man awkwardly balancing a young child on his knees. The child utters an improbable text in celebration of its carefully planned existence. Whilst targeting men and offering a revised construction of fatherhood through the image, the text ensures that the father retains his distance from the business of reproduction and child-rearing. But a current leaflet (1991) issued by the Department of National Health and Population Development and displayed in municipal offices is headed 'Information for Men'. The text starts as follows: 'The man is the head of the family and has the responsibility to make important decisions about his family.'

REFERENCES

Anderson, B. (1983) *Imagined Communities: Reflections on the origin and spread of nationalism*, London: Verso.

Barthes, R. (1977) *Image–Music–Text*, London: Fontana.

Burgin, V. (1983) 'Seeing sense', in H. Davis and P. Walton (eds) *Language, Image, Media*, Oxford: Blackwell, pp. 226–44.

Dyer, G. (1982) *Advertising as Communication*, London and New York: Routledge.

Fairclough, N. (1989) *Language and Power*, London: Longman.

Fish, S. (1980) *Is there a Text in this Class? The authority of interpretive communities*, London and Cambridge, MA: Harvard University Press.

Halliday, M. A. K. and Hasan, R. (1976) *Cohesion in English*, London: Longman.

Kuhn, A. (1982) *Women's Pictures: Feminism and cinema*, London and Boston: Routledge & Kegan Paul.

Levinson, S. (1983) *Pragmatics*, Cambridge: Cambridge University Press.

Linker, K. (1984) 'Representation and sexuality', in B. Wallis (ed.) *Art after Modernism: Rethinking representation*, New York: The New York Museum of Contemporary Art Publications, pp. 391–415.

Myers, K. (1983) 'Understanding advertisers', in H. Davis and P. Walton (eds) *Language, Image, Media*, Oxford: Blackwell, pp. 205–23.

Pateman, T. (1983) 'How is understanding an advertisement possible?' in H. Davis and P. Walton (eds) *Language, Image, Media*, Oxford: Blackwell, pp. 187–204.

Pêcheux, M. (1982) *Language, Semantics and Ideology*, London: Macmillan.

Pratt, M. (1987) 'Linguistic utopias', in N. Fabb, D. Attridge, A. Durant and

C. McCabe (eds) *The Linguistics of Writing*, Manchester: Manchester University Press, pp. 48–66.

Said, E. (1983) *The World, the Text, and the Critic*, Cambridge, MA: Harvard University Press.

Sperber, D. and Wilson, D. (1986) *Relevance: Communication and cognition*, Cambridge, MA: Harvard University Press and Oxford: Blackwell.

Wicomb, Z. (1991) 'Tracing the path from national to official culture', in P. Mariani (ed.) *Critical Fictions*, Seattle: Bay Press, pp. 241–50.

Williamson, J. (1978) *Decoding Advertisements: Ideology and meaning in advertising*, London: Marion Boyars.

Chapter 5

The Woman, the Man and the Filofax
Gender positions in advertising

Joanna Thornborrow

INTRODUCTION: OBJECTIVES AND THEORETICAL FRAMEWORK

In this essay I want to examine how the language used in two advertisements functions to construct an ideal reading position based on gender stereotypes. The linguistic analysis which follows examines some of the syntactic, semantic and pragmatic features of two advertisements for Filofax personal organisers, focusing particularly on aspects of transitivity, modality and address, as well as lexical collocation and contrasting semantic fields in the texts.[1] I then relate these stylistic features to specific discourse genres, and discuss how they construct an 'ideal' readership based on common-sense assumptions about gender-based social roles and stereotypes.

Through this analysis I argue that the discourse of the two Filofax advertisements differs considerably according to whether they are aimed at male or female consumers, and that it is not only these differences in themselves which are significant, but the attitudes to social roles and the perception of status that they convey and perpetuate. I believe that the language used in these advertisements has wider implications for the way women are represented in advertising, in so far as we are still frequently excluded from male-associated concepts of power and economic status, and constrained within common-sense notions of female stereotype roles.

As a theoretical framework for this analysis I draw on a range of work in stylistics and feminist linguistic theory, as well as work in critical discourse analysis. The use of linguistic theory to examine how different types of discourses represent and position people into particular social roles began with early studies by Fowler *et al.* (1979) into the relationship between language and ideology; the role of language in maintaining

128

asymmetrical social relations through patterns of representation, as well as through the organisation of talk, continues to be the subject of much research (see, for example, Harris 1984; Fairclough 1989, 1992; Thornborrow 1991). All these studies have in common the basic precept that by looking closely at the linguistic structure of any given text or discursive interaction, we can 'denaturalise' the ideologies which underlie it. The work of Cameron (1985) on feminism and attitudes to linguistic theory, as well as of other linguists who are concerned with gender differences in language use, (particularly Coates 1986, 1988) and with how discourse functions as a vehicle for maintaining asymmetrical relations of power (Coates and Cameron 1988), has continually informed this particular study. Another important influence has been the study of the representation of women in literary texts as well as in advertisements (Williamson 1978; Wareing 1990).

In undertaking a critical stylistic analysis of this kind, it is possible to make some very specific observations about the type of language used in a text, and the effect particular linguistic features may have on readers. It has been claimed that for any given text there is a range of possible reading positions (Mills, and Christie, this volume) and in this essay I want to examine how an ideal reading position is constructed in the two Filofax advertisements through the use of particular stylistic devices. This is not to say that readers have to take up the position inscribed by the text in order to make sense of it, and these advertisements will inevitably affect different readers in different ways. Nevertheless, in undertaking this kind of analysis, it is possible to demonstrate how selections in form, style and lexis in these advertisements differ according to the consumers they are targeting and, in particular, in the way they address male and female readers.

I will be looking in particular at the selections in representation in these advertisements with regard to transitivity, that is, 'who (or what) does what to whom (or what)' (Montgomery 1986a: 184), modality and vocabulary. I also look at patterns of lexical collocation in the advertisements, that is, the organisation of vocabulary in terms of lexical items which co-occur in a text (Halliday and Hasan 1976), and at the semantic fields to which they belong. Another important feature of these texts is their form of address (Montgomery 1986b; Mills, this volume), which plays a crucial role in the way readers are positioned in relation to the 'voice' of the text.

Two further concepts I draw on in this analysis are the notions of common-sense background knowledge, and of social stereotypes. For the purposes of this essay, common-sense background knowledge, or assumptions, can be defined as those 'whose "truth" is proposed as obvious, natural, inevitable and unarguable' (O'Sullivan *et al.* 1978). Stereotypes, which 'operate to define and identify groups of people as generally alike in certain ways' (O'Sullivan *et al.* 1978), play an important role in organising common-sense 'knowledge', and classifying groups of people according to often highly generalised or simplified criteria. Advertising mobilises common-sense assumptions about social stereotypes, that is, the way certain groups of people 'stereotypically' behave, their characteristics, etc., in order to set up connections between groups of consumers and certain products (Williamson 1978). In this analysis of the two Filofax advertisements I examine how these assumptions both shape the discourse and construct a 'naturalised' position for readers as the text is processed.

THE ADVERTISEMENTS: FIRST IMPRESSIONS

The two Filofax advertisements in Figures 5.1 and 5.2 appeared in Sunday newspaper supplement magazines in December 1989.[2] While they both advertise the same product, and have some features of layout and text in common, the discursive style of each advertisement is very different. One is explicitly aimed at women readers, the other is implicitly aimed at men. In the one aimed at women, this targeting of the reader is achieved on an interpersonal level through features of direct address in the text. In the advertisement aimed at men, it is achieved on an inferential level through assumptions accessible to readers in making sense of the text (see Christie, and Wicomb, this volume, on inferencing).

Before going on to analyse these differences, and other stylistic features of the two advertisements, I look first at the similarities between them, henceforth to be referred to as advertisement A (Figure 5.1, targeting women) and advertisement B (Figure 5.2, targeting men). There are some shared features of layout: the text is set out in three columns, with the same italicised typescript, the first letter is highlighted in the same way, and both advertisements contain a square frame insert – at the centre of the page in A, slightly higher in B. Both advertisements contain visual elements around the margins and embedded in the text itself. Certain textual elements are also common to both advertisements, as follows:

The answer is Filofax.
Quality stationers everywhere can show you all the practical benefits with its uniquely useful pages.
The most famous name in personal organisers.

busy mother seeks

SECRETARY
ACCOUNTANT
TRAVEL AGENT
DIETICIAN
& LINGUIST

to help organise successful family

...hings get hectic at times, don't they? All that professional help could keep control of the busiest life – no matter how complicated it gets. But let's be practical – a Filofax Personal Organiser, with its uniquely useful pages, is a more realistic answer. If you must ring that neighbour who's ferrying your eldest to school, you can find the number. If your husband wants that suit cleaned by Thursday, Filofax will help for you remember to take it, and to find the receipt. Because Filofax produce special memory-jogging pages, and neat storage sleeves for fiddly bits such as tickets and stamps. Filofax is the most famous name in personal

organisers, and still the finest. The top-quality cover is made to last, because unlike a conventional diary, Filofax retains information such as birthdays and anniversaries, year after year. Only Filofax offers you such a wide choice of cover styles and finishes, plus the biggest range of insert pages. There are several types of diary layout to choose from, as well as

practical planners to show school holidays and other forthcoming events, at a glance. Our Home Entertainment pages help you arrange ideal combinations of guests, and record their favourite food and drink. With the unique Filofax shopping, budgeting and dietary pages, you can keep control of pennies or calories equally easily. The Travellers Checklist, another original from Filofax, simplifies holiday planning. And while you're there, foreign phrases are at your fingertips in Filofax Phrasefiles. Quality stationers everywhere can show you all the practical benefits of Filofax. The only name that means so much in personal organisers – for yourself, or as gifts that show you care.

THE ANSWER IS
ƒILOFAX®
PERSONAL ORGANISERS

Filofax plc, Filofax House, Forest Road, Ilford, Essex IG8 3HP

Figure 5.1 Filofax advertisement (A), 1989

Figure 5.2 Filofax advertisement (B), 1989

These are the only shared elements of the advertisements. In A, the photograph takes up nearly half the page. In B, the graphics are either sketches of various objects, or pictures of maps and guides. The Statue of Liberty holds her torch high up towards the top of the page, where there is no closed margin. In A, the text is densely packed into the space between the paragraph at the top, the margins at each side, and the row of Filofax at the bottom. There are no paragraphs. The effect of the layout in A is to compress the text into one, unbroken unit, and just as the woman in the photograph is shown inside the kitchen, the text is 'walled in' by the margins. This closing in of the text does not occur in B, where there is more space between the different sections. A further impression of space is created by the sketches, dotted around the page and breaking through the margins on either side. The section headings are capitalised, creating a contrast with the rest of the text, and the layout creates an overall impression of variety and openness, rather than compressing the text into a confined space. The page seems to open out to the rest of the world, whereas in A the focus is inward, leading the gaze from the photograph to the centre frame and into the text.

The colours in A are strong primary reds and blues, whereas in B the colours are subtler blues, browns and greys. The colours of the Filofax covers at the bottom of the page in A are present in the photograph: there is a red teapot, toastrack, telephone and spoon. The woman's nail varnish and lipstick are red, as is the noticeboard frame. The red Filofax is open to show a man's picture, next to the red wrappings of the present. There is a blue Filofax open by the telephone, and the woman's jumper is blue, so is the rim of the clock. In B, the only visual representation of a Filofax is in a sketch where it is closed, with what looks to be a leather binding, next to an expensive-looking piece of luggage (see Wicomb, this volume, for scripto-visual analysis).

From a first glance at the visual features of these advertisements, it is obvious that A is explicitly aimed at women readers, both from the situation depicted in the photograph and from the text of the 'small ad' within the inserted frame:

Busy mother seeks secretary (etc.)

B, with its eclectic images of a duck, cupid, contact lenses etc., does not immediately appear to target male or female readership. The symbols do not have specific gender associations, nor does the text of the inserted frame:

You can find it all in Filofax.

Both advertisements, however, set up expectations for readers through the use of these visual elements, against which the rest of the text will be processed.

Looking at A first, readers can make some preliminary assumptions about the woman in the photograph. These assumptions are based on readers' culturally based, background knowledge of social stereotypes and behaviour. Among them the following could be listed:

She works; she is well dressed, made-up, hair neat at 8 a.m.
She is health-conscious: brown bread, fruit juice, milk on table.
She is assertive: she is telling a man not to interrupt.
She has a high-powered job: she gets telephone calls at 8 a.m.
She is angry about something: she is frowning.

From this visual information in the photo, readers can infer that the woman is probably a middle-class, professional working mother. The assumption that she works outside the house is reinforced by the small advertisement for home help: she is 'busy' because she goes out to work. At the same time, the listed occupations in the advertisement elevate the status of domestic work within the home by implying that it requires a whole range of professional skills (although, apart from the accountant, the other four are stereotypically occupations which are associated with women). These assumptions, triggered by the photograph, enable readers to make certain predictions about the text in advertisement A. The most prominent of these seems to be that the text will probably be concerned with the problems facing a working mother, who needs a Filofax to help her organise her time as effectively as possible.

In B, the illustrative sketches have cultural connotations, although their combination here does not immediately trigger the same kind of specific assumptions as those produced by the photograph and small advertisement in A. The referents of 'it all' can be interpreted, on one level, at the various objects depicted on the page. Some of these are well-established signifiers:

Cupid = love.
Statue of Liberty = New York, America, freedom.
Mortar board = academic success.

The snail and the shopping bag containing French bread and a bottle of wine, the expensive luggage and the maps and guides all have associations with high-status, luxury lifestyles. The contact lenses and the scales are less obvious signifiers, and readers may wonder how they relate to the others. The main expectation set up by these visual elements and by the text of the framed insert is that all will be revealed on reading the text – the 'puzzle' will be solved. This juxtaposition of random images on the page also has connotations of the postmodern, and signals an awareness of art and fashion, which contrasts with the use of a photograph depicting a 'real-life' domestic scene in A.

The predictions readers can make about the text of the advertisements, based on this visual information, are different for each one. In A, a specific, detailed situation is presented at first glance, and it can be predicted that the text will probably provide further information about the benefits of owning a Filofax for the woman portrayed. In B, however, there is no specific situation, only a set of apparently unrelated objects. In this case, readers can predict that the relationship between them will be made explicit by the text. We will return to these expectations and the ways in which they are confirmed or disconfirmed later in the discussion.

MODES OF ADDRESS: CONSTRUCTING TEXTUAL SPEAKERS AND HEARERS

I want now to consider how these advertisements gender their readers through the stylistic device of address in the text. The role of direct and indirect address in positioning readers/listeners has been discussed by Montgomery (1986b) and Mills (1992 and this volume). The use of second-person pronouns positions the reader as the ratified 'hearer' of the textual voice, whereas indirect address can operate on other linguistic levels. A significant form of indirect address is the assumed sharing of background knowledge between text and reader, where 'certain information is posed to the reader as if it were self-evident' (Mills, this volume).

Both these advertisements contain instances of direct address in the use of second-person *you* pronouns, and one sentence is common to A and B:

Quality stationers everywhere can show *you* all the practical benefits.

Through this direct address, the text positions readers as potential consumers of the product. In advertisement A, there are twelve further uses of second-person pronouns, in both subject and object positions, and in the possessive form *your*. These are as follows:

you must ring	your eldest
help you remember	your husband
help you arrange	for yourself
while you're there	at your fingertips
to show you care	Filofax offers you
you can keep control	you can find

In advertisement B, there are three instances of second-person forms:

You can find it all in Filofax.
Even when you have to pack a lot in.
Questions that would defeat your diary.

In A, the reader is overtly positioned as the 'hearer' of the text, in so far as the textual 'voice' directly addresses the reader in a one-to-one, speaker–hearer relationship. In contrast, the reader of B is directly addressed only three times; once by the text of the inserted frame:

You can find it all in Filofax.

and twice at the end of the text:

To . . . questions that would defeat your diary.
Quality stationers everywhere can show you all the practical benefits.

The other instance of the second-person pronoun is generic rather than direct address to the reader, in so far as it includes both narrating voice and possible readers as its referents. Its position in a sentence which occurs between two other sentences containing first-person subject pronoun forms:

What do I check in?
Even when you have to pack a lot in.
It's my personalised data bank.

supports this interpretation since the referent of 'you' here is anyone who packs a case, including the narrating 'I', rather than an identifiable addressee.

In A, there are further stylistic features of the text which reinforce the direct address of the second-person pronouns. For example, the opening tag question:

Things get hectic at times, don't they?

referring exophorically to the scene in the photograph, establishes a dialogic structure, where the reader is the ratified hearer of the textual voice in a person-to-person conversation. The tag question is a grammatical form which has been associated in particular with 'women's speech', expressing lack of confidence or hesitancy (Lakoff 1975). While this theory has been critically examined by Cameron et al. (1988), one function of tag questions in certain contexts leads to a 'co-opting' of the hearer into agreeing with, or, sharing, the declarative proposition (Harris 1984). This particular function of tag questions is particularly noticeable in their use by dominant participants in asymmetrical discourse (e.g. in the magistrates' court setting examined by Harris) as 'highly assertive strategies for coercing agreement' (Cameron *et al.* 1988) rather than as expressions of tentativeness.

In A, the tag question posits a shared recognition (between speaker and hearer) of the scene in the photograph as 'hectic', and having established that recognition, goes on to address the reader as if she were the woman portrayed. The chatty, empathising tone of the discourse is maintained by the suggestion in the sentence:

But let's be practical.

which signals that some advice will follow, and again positions the reader as the recipient of that advice. The use of *let's* here is another discursive feature associated with 'women's talk'. In a study on the organisation of peer-group play (Goodwin 1980), it was found that girls favour 'suggesting' moves while boys used direct imperatives. These co-opting strategies not only draw the reader into the discourse as the direct addressee of the textual 'voice', but the use of items such as tag questions and *let's* also imitates the co-operative, empathising characteristics which have come to be associated – folk-linguistically – with women's talk.

In B, the text takes the form of a personal diary or journal, with a first-person narrator. The pronoun forms are therefore predominantly first person. 'I' occurs seven times, 'my' five times, 'me' three times and 'we' once. Other than the direct address to the reader as potential consumer mentioned above, there are no further instances of direct address. The directive sentence:

Imagine Manhattan without contact lens solution.

has no specifically designated addressee within the context of the first-person diary narration, and like the generic 'you' discussed above, seems to include the narrating 'I' in its range of address. What then is the position of the reader in relation to the narrating 'I' of the text? I suggest that the targeted readers of B are those who either identify with or aspire to the type of lifestyle described in the diary entries, and that they are male. This is signalled on a pragmatic level through inferences made while reading the text, rather than by direct address to a gendered reader as in A. The first of these inferences is triggered by the heading of the first diary entry, the question:

Will I be stumped between Ongar and Oval?

The pun based on the cricket term 'to be stumped', and reference to the Oval cricket ground in London, lead the reader to infer that the narrator is male, since cricket, according to socially based stereotypes, is a game predominantly played and watched by men. This assumption that the narrator is male is later confirmed by the reference to 'Suzi':

Suzi – 6pm, Freuds.

Readers make these assumptions because these seem most relevant to common-sense knowledge of the social context in which actions of this kind take place. Watching cricket and wining and dining women are, in general, associated with men. Other inferences could be made, for instance that the narrator is a woman cricket fan, or that Suzi is a business colleague, and these inferences are not specifically excluded by the text. The fact that they are not preferred inferences here may be due to the semantic tendency for male forms to be posited as the 'norm', or neutral, while female forms are marked in some way. As Cameron puts it, 'words are neutral on the surface, masculine underneath'. Examples of this surface neutrality can be found in sentences such as the following:

Fourteen survivors, three of them women.
People are much more likely to be influenced by their wives than by opinion polls.
(Cameron 1985: 69)

Similarly, texts which claim to address a universal audience are often addressed really to men (see Mills, and Wicomb, this volume), while texts that are addressed to women always specify the fact. The texts under discussion here exhibit the features of marked and unmarked discourse with regard to address. The direct address to a woman reader in A, and the use of linguistic forms related to women's talk, contrast with the absence of a direct addressee in the narrated text of B. However, this advertisement's initial neutrality of address to all potential consumers, expressed by the most prominent 'you' form in the inserted frame:

You can find it all in Filofax.

becomes exposed as address to men through the inferences triggered by reading the rest of the text. The background assumptions available to readers, in the form of knowledge of heterosexual stereotypes, enable us to infer that both the narrator of this text, and its indirect addressee, or 'ideal reader', are male.

PATTERNS OF TRANSITIVITY: AGENTS AND ACTIONS

The next aspect of language use I want to consider in these advertisements is that of transitivity. Transitivity is the linguistic function which shows 'types of processes, participants and circumstances' (Halliday 1981: 330), or, more simply, 'the arrangement of lexical items into sentences' (Montgomery 1986a: 184). For any given clause, there will be an agent, a process and possibly an affected entity. I want to focus in particular on the agent and affected entity positions for the textual addressee in advertisement A, and for the narrating subject in advertisement B.

The second-person pronouns in the following verb phrases position the the addressee of A as the agent of specific processes, or actions:

> You ring that neighbour.
> You find that number.
> You remember to take [that suit to the cleaners].
> You arrange ideal combinations of guests.
> You keep control of calories.

However, these actions are mitigated through their embedding in conditional or modal structures, or by their embedding in a main clause. For example, in the following sentences, 'you' is in the affected position of the main clause in the sentence:

> Filofax will help you remember to take it.

where the subject, or agent, of the main verb 'help' is 'Filofax'. Similarly, in the sentence:

> Our home entertainment pages help you arrange ideal combinations of guests.

the subject of the main clause is 'our home entertainment pages', the main verb is 'help' and 'you' again occupies the affected object position. The same pattern is repeated in the sentence:

> Only Filofax offers you such a wide choice of cover styles.

where 'you' is in the affected position, while at the same time being the agent of the nominalised action:

> You choose cover styles.

This structural embedding of clauses of which the agent is 'you' into main clauses of which the agent is 'Filofax', positions the addressee of the text as the agent of a set of actions. However, these actions are in some way initiated or enabled by 'Filofax', as the head noun phrase occupying the agent position of the main clause.

Another instance of mitigated action in advertisement A occurs in the conditional sentence:

> If you must ring that neighbour who is ferrying your eldest to school.

where the necessity, or obligation, expressed by the modal 'must' is mitigated by the conditional structure 'if you must'. This structure often functions in talk to imply that the necessity for action is perceived by one participant in an exchange, but not by the other, such as in the example:

A: Can I open the window?
B: If you must.

It can be interpreted in this way here, that is, the necessity to ring the neighbour is not perceived equally by the speaker and hearer in the text. The difference can be demonstrated by substituting the verbs 'have to' or 'want', which do not produce the same interpretation:

If you have to ring that neighbour.
If you want to ring that neighbour.

Here, there is no marked difference in the perception of necessity by the participants. The use of 'if you must' contrasts with the obligation expressed in the other conditional sentence in advertisement A:

If your husband wants that suit cleaned.

where, as above, there is no difference in the degree of necessity perceived by the addresser and addressee. The effect of these conditional sentences in the discourse is to represent the woman's ringing the neighbour as not really necessary, and the man's wanting his suit cleaned as necessary.

These patterns of transitivity and embedded clauses contrast with those in advertisement B, where the narrating voice of the text is the agent of most of the main clauses. The first-person pronoun 'I' occupies the agent position of the following verb phrases:

I slip quietly to the coast.
I'm flying off to NYC later.
I had this city in my pocket.

and the first person is the elided agent in the abbreviated forms:

soon spotted an easy run
just bowled over
phone Marina
consult traveller's checklist
arrive JFK
consult day planner

The frequency of the first-person 'I' as the subject of main clauses in the narration contrasts with the mitigated actions of the textual addressee in A, where the second-person 'you' never occurs as the agent of a main clause unless it is embedded within a conditional or modal structure. Similarly to

A, Filofax also occurs as the agent of the enabling verbs 'lets', 'help' and 'assist' in the following:

My data set lets me verify flight times.
Filofax helps avoid anxiety and neurosis and assists me in booking a table for two.

and in the agent position of the sentence:

Filofax exercise and diet pages reduce excess bulk.

The difference between the two advertisements is in the type of actions which are enabled in each case. In A, the types of processes represented are confined to the domestic domain: taking husband's suit to the cleaners, arranging dinner parties, remembering family anniversaries and keeping control of *pennies and calories*. In B, the processes of which the narrating subject is the agent represent unconstrained movement: *easy run*, *bowled over*, *slip to the coast*, *flying*, and the type of actions enabled by Filofax include booking tables in restaurants and making airline reservations. All these processes comprise a lifestyle which is very different from that of the domestic sphere represented in A. They relate to the outside world of work and leisure activities, long-distance travel and expensive food. There is no reference to 'control' in B, the problem of losing weight is represented in terms of action, *battle of the bulge* and playing squash, rather than in terms of dieting and control, as in A.

The patterns of transitivity discussed here seem to reinforce two behavioural stereotypes. On the one hand, the woman addressed by the text is represented only in activities which are limited to the home and family. Through the syntactic embedding of clauses where she is the agent, she is not the initiator of any action, but is involved in processes which are enabled by Filofax, and which are entirely domestic in nature. On the other, the narrating male subject of B is the unmitigated agent of the rapid succession of different actions, all related to high-status, executive travel and 'play' (going to concerts, restaurants, etc.). The domain of the woman is represented as the confined space of home and family, while the domain of the man is represented as the outside world.

CONTRASTING DISCOURSE GENRES

The choice of discourse genres for the two advertisements, informal chat in A, first-person narration in the form of a personal diary in B, functions to position readers as the recipients of the discourse according to two different criteria. In A, the emphasis is on offering practical solutions to domestic problems, the voice of the text gives practical advice on how the woman can 'control' her life. In B, the reader is positioned as the consumer of a 'literary' text, reading for pleasure, not for advice. The language of the diary entries and the first-person narration in B echo the discourse of popular fiction, and the 'literariness' of the text is produced by a series of literary and poetic devices such as punning and wordplay, for instance the pun on 'stumped' discussed above. The entry which follows that first heading is an extended play on cricket terminology, with the expressions 'an easy run', and 'bowled over' used to refer to travelling across London, while 'lamb out for duck' refers to what the narrator chose for lunch, and also the cricketer Lamb being caught out for no score. There are other puns in the text, for example:

> New York's all night chemist is indispensable [dispensing chemist].
> White Burgundy, 1978, a tasteful choice [the wine tastes good, showing good taste].
> Work out and make it count [mathematical calculation, physical exercise].

Further poetic devices in the narration of B include the alliterative phrases 'Brighton to Birmingham' and 'the city that never sleeps'. There are rhymes, as in 'work out/count', 'wide/eyed' and in the more complex patterns of:

> I slip quietly to the coast

with the repetition of vowel sounds [ai] and [i], and the consonants [k], [l], [s] and [t]. The third question:

> What do I check in before I check-in?

contains a play on the two meanings of the verb phrase 'check in', and the fifth question:

> Out of milk, coffee and time at 4.00 am?

exploits the possibility of both abstract and concrete complements for the verb phrase 'run out of'. Other literary effects are produced through the use of proverbs and poetic expressions which are transformed in various ways. 'Body willing but spirits dampened' is a variation on *The spirit is willing but the flesh is weak*, 'breadless' replaces the more predictable *breathless*, and in the final paragraph, 'for business or leisure' the word *leisure* is substituted for the more usual *business and pleasure*.

The literary register of the language in B emphasises the pleasurable nature of reading, together with the pleasure of completing a puzzle by fitting together the visual 'clues' of the advertisement into a complete picture. This playful, pleasurable aspect of the text of B is notably absent in A, where the emphasis is on practicality and being *realistic*, not on enjoyment. The same device of alliteration used in the context of the conversational, chatty discourse in A produces a different effect:

Foreign phrases are at your fingertips with Filofax phrasefiles.

There is no poetic effect here, but rather one of overstatement through repetition of the consonant [f] of Filofax: a device from the domain of advertising rather than literary discourse. The visual elements of the advertisements also serve to reinforce their discursive genres: in A, practicality is emphasised through the realism of the photograph of an 'everyday' scene; in B, the 'literary' effect is created through the symbolism of the various objects representing desirable states or activities such as academic success, long-distance travel and eating expensive food, and the appeal to the postmodern in their random combination.

In A, the chatty style of the discourse relies on stylistic features which reinforce the personalised, advisory voice of the text, in particular the use of deixis. Deictic words are those which take some element of their meaning from the context in which they are uttered, such as the time or the place of an utterance (Hurford and Heasley 1983). The use of deixis in direct address has been examined by Montgomery (1986b) in relation to disc jockey talk. He argues that it functions as a device for 'erasing a sense of distance between speaker and audience', by referring to 'the immediate environment of the speaker as if details were visible to the audience' (Montgomery 1986b: 429). An example of this use by a disc jockey is:

'Er got my pumpkin in the studio *here*.
Can you see *that*?
A real hallowe'en pumpkin.

where the use of deictic terms 'here' and 'that' simulate a co-presence between speaker and hearer. In advertisement A, the deictic *that* occurs three times in the opening sentences of the text. The first instance is in the phrase:

all that professional help

which co-refers to the list of occupations in the inserted 'small-ad', and places the addresser and addressee of the text in the same deictic relation to the information contained in the inserted frame. The referent of 'that professional help' is equally accessible to both textual voice and readers, and a position of deictic proximity is set up between 'speaker' and 'hearer'.

The other two instances of deixis which create an effect of familiarity, or closeness, between speaker and hearer of the text are in the phrases:

> that neighbour
> that suit

These again reinforce the personalisation of the discourse through shared recognition of particular referents, a feature of informal, chatty, person-to-person talk. Moreover, there is not only shared deictic space, but also shared time: 'by Thursday' places both speaker and hearer in the same relation to a given point in time, i.e. the immediate present, now. The discourse of A thus positions readers unambiguously as the recipients, or hearers, of the textual voice. It does this not only through the use of direct address, but also through the deictic proximity which is set up in terms of shared knowledge between speaker and hearer of the situation described, creating an informal register of one-to-one chat.

On the one hand, then, the discourse of B features literary devices of first-person narration, wordplay, alliteration and rhyme, which make reading the text a pleasurable experience (compared to other types of reading, for information or advice; a report for instance). On the other hand, the discourse of A is chatty, personalised and empathetic, giving 'realistic' advice to solve 'practical' domestic problems, not a text to be read for pleasure.

LEXICAL COLLOCATION AND SEMANTIC FIELDS

I want now to look at the patterns of lexical collocation in the advertisements, including selections in vocabulary from specific semantic fields. Collocation refers to the organisation of vocabulary in any given text (Halliday and Hasan 1976; Halliday 1981), which produces textual cohesion through 'the association of lexical items that regularly co-occur' (Halliday and Hasan 1976: 286). This association depends on a tendency for certain terms to share the same lexical environment, rather than on any direct semantic relation between them.

There are a range of words and phrases in A which frequently occur in relation to advertisements for home furnishing, for example in the type of language used to sell fitted kitchens or dining-room furniture:

> a wide choice of cover styles and finishes
> top quality cover
> neat storage sleeves

made to last
the biggest range of insert pages

with the emphasis on choice, quality and colour (the covers of the Filofax at the bottom of the page are the same as the colour scheme of the kitchen in the photograph). In B, there are many terms which are associated with the world of business, finance and information technology:

data set
data bank
fitness account moving into credit
tap into 24 hour cashpoint
consult
verify

The features of Filofax are represented differently, according to who is being targeted by the advertisements, through the use of vocabulary from the contrasting semantic fields of domesticity on the one hand and business on the other. The same topics are present in each advertisement, for example food, travel, money and shopping, but they are not represented in the same way. For example, in A the topic of food and drink relates to planning dinner parties at home:

our home entertainment pages
ideal combinations of guests
record their favourite food

whereas in B it relates to eating out in restaurants:

a table for two
a recommended restaurant nearby
white Burgundy 1978

Here again, the contrast is between the practical task of cooking and preparing food, and of the pleasure of having it prepared for you in restaurants.

In the same way, the travel in B is undertaken by the narrator. It is long-distance and high-status:

I slip quietly to the coast.
Birmingham is the next port of call.
I'm flying off to NYC.

In A, the travel pages are for planning family holidays, with no mention of specific destinations:

The Traveller's Checklist simplifies holiday planning
while you're there.

The term 'shopping' occurs in the same sentence as 'budgeting' and 'dietary':

with the unique Filofax shopping, budgeting and dietary pages

placing this activity on the same level as other domestic constraints, something which the woman must keep in control. In B, however, the narrator uses the 'All night London guide' to go to a more exotic 'dusk-til-dawn shopperama', a spontaneous, more pleasurable activity than the banality of shopping for a family. The woman in A has to 'keep control of calories', whereas the narrator of B plays squash to burn them, again a more pleasurable, high-status activity which has greater social value than the notion of self-control and restraint involved in dieting. For the narrator in B, a Filofax is a 'data set', a 'personalised data bank', while for the woman in A it has simply mundane 'memory-jogging pages'.

A further contrast between the two advertisements is the frequency of names in B compared to their absence in A, where members of the family are referred to as 'your eldest' and 'your husband'. The holiday destination is not given, only referred to as *there*. In B, on the other hand, names proliferate:

Marina	Suzi
Clapton	Freuds
NEC	NYC
JFK	England
Brighton	Birmingham
London	L'Escargot

These names collocate within a specific type of discourse, and they produce a lexical code which demonstrates membership of a social class and enables recognition between its members. Their use here, especially the use of initials (NEC, JFK) and familiar forms (Clapton, Suzi), infers that readers will be able to identify their referents, and thus positions those readers within the same social group as the textual narrator. To someone who shares this lifestyle, the reference to concert venues, international airports, expensive London bars and restaurants, will be meaningful. It is the language of young, single, successful businessmen, a form of executive 'yuppie-speak'. Even the names Marina and Suzi tend to be associated with the particular social class to which the narrator belongs.

In A, the lexical collocation produces a different effect. The terms listed below contrast strongly with the high-status codes of the discourse of B discussed above:

ferrying
fiddly bits

tickets and stamps
pennies
foreign phrases

These are all trivialising selections in so far as they reduce the actions and objects they represent to their smallest, most reductive units. 'Ferrying' is a short journey backwards and forwards between the same points; 'fiddly bits' are small difficult items; 'tickets and stamps' are small pieces of paper; 'pennies' are the lowest unit of currency; and 'phrases' are small chunks of language. The use of these terms minimalises the objects and actions which make up the woman's 'busy life'. The type of actions that a Filofax helps her carry out are also of a purely domestic nature:

ring that neighbour
take that suit to the cleaners
remember holidays and anniversaries
arrange dinner parties
shop, budget and diet
plan family holidays

whereas the Filofax helps the narrator of B to carry out actions which form part of a high-status, jet-set lifestyle:

watch cricket matches
make flight reservations
go to concerts
play squash
wine and dine women
shop at 4 am.

However, the mundaneness of the domestic tasks performed by the woman in advertisement A is nevertheless represented as part of a different type of high-status lifestyle. The woman in A belongs to a very small group of women who are white, middle-class and who do not have any financial necessity to work to earn a living. The type of activities she engages in, arranging dinner parties, running around after her husband, providing healthy food, etc., are presented in this advertisement as a lifestyle model for women to aspire to, a lifestyle that owning a Filofax will produce by enabling women to control all these tasks efficiently.

There is no mention of control in B, where the emphasis is on movement from one pleasurable activity to another, from a cricket match to a Clapton concert to New York and back. These are the kind of activities which stereotypically constitute the lifestyle of successful, single males, who need a Filofax to enhance this already high-status existence, rather than to produce it for them.

The implications of the use of these different discourses in the two advertisements are significant. On the level of social stereotypes, A reinforces the role of the woman in a heterosexual relationship as being solely in the domestic domain. The man goes out to work, the woman assumes all domestic responsibility, and moreover does not work outside the home herself.

In the inserted small advertisement, it is the *family* who is successful, not the mother. The expectations set up for readers by the photograph and the inserted frame are thus totally contradicted by the text. The implication that the woman works outside the home is not confirmed, nor is the implication that even within the home domestic tasks can be complex and demanding. The professional skills listed in the small advertisement contrast with the trivial nature of the activities listed in the text, and the reductive selections in vocabulary used to describe the woman's tasks. In the photograph, she is not making a business call after all, but *ringing the neighbour*. The man is telling her not to forget to take his suit to the cleaners. The woman's *busy life* consists of organising dinner parties and running round after other family members, planning holidays and remembering anniversaries, not trying to juggle responsibilities at work with demands at home. These are the type of actions which are presented as status-producing for women. Owning a Filofax will enable her to achieve this by helping her keep control of mundane domestic details which define her success, and not at all, as the first interpretation of the photograph implied, to help her organise a busy professional working schedule.

In B, however, the expectations set up by the visual sketches and symbols of the advertisement are confirmed by a subsequent reading of the text. The various objects depicted on the page all fit together as characteristic elements of the narrator's lifestyle: young, single, successful and male. The discourse of the advertisements is thus very different in terms of how they position their targeted readers. In A, the fraught woman needs a Filofax to help her control the mundane details of domestic life and create a 'successful' family. In B, the already high-status lifestyle described by the narrating 'I' is made even more enjoyable through owning a Filofax, which in this case is status-enhancing rather than status-producing.

In conclusion, then, having compared the discourses of these two advertisements, I have claimed that the stylistic features of the texts work to position readers in very specific ways. Although a first glance at the advertisements creates an impression, on the one hand, of a recognition of the changing role of women, and on the other, of a non-gendered readership, a close reading of the texts does not confirm this interpretation.

In A there is one level of address, the reader is the recipient of the 'chatty' discourse, a genre that has been primarily associated with women: familiar, empathetic, echoing the language of advice columns in women's magazines and offering practical solutions to domestic problems. The addressee of the text is placed in the affected object position within most of the main clauses of the text, and her actions are mitigated through modal or conditional structures. The semantic fields in the text relate to the domains of colour schemes and home furnishings; the lexical selections are reductive, trivialising the objects and tasks which make up the woman's supposedly 'busy life'. The textual voice of the advertisement appeals to practicality, reasonableness and being 'realistic', all qualities women are supposed to exhibit in order to organise domestic life successfully.

In B, on the other hand, there is no appeal to practicality or realism, even though the product being advertised is the same. The narration is primarily concerned with ease of movement, pleasure and luxury, and the literary devices in the text emphasise the pleasurable aspects of the lifestyle it describes. There are two levels of textual voice, one which directly addresses the reader as consumer, in the final two paragraphs, and the other, the narrating subject, which positions the reader on an inferential level through recognition of, and association with, the actions it describes. The narrating voice is the unmitigated agent of these actions, and the semantic fields of the text relate to the world of finance, travel and pleasure, a world which is predominantly male-dominated.

In a report of a survey carried out by the Advertising Standards Authority (Olins and Rafferty 1990), it was stated that according to three-quarters of those questioned, 'advertising still fosters unrealistic ideas about the way women should look and behave', while advertising executives claimed that 'women are pictured as strong, independent and successful'. The social stereotypes represented in these Filofax advertisements, and the discourse genres selected for their corresponding textual elements, seem to indicate that the common-sense assumptions upon which they are based have not taken account of the changing status of women at work or within the family unit. On the contrary, they perpetuate images which position women very clearly in the domestic domain, and posit this as a desirable state, rather than as successful professionals with equal status to men, sharing family responsibilities. The contradictions in advertisement A between the initial interpretation of the photograph and the content of the text are all the more disturbing, since the first impression is precisely that of a 'strong, independent and successful' woman. This impression of a working mother is subsequently undermined by the representation of what constitutes a 'busy mother' in the text, and by the trivialisation of the tasks she assumes through the stylistic features of the discourse.

Although the representation of women in advertising is constantly being challenged, and it is claimed that the stereotypical images of women as either sex-objects or mothers (or sometimes both) are being replaced by more positive images of women as 'smart career girls' (*Sunday Times*, 11 February 1990), there is still a long way to go. As I hope to have shown in this chapter, language of this kind in advertisements still tends to reinforce common-sense assumptions about the role of women, positioning them firmly within the domestic domain, and excluding them from other types of activity which remain predominantly male. Although it is perfectly conceivable for women to do all of the things described in advertisement B, they are not addressed by the text and cannot share the subject position of the narrating 'I' of the discourse. The marked address of advertisement A, specifically targeting women, continues the tendency to separate women out from the male world of action and power, and to foreground the gender stereotypes of wife and mother, while the ubiquitous nature of advertising serves to embed these stereotypes even more deeply into structures of common-sense knowledge. By undertaking a systematic analysis of the language used in advertisements, and particularly, in this case, by examining the differences in the discourse genres used to sell the same product to both men and women, I hope to have demonstrated the validity of linguistic analysis as a crucial step in the process of exposing and challenging these stereotypes.

NOTES

The author would like to thank Sally Robertson for providing initial impetus for this chapter, and Shân Wareing for helpful comments during rewriting.

1. For those readers who are not familiar with these linguistic terms, I give a brief account of what they mean and how they function in discourse at each relevant section of the analysis.
2. The advertisements were originally supplied by Sally Robertson, whose initial discussion of background assumptions and inferencing in relation to these advertisements gave rise to this chapter.

REFERENCES

Cameron, D. (1985) *Feminism and Linguistic Theory*, London: Macmillan.
Cameron, D., McAlinden, F. and O'Leary, K. (1988) 'Lakoff in context: The social and linguistic functions of tag questions', in Coates and Cameron (eds), pp. 74–93.
Coates, J. (1986) *Women, Men and Language*, London: Longman.
Coates, J. (1988) 'Gossip revisited: Language in all-female groups', in Coates and Cameron (eds), pp. 94–122.
Coates, J, and Cameron, D. (eds) (1988) *Women in their Speech Communties*, Harlow: Longman.
Fairclough, N. (1989) *Language and Power*, London: Longman.
Fairclough, N. (ed.) (1992) *Critical Discourse Analysis*, London: Longman.
Fowler, R., Hodge, R., Kress, G. and Trew, T. (1979) *Language and Control*, London: Routledge & Kegan Paul.
Freeman, D. (ed.) (1981) *Essays in Modern Stylistics*, London: Methuen.
Goodwin, M. H. (1980) 'Directive–response speech sequences in girls' and boys' task activities', in McConnell-Ginet, Borker and Furman (eds), pp. 157–73.
Halliday, M. A. K. (1981) 'Linguistic function and literary style: An inquiry into the language of William Golding's *The Inheritors*', in Freeman (ed.), pp. 325–60.
Halliday M. A. K. and Hasan, R. (1976) *Cohesion in English*, London: Longman.
Harris, S. (1984) 'Questions as a mode of control in magistrates' courts', *The International Journal of the Sociology of Language*, 49: 5–27.
Hurford, J. and Heasley, B. (1983) *Semantics: A coursebook*, Cambridge: Cambridge University Press.
Lakoff, R. (1975) *Language and Women's Place*, New York: Harper & Row.
McConnell-Ginet, S., Borker, N. and Furman, N. (eds) (1980) *Women and Language in Literature and Society*, New York: Praeger.
Mills, S. (1992) 'Knowing y/our place: Marxist feminist contextualised stylistics', in M. Toolan (ed.) *Language, Text and Context: Essays in stylistics*, London: Routledge.
Montgomery, M. (1986a) *An Introduction to Language and Society*, London: Methuen.
Montgomery, M. (1986b) 'DJ talk', *Media, Culture and Society*, 8, 4 (October): 421–40.
Olins, R. and Rafferty, F. F. (1990) 'No to the sexy sell', *Sunday Times*, 11 February, p. 5.
O'Sullivan, T., Hartley, J., Saunders, D. and Fiske, J. (1978) *Key Concepts in Communication*, London: Routledge.
Thornborrow, J. (1991) 'Orderly discourse and background knowledge', *Text*, 11, 4: 581–606.
Wareing, S. (1990) 'Women in fiction – stylistic modes of reclamation', *Parlance*, 2, 2: 72–85.
Williamson, J. (1978) *Decoding Advertisements: Ideology and meaning in advertising*, London: Marion Boyars.

Part III

Reception-theory/ Reader-response Analyses

Chapter 6

Pre-Raphaelite Painting and the Female Spectator

Sexual/textual positioning in
Dante Gabriel Rossetti's The Beloved

Lynne Pearce

This chapter, like Kay Boardman's (see Chapter 8), addresses the question of how twentieth-century feminist readers and viewers are positioned by texts from an earlier historical period: to what extent are they able to challenge the conditions of production and consumption by which such texts are historically inscribed? To what extent can they create an 'alternative' reading position? My conclusion, based on my earlier work with the Pre-Raphaelites and reviewed and revised in the reading of the Rossetti painting which follows, is that such recuperation is extremely problematic. While it might be possible for feminists to be active in writing and rewriting the 'scripts' of contemporary art works (Madonna's song lyrics, for example: see Bradby, this volume), there are more theoretical and political obstacles to reading nineteenth-century texts 'against the grain'. While we are the historically specified audience of the one (even allowing for our exclusion/marginalisation on the grounds of gender), we cannot intervene in the meaning production of the other without overriding the particular set of historical circumstances in which that work was first received. Such constraints would seem especially important when dealing with 'high art', moreover, since the cultural values of the institutions in which such texts first circulated are not easily displaced; indeed, they persist, very visibly, in the nineteenth-century art galleries in which Rossetti's and other paintings continue to be viewed. Therefore, while we may (as twentieth-century feminist viewers) *desire* to 'usurp' the reading position originally authorised by Rossetti and his patrons, we are seriously circumscribed. The reading which follows instances a number of ways in which the ropes (metaphorical as well as literal) drawn round the nineteenth-century art work are effective in keeping feminists out.

Dante Gabriel Rossetti's *The Beloved* is probably not a painting you would want to own. I remember that once, when the Tate Gallery shop was selling off copies of this particular print for 25p, I bought two, for myself and a friend. Yet while assorted other Pre-Raphaelite images found their way onto our walls, this one never did. Looking at it again now, I can understand why: aesthetic considerations aside (that loud conjunction of orangey-red and yellowy-green would jar uncomfortably with most modern domestic spaces), what has this image to say to the twentieth-century feminist viewer that is at all salutary? A century of ideological self-consciousness has wedged itself between ourselves and this text's production so successfully that a canvas representing six female subjects (the most Rossetti ever included on a single canvas), must now be seen as excluding the female viewer. Our education as feminist readers/viewers will have enabled us to recognise, in a moment, that the gaze of these six pairs of eyes *is not for us*, but for some nineteenth-century male voyeur. Exactly *who* he is, and exactly how *we* (the twentieth-century female/feminist spectator) are positioned outside this text will be the subject of the following chapter.

Before I engage with these questions directly, however, I should perhaps say something about the theoretical and political reasons for my choice of such a recalcitrant text.

First, it was a choice made somewhat wearily and cynically soon after the completion of my book *Woman/Image/Text: Readings in Pre-Raphaelite art and literature* (1991). After many years probing Pre-Raphaelite representations of women for the Machereyan 'gaps and silences' that would allow us, as feminist readers and viewers, to intervene in a text's 're-production' and appropriate a meaning and/or pleasure 'against the grain', I had concluded that such reading strategies, while theoretically possible, were politically dubious.[1] I ended my book with the rather depressing qualm that to read *against* the historical context of a text's production was, in many cases, to excuse the inexcusable. How could I justify the revelation of a painting's 'competing discourses' or 'hidden subtexts' if the dominant discourse, the one exchanged between the historical producer and consumer (i.e., male patron/purchaser or nineteenth-century viewing public) was as distressingly demeaning and misogynistic as these often were? My book concluded that only two of the eight poem–painting combinations I had considered were of 'sufficient ideological complexity' to allow for a *positive* feminist appropriation. In all other instances, I found the dominant discourses which overlaid the

Figure 6.1 Dante Gabriel Rosetti: *The Beloved*, 1865

text too securely dominant: reclaiming these representations as subversive and/or 'heroic' was certainly possible, but not ethically legitimate (cf. Mills, and Christie, this volume).

And so, in writing this chapter, I decided to put all pretensions of feminist appropriation behind me. I picked up the Tate Gallery catalogue with an eye not for complexity, but for cliché. After reclaiming Pre-Raphaelite paintings against the odds, I would attend, once more, to their surfaces: to their predominant ideologies. The remit of the present volume was after all, 'positioning the reader' and, no matter how dextrous the feminist reader/viewer might be in usurping that role, it was clear she was not meant to be there. Pre-Raphaelite painting is, by and large, a canon of art made by men, for men: or (to phrase the point a little less essentially), these are texts which were inscribed by, and are re-productive of, patriarchal discourse. With these cynical criteria in mind, The Beloved selected itself without too much difficulty. This is Rossetti's work at its worst, I thought: its most parodic, its most unfascinating.[2]

POSITIONING AND CONTEXT

Perhaps the first thing to observe about the 'art history' of this painting is that my criticisms would probably go unchallenged by even the most devoted Rossetti scholars. Painted in 1865–6, it is a canvas from Rossetti's 'decadent' middle period: the decade in which, following Elizabeth Siddal's death in 1862, he took up his paint-brush once more (during the 1850s he worked almost exclusively in pen and watercolour), and began manufacturing a series of bust-length 'portraits' of beautiful women which are variously described as 'sensuous', 'decorative' and 'degrading'.[3] The appearance of these paintings – which include such titles as Venus Verticordia (1864–8), The Blue Bower (1865), Regina Cordium (1866) and Monna Vanna (1866) – has traditionally been explained, in biographical terms, as part of Rossetti's reaction to Siddal's death (see e.g. Dixon-Hunt 1968; Marsh 1984). Siddal, who mythologically has always represented the virginal/spiritual pole of Rossettian womanhood, had become, during the early 1850s, virtually his only model. Her face figures again and again in the drawings from this period, frequently as a representation of Dante's Beatrice.[4] Although Rossetti had, in fact, already begun to use other models before Siddal's death, the popular story-line is that his 'descent' into the 'fleshly' was an emotive response to Siddal's loss.[5] With his icon of purity gone, the despairing artist turned (both personally and professionally) to the pleasures and comforts of the flesh: Fanny Cornforth, Alex Wilding, Marie Ford (sitter for the bride in *The Beloved*) became his new models, while Jane Morris, muse of his later years, waited in the wings. Closer attention to Rossetti's output during these years will reveal that this chronology is wrong (see note 5), but the narrative is an appealing one. Read in this way, the new eroticism of the portraits from the 1860s is seen as a confrontation not only with carnality, but also with *mortality*. Instead of mere degeneration into the 'fleshly', we see a preoccupation with the *carpe diem* motif.

This biographical context has subsequently 'permitted' aesthetic criticism of paintings like *The Beloved*: they are seen to represent a period of technical experiment and emotional re-adjustment, in which the lack of anything to say is noted but excused.[6] This assessment nevertheless conceals two important facts about the paintings: first, Rossetti's own high esteem of them, and second, their market success.

Rossetti's own pleasure in his successful return to oil painting is most triumphantly expressed in his comments on one of his 'Venetian' subjects from 1866. Of this painting he wrote:

> I have a picture close on completion – one of my best, I believe, and probably the most effective as a room decoration which I have ever painted. It is called 'Venus Veneta', and represents a Venetian lady in a rich dress of white and gold, – in short the Venetian ideal of female beauty. (Doughty and Wahl 1965–7, quoted in TGC, p. 215)[7]

Notable in this proud self-assessment is, of course, the conjunction of 'success' with 'decorative quality'. Read cynically, the statement could be taken as tacit acknowledgement that the function of 'art' is ultimately no more than 'decoration'; a criterion that most artists and art-historians would reject as profoundly heretical. For the feminist reader, however, this bald reduction of art to decoration is made disturbing by the fact that the decorative commodity is 'woman': 'the Venetian ideal of female beauty'. With art reduced to its material function, the representation of the female body is similarly demystified: the nexus woman/art/commodity gives 'female beauty' an unambiguous market value.

The actual market price of *The Beloved* was £300.[8] As with many of the paintings from this period, it was a commissioned piece, and its price was negotiated in advance by one of Rossetti's principle patrons, George Rae. In 1863 (when this picture was first started) £300 was a considerable fee for a canvas of these modest dimensions ($32\frac{1}{2}'' \times 30''$) as comparative pricings show, but its market value is probably best understood in terms of the *demand* that arose for Rossetti's paintings of this kind. The exhibition 'The Pre-Raphaelites; Painters and patrons in the north east', held in the

Laing Art Gallery, Newcastle, 1989–90, revealed the vogue Rossetti's work had gained with collectors (in this case, mostly wealthy industrialists) by the mid-1860s. Alexander Stevenson, for example, partner in the Jarrow chemical company, paid 150 guineas for the small watercolour of *Lady Lilith*, being unable to afford the 500 guineas being asked for the oil painting of the same subject.[9]

While the collectors of Pre-Raphaelite art were not *exclusively* male, it is hardly surprising to discover that they were predominantly so. Although Rossetti, during this middle period, undertook a number of commissions for family portraits, and although the wives of his patrons (for example, Margaret Smith of Newcastle) sometimes played a prominent role in the selection process, it was invariably the male heads of the households who held the purse-strings.[10] The relationship between the wives of these collectors and the images of women that found their way into their households is, indeed, a curious one: positioned, on the one hand, to share in their husbands' pleasure in acquiring the desired purchase, they were, at the same time, excluded by their economic superfluity to the transaction. Thus, while we may never *know* if, and what, George Rae's wife thought when she saw *The Beloved* being mounted on her wall, we do know that she had no *material* means of intervening in a transaction that was between her husband and the artist or his dealer. Whether the painting delighted or offended her, whether she received it as an image commensurate with her husband's feelings for her or of his dissatisfaction, it hardly matters, since his *ownership* of the canvas meant that it was ultimately his to do what he liked with. George Rae might have been a generous and discriminating man who, like Thomas Smith, consulted with his wife on all such purchases. If, on the other hand, he was not, his wife's moral/aesthetic preferences would not necessarily be taken into account.

POSITIONING AND TEXT

I want to move now from the man who may be positioned as the historical legatee of the painting to his hypothetical brother, the 'implied' reader/viewer. My thesis here, as I expressed in my opening remarks, is that this is a text which unequivocally addresses itself to a male audience (see Thornborrow, this volume). Even were *The Beloved* painted by a woman (and, as is noted below, there were several women artists producing similar images by the end of the century), and even were it bought by George Rae's wife with her own money, I would argue that the semiotics of the text position the reader as a white, heterosexual, middle-class male. To this extent, I am therefore allowing that in matters of address, text and context may be at variance; that the expectations raised by our information about the historical producers and consumers of a text might not be realised by our examination of the text itself. Such deviance is possible, I believe, because the ideological discourses of any society, and at any historical moment, cut across the biological sex of its producers and consumers. As we see in the case of the *fin-de-siècle* women followers of the Pre-Raphaelites (for example, Henrietta Rae and Evelyn de Morgan), it is quite possible for a woman artist to position a male viewer as the audience of her painting: to reproduce images of women that are the objects of the male gaze.[11] In the case of *The Beloved*, however, text and context concur: the patriarchal hegemony of the painting's production and consumption are replicated in its textual politics. In the second half of this chapter, I am therefore going to deal with four of this text's positioning devices: namely, (1) the verbal text inscribed on the frame of the painting; (2) the gazes and gestures of the women in the painting; (3) the painting's formal properties; (4) the inscription of ethnicity and class.

The verbal text

As I argue in *Woman/Image/Text* (1991: 31–45), the appending of verbal texts to a painting is clearly the most explicit of the ways in which its potential 'meaning' is directed and circumscribed. Although the conjunction of the visual and the verbal is often a suggestive interface, there is little doubt that the Victorian artists' penchant for this device was part of an attempt to prevent ambiguity. The addition of a literary inscription (in Rossetti's case, frequently one of his own poems) to frame or canvas has the effect of pre-empting the viewers' own attempts at interpretation; it also positions the reader, as we shall see, in terms of class, education and gender.

As is the case with many of Rossetti's paintings, the inscription for *The Beloved* was added some time after the completion of the actual painting, when a new frame (dated c. 1873) was supplied.[12] The text itself is a conflation of the Song of Solomon 1.2 and 2.16 and Psalms 45.14:

My Beloved is mine and I am his,
Let him kiss me with the kisses of his mouth:
for thy love is better than wine.
She shall be brought unto the King
in raiment of needlework: the virgins
that be her fellows shall bear her
company, and shall be brought unto thee.

These lines, which focus on the bride's dedication of herself and her attendant virgins to her future husband, are an exemplary instance of reader positioning. First, and most dramatic, is the opening invocation in the first person. Here, a statement of sexual abandonment ('My Beloved is mine and I am his') is followed by the erotic appeal: 'Let him kiss me with the kisses of his mouth' (but not, significantly, 'let *me* kiss *him*). Freed from their biblical context, the invitations of Solomon's future wife address themselves provocatively to the viewer of the painting. This, of course, positions 'him' as a heterosexual male, and offers anyone in that category an immediate rapprochement with the woman represented in the painting. Those of us who are not heterosexual males are simultaneously excluded or marginalised: we are consigned merely to *overhear* what is being said. As with the verbal texts which accompany visual representations in popular pornographic magazines today, the reader/viewer is made to feel wanted: he is positioned in such a way that he 'believes' himself and the woman represented in the picture to have formed a 'special' relationship. Her use of the first-person pronoun constitutes *him* as the second-person singular addressee, and the success of the provocation depends very much on how 'exclusive' the reader/viewer feels this relationship to be.

But Rossetti's text – cleverly culled from different biblical sources – underwrites this invocation/provocation with another dynamic. The five lines from Psalms, which represent a movement from the first-person to the third-person pronoun ('She'), also register the commodity status of the 'Beloved'; an impotence further endorsed by the passive verbal construction: 'shall be brought'. In this way, the reciprocity of power implicit in the opening invocation ('My beloved is mine and I am his') is neatly circumscribed, and the addressee is positioned not only as 'desired object' but also as 'master'. Needless to say, this 'mastery' is enhanced by the fact that the bride is attended by virgins who 'shall be brought' in the same manner. Meanwhile, the re-appearance of the second-person singular pronoun in the final word of the inscription ('thee') re-establishes the intimacy formulated in the opening line.

Gesture and gaze

The positioning of the reader/viewer effected by the verse inscription is replicated and reinforced in the gestures and gaze of the bride and her attendants in the painting itself. In common with the other bust-length 'portraits' painted during the 1860s, the subject of *The Beloved* looks directly out of the canvas to engage the viewer. This 'eye contact' is very much in contrast with Rossetti's drawings and watercolours of the 1850s, where the women are nearly always represented with their eyes averted, and for which Siddal's *Beata Beatrix* ('rapt' towards death with her eyes closed) may be seen as the culminating symbol.[13] The sexual politics of eye contact is, however, no straightforward matter. Although we might read the direct gaze of the woman in *The Beloved* as more sexually provocative simply because she *is* engaging her viewer, the 'unconsciousness' implicit in the averted gaze (i.e., this woman does not know she is being looked at) permits the voyeuristic pleasure that is denied by direct eye-to-eye confrontation.[14] Direct eye contact, then, is ambiguous in its sexual import: it betokens challenge at the same time as registering the classic 'come on'. Both these messages are, I would suggest, present in Rossetti's representation of King Solomon's bride. Her *faux-naïve* invitation is mixed with artful self-consciousness. As she unveils herself for her viewer, so is she exercising a degree of power over him; the element of confrontation mitigates her passivity.

The sexual–political significance of the act of veiling/unveiling has recently been probed by Ludmilla Jordanova in her book, *Sexual Visions* (1990). With reference to its representation in the history of western art, Jordanova shows the 'powerful moral ambivalence' attached to the actions of veiling/unveiling to be commensurate with 'the absence of any stable value attached to the female body and hence its visibility or concealment' (p. 89). The veil is the paradoxical signifier of both innocence and corruption: vulnerability and (sexual) threat. Although ostensibly there to protect the wearer, the veil also protects the viewer. Removing the veil removes the protection. It is a profoundly risky act. Jordanova writes:

> Why, then, must we ask, is it the *female* in particular that is to be (un)veiled? Un/covering women's bodies has two implications that may be pertinent here. First, covering them implies shame and modesty. . . . Secondly, veiling implies secrecy. Women's bodies, and by extension feminine attributes, cannot be treated as fully public, something dangerous might happen, secrets be let out, if they were open to view. (1990: 92–3)

The gender-specific nature of veiling is further explained by Jordanova as an indication of the massively overdetermined symbolic significance of the female body and the fact that: 'By contrast, the idea of unveiling men is comic, implausible and unthreatening, presumably because their bodies are not the symbolic carriers in modern society of either creative or destructive forces' (p. 96). While un/veiling, then, is an action which discloses the disturbing connotative ambivalence of the female body in modern western culture, it also signifies the way in which the threat has been contained.

One way in which this particular painting is exceptional in Rossetti's *œuvre* is, as I indicated at the beginning of the chapter, in the presence of the supporting cast. The bride's attendants consist of four dark-haired women and a black (African) child. The sex of the latter is a matter of uncertainty for most viewers, although Virginia Surtees (1971: 42) reveals that late improvements to the painting in 1865 included the replacement of a mulatto slave girl with a black slave boy. Like the bride, all these attendants (with the possible exception of the one on the far right) look *out* of the canvas, although the 'direction' of their gaze (both literal and metaphorical) is different. While the bride looks directly into the eyes of the husband/viewer, the attendants are examining his face and body for its 'reaction'. They are, in effect, *mirrors* for the impression of her beauty upon its recipient.[15] The fact that they are looking at him from slightly different angles helps to distinguish the import of their looks from hers; it also lends a certain sense of movement to an otherwise static composition. While the bride's gaze fixes her husband/viewer in space, those of her attendants register the fact that he has just appeared and is walking towards them.

Returning to the sexual politics of these positioning devices, it may consequently be argued that where the directness of the bride's gaze replicates the invocation/provocation of the literary text ('Let him kiss me . . .' etc.), those of her attendants preserve her passive role as the third-person *object* of the (male) viewer's gaze. Her commodity status is, moreover, reinforced by the slave child's 'offering' of the vase of roses which, in semiotic terms, functions as her 'supplementary signifier'.[16] According to the system of exchange expounded by Judith Williamson in her work on advertisements (1978), the face and flowers in this text would, indeed, become interchangeable signifiers revealing a mutual signifier that might be translated, without too much trouble, as 'beautiful gift'. According to these hermeneutics, the position of the husband/viewer is equally simple: if she is the gift, he is its honoured *recipient*.

The formal properties

It may be argued, however, that the sexual provocativeness of paintings like *The Beloved* risk threatening their male audience. Notwithstanding the various strategies to undermine the threat by emphasising the female subject's essential passivity, there remains the danger of the eroticism being *in excess* of the means of controlling it. Sex and sexuality are so overdetermined in these paintings (Rossetti's series from the 1860s is arguably 'about' nothing else), that the positioning described above may not be sufficient to keep the male viewer in a position of power. It is for this reason that the formal properties of such paintings become as important as their representational content. As I argue in *Woman/Image/ Text*, the viewpoint, surface detail, two-dimensional flatness, colour and decorative symbolism of Pre-Raphaelite art can all be seen as devices to undermine the *material presence* of the female subject and hence 'neutralise' her (sexual) threat.[17]

In this respect, as in so many others, *The Beloved* is a prototypical text. As in all these 'portraits' from the 1860s, the 'subject' of the painting (the representation of a beautiful woman) vies, aesthetically, with the decorative appeal of the composition. In line with Rossetti's own comment on *Monna Vanna* as a successful 'room decoration', paintings like *The Beloved* can, one feels, be 'enjoyed' purely in terms of their rhythm of colour and line. They work, on one level, as little more than successful 'patterns'. *The Beloved* is especially conservative and formulaic in this respect. With the palette reduced to two contrasting spectrums of red and green, the composition is structured according to a predictable system of chromatic counterpoint: an area of green here, necessitates an incidence of red there. Hence, the green sleeves of the bride's dress are balanced by the red roses and lilies held by her attendant, and the red brocade of their dresses (which form the background to the bride's own) are complemented by the greenery that floats, gratuitously, in the space at the top of the picture. In sexual–political terms, it is also interesting to observe that, while the reds of the flowers, the jewels hung about the slave child's neck and the bride's own coral headress all, on one level, serve to draw attention to her mouth (which is the same colour), they simultaneously diffuse its sexual connotations by making it part of the pattern. This can, in terms of the hypothesis I am proposing, be read as a protective device for the male viewer, whereby the most erotic constituent of the painting is thus safely fetishised. The careful balance of colour is also underwritten, in this particular painting, by its almost square dimensions ($32\frac{1}{2}'' \times 30''$) and the 'mirror-image' distribution of forms. Indeed, it is only the slight tilt of the bride's head, and the fact that it is situated a little high, which prevents this from becoming the dead-centre axis around which all the other forms and colours are arranged.

Concomitant with the aesthetics of decoration is the tendency of these paintings towards two-dimensionality. As I argue in *Woman/Image/Text vis-à-vis* Burne Jones' *Laus Veneris* (1991: 130–41), the attention to surface detail is correspondent with a lack of perspective: a feature usually explained technically by the fact that the Pre-Raphaelite artists used to work in a 'fresco' manner, applying small patches of colour to a wet, white ground. Building up a painting in this 'patchwork' manner inevitably made it difficult to create a sense of depth successfully, and paintings like *The Beloved* avoid the problem by cramming everything into what is virtually a single plane. Although the painting represents three rows of figures (slave child, bride and rear attendants) they are all distributed within a single dimension. The politics of this two-dimensional representation of space is similar to the decorative distribution of colour: like the latter, it effectively undermines the (three-dimensional) materiality of the women represented and hence mitigates their sexual 'presence'.[18]

A similar mechanism can, moreover, be inferred in the painting's use of symbolism. As in many of the portraits from the 1860s, *The Beloved* juxtaposes its female subject with flowers that are representative of her sexuality. Honeysuckle and roses (*Venus Verticordia*) and passion flowers (*The Blue Bower*) are symbols of sexual seduction, and it is, of course, significant that the lily included in *The Beloved* is not 'virginal' white, but red. Like the formal devices, such symbols have the effect of converting the female subject's pretensions to a material reality 'beyond the canvas' back into abstract signification. The male viewer is thus, once again, granted a means of controlling the sexual potency of an image which he simultaneously desires and fears.

Ethnicity and class

I want, finally, to move from discussion of how the text positions its reader in terms of gender and sexuality, to positioning in terms of ethnicity and class.

Although most Pre-Raphaelite paintings are notable for the *absence* of racial groups except the white European, *The Beloved* registers an implicit politics of colour. An important hidden subtext to the representation is, first of all, its biblical source, in which the bride claims beauty *in spite of her blackness*:

> 5   I am black, but comely, O ye daughters of Jerusalem, as the tents of Kedar, as the curtains of Solomon.
> 6   Look not upon me, because I *am* black, because the sun hath looked upon me: my mother's children were angry with me: they made me the keeper of the vineyards, *but* mine own vineyard I have not kept.

Rossetti's portrayal of her as unequivocally white therefore places the painting firmly in the tradition of white Eurocentric representations of biblical subjects: the textual evidence that King Solomon and his bride were black is set against the contrary expectations of the white audience. In this instance, a particular prejudice revolves around the meaning of the word 'fairness' used repeatedly to describe the bride. In the Bible, the epithet clearly means 'beautiful':

> 4.1 Song of Solomon: Behold, thou *art* fair, my love, behold, thou *art* fair: thou *hast* doves' eyes within thy locks: thy hair *is* as a flock of goats, that appear from mount Gilead.

Rossetti, however, has clearly inferred the secondary, Western European sense of 'blondness'. The irony of his misreading is enhanced by the information that the painting began life as a Beatrice subject, which was changed to the Song of Solomon when Rossetti found the model's complexion *too bright* for his conception of Dante's Beatrice (see TGC, p. 210). Her 'ultra-fairness' is, moreover, compounded in the painting by her juxtaposition to the slave child and the attendants. The latter, presumably of Mediterranean or Middle-Eastern race, are all dark-haired and darker skinned in comparison with the bride.

This disturbing conflation of sexual and racial politics (the 'whiter' the woman is, the more desirable) positions the reader/viewer most revealingly. While on a textual level we may still infer that the bride's husband, King Solomon, is black (as he is in the Bible), the Eurocentric logic which led Rossetti to paint a white bride clearly presupposes a like-minded and like-skinned nineteenth-century audience. It is possible, then, for *The Beloved* to have *two* implied viewers in this respect: the narrative subject, *King Solomon*, who is black, and the contemporary nineteenth-century viewer, who is white. Although positioned differently in terms of their own skin colour, both viewers are therefore assumed to concur in their racial politics ('white is beautiful'), especially since blackness so clearly equals slavery.

Where this racial positioning leaves the contemporary feminist is rather more complex. While the explicit gendering of the painting might have excluded or marginalised the female spectator, both black and white, it is important to recognise that the issue of colour represents a counter-politics, inviting new processes of identification and alienation. While for the white feminist this might take the form of an invisible/unconscious alignment with the bride and a shortsighted assumption that the text's colour politics are concentrated in the representation of the black slave, the black feminist is likely to experience the explicit privileging of whiteness much more consciously: perhaps, indeed, to the extent that this, and not gender, represents the painting's most overt exclusionary practice. Recent work in the area of white racism has revealed that, for too long, white feminists have considered colour politics to be simply an issue of black representation, and in their discussion of such matters have failed to register the significance of their own whiteness.[19]

The implied social class of the viewer of this painting is probably the least remarkable aspect of its positioning. *All* nineteenth-century painting presumed a largely middle- to upper-class audience; the Pre-Raphaelites distinguishing themselves only (as I noted earlier) by the high proportion of *nouveau-riche* industrialists amongst their patrons. Extratextually, the class of *The Beloved*'s viewers would have been determined by its market value (discussed at the beginning of this chapter) and the place of its exhibition: in this case, the Arundel Club, London, where it was shown for one day only on 21 February 1866. Intratextually, class positioning is implicit in the 'cultural capital'[20] necessary to make sense of the subject: a certain degree of education is necessary to interpret most of Rossetti's works whose textual referents range from the Bible, as here, to classical mythology, and early European literature (for example, Dante).

CONCLUSION

Were we to construct an ideological photo-fit of the 'implied' reader/viewer of Rossetti's painting, these readings seem to leave little doubt that he would be the prototypical white, middle- or upper-class, heterosexual male that I hypothesised at the beginning of the chapter. Both textually and contextually, everything we (as twentieth-century feminist readers and viewers) are able to deduce supports this conclusion.

Nor is this a text which can be easily read 'against the grain'. As I noted in my opening remarks, it is now my feeling that feminist attempts to appropriate texts like *The Beloved* – to usurp the male reader/viewer and insert ourselves in his place – are, in many instances, misguided. *The Beloved* is, for me, one such instance. While it could be argued that the sexual threat posed by the bride means that her gaze is directed, ironically, at us, her feminist sisters, *as well* as at her male admirers, it is a dubious intervention.[21] The reader positioning of Rossetti's painting is so grossly caricatured in terms of gender that I see few feminists *wanting* to stake a claim.

To construct an alternative woman-to-woman relationship between this text and a feminist audience necessarily overrides the politics of its production and consumption: suspends (albeit temporarily) knowledge of the patriarchal/heterosexist ideologies by which it is so blatantly informed. To this extent I would propose that it is more problematic to intervene in the meaning production of a nineteenth-century text than a contemporary one: the discourses by which it is inscribed are not 'open' to us in the same way.

At the beginning of my work on the Pre-Raphaelites, the fact that a text (any text?) could elicit a range of contradictory reading positions seemed to me exciting and politically liberatory. I believed it was quite possible to make a pro-feminist reading of a text without losing sight of its gendered specificity or historical context. Like many post-structuralist critics, I thought the days of making those sort of 'either/or' choices were long past; that truly radical critical practice was to extend and multiply the range of possible meanings/reader positionings in whatever texts we dealt with. Now I am not so sure. While it is hypothetically true that no text is restricted to a single readership any more than it is restricted to a single meaning (see Mills, this volume), it is surely difficult to foster multiplicity at the same time as retaining a proper sense of a text's controlling discourses and address.

For this reason, I find myself coming back to a position which advocates feminist intervention in such texts as 'critique' rather than 'appropriation'. This is a subtle difference of methodology that was for a long time confused in my own work, but which may be explained as the difference between privileging the 'alternative' and 'oppositional' discourses of a text ('appropriation'), and deconstructing the dominant ones ('critique').[22] This means, in practice, that although it would be quite possible to read Rossetti's *The Beloved* as a pro-feminist celebration of female sexuality addressed to a female audience, it remains more politically urgent that we intervene to expose its dominant ideologies and gendered specificity of address. This is the sort of transgressive intervention that Cindy Sherman's photographic montages achieve so superbly, and that Zoe Wicomb advocates at the end of her chapter on advertising (see Wicomb, this volume).[23]

Many critics, I am aware, will insist that this sort of radical critique can be performed alongside a more positive appropriation of the texts concerned. They might be right, but for me the fact remains that these alternative readings demand that we *transcend* our positioning as historical and/or gendered readers. To read *The Beloved* as a call for female sexual liberation we have to, albeit temporarily, oust the historical male audience and assume that the text is, indeed, speaking to (and for) us. Post-structuralist theory has led us to believe that this is precisely the sort of mutability we can, and should, aspire to. I still aspire, but I cannot quite believe.

NOTES

1. For an account of Pierre Macherey's 'symptomatic' method of reading texts, see Pearce (1991: 5–11).

2. See Jackie Stacey's ground-breaking essay on what female spectators have found compelling about women stars in Hollywood cinema (1988). Stacey argues that 'the rigid distinction between *either* desire *or* identification, so characteristic of psychoanalytic film theory, fails to address the construction of desires which involve a specific interplay of both processes' (p. 129), and proposes a third term, 'fascination', to account for the pleasure the female spectator takes in the 'idealised female other' (p. 115).

3. The first two adjectives are used extensively in texts describing Rossetti's paintings from this period (e.g., the 1984 Tate Gallery exhibition catalogue, *The Pre-Raphaelites* (hereafter TGC)), while it was John Ruskin who found them 'degrading' and 'coarse' (Cook and Wedderburn 1909: 491).

4. See my chapter, 'Beatrice: Hazy outlines' (in Pearce 1991) for a full account of Rossetti's treatment of this subject.

5. Marsh corrects the chronology of these events (see especially 1984: Chapters 9–12). She notes that Rossetti 'never really lost touch' with Fanny Cornforth during the years of his marriage, and that she modelled for a number of figure drawings in 1861–2 (i.e., before Siddal's death). Jane Morris, whom Rossetti first met in 1857 before her marriage to William Morris, also sat for Rossetti in 1860, although she did not become his principal model until 1867.

6. F. G. Stephens, writing in the *Athenaeum* (21 October 1865) observed of *The Blue Bower* that

   > there is nothing to suggest subject, time, or place. Where we thus leave off, the intellectual and purely artistic splendour of the picture begins to develop itself. The music of the dulcimer passes out of the spectator's cognizance when the chromatic harmony takes its place in appealing to the eye. (pp. 545–6)

7. For full details of the provenance of the paintings from this period see the TGC. Some prices include *The Blue Bower* (1865), 210 guineas (sold a year later for 500 guineas); *Regina Cordium* (1866), 170 guineas; *Mariana* (1868–70), £500; *The Bower Meadow* (1871–2), £735.

8. The cost of *The Beloved* is cited in the TGC, p. 211.

9. For comparative pricings see the exhibition catalogue *The Pre-Raphaelites* (1989).

10. See *The Pre-Raphaelites* (Laing Art Gallery 1989: 129–30) for full details of Margaret (Eustacia) Smith.

11. See Greer (1981) and Deborah Cherry's exhibition catalogue (1986) for discussion of the women artists associated with the Pre-Raphaelite movement.

12. See TGC, p. 210, for details of the frame upon which the verses are inscribed,

13. In his famous statement on *Beata Beatrix* Rossetti wrote that:

   > The picture must of course be viewed not as a representation of the incident of the death of Beatrice, but as an ideal of the subject, symbolizing a trance or sudden spiritual transfiguration. Beatrice is rapt visibly into heaven, seeing as it were through her shut lids. (TGC, p. 209)

14. Several of the essays collected in Rosemary Betterton's *Looking On: Images of femininity in the visual arts and media* (1987) address the politics of body language and 'the gaze' in visual representations of women. See especially Kathy Myers 'Towards a feminist erotica' (in Betterton 1987: 189–202).

15. F. G. Stephens noted in the *Athenaeum* (21 October 1865):

Coming near, she draws from before her face, with a graceful action of both hands, the bridal veil of blue [?*sic*] and white. . . . As she unveils, they (the attendants) look with different expressions for the effect of the disclosure on the coming man. (p. 546)

See TGC, p. 211.

16. See Williamson (1978). According to Williamson, the majority of advertisements work by juxtaposing an image of the product (e.g. a car) with a supplementary signifier (e.g a cheetah) in order to reveal the concept/'signified' being sold (e.g. speed).

17. See especially Pearce (1991: 46–58). Griselda Pollock discusses the two-dimensionality of Pre-Raphaelite paintings and the sexual threat they present in her chapter 'Women as sign: Psychoanalytic readings' (1988: 120–54)

18. See Zoe Wicomb's chapter (this volume) for similar discussion on the politics of representation.

19. See, for example, Helen (charles)'s essay, '"Whiteness": The relevance of politically colouring the "non"' (1992: 29–35).

20. 'Cultural capital' is a concept invented by the theorist Pierre Bourdieu to explain the way in which power is relayed in capitalist societies through the individual's access to/exclusion from the practices of 'High Culture' (e.g. a familiarity with opera, a knowledge of expensive wines). One of the best introductions to Bourdieu's work now available to the feminist reader is Toril Moi's article (1990–1: 1017–49). Associated with the notion of 'cultural capital' is that of 'symbolic violence': the means by which the possessors of cultural and symbolic capital (a closely related concept) assert their power over others. On this point Moi writes: 'In late capitalist societies . . . symbolic violence flourishes most perniciously in the domains of art and culture, perceived as sacred refuges for disinterested values in a hostile, sordid world dominated by economic production.' (p. 1023)

21. See the Introduction to Pearce (1991) for a full discussion of the problems and possibilities of 'interventionist' readings.

22. For an explanation of these terms, 'alternative' and 'oppositional', see my account of Raymond Williams' four types of ideology (1991: 8). One possible way of mediating between a reading practice which privileges the apparent dominant ideology of a text and one that seeks to 'release' its alternative/oppositional ideologies is to argue for there being a *hierarchy* of such discourses in every text. By recognising this hierarchy the reader can liberate the oppositional and alternative ideologies of a text without disavowing the presence of the dominant one. Stuart Hall proposed this model in his article on 'Encoding and decoding the TV message' (1973), and I consider its implications for the feminist reader in a paper called '"I" the reader: Text, context, and the balance of power' (forthcoming).

23. A recent exhibition catalogue of Cindy Sherman's work reproduces a wide selection of her work, and also offers insightful commentary on the rationale behind her work (Kellein 1991).

REFERENCES

Betterton, R. (ed:) (1987) *Looking on: Images of femininity in the visual arts and media*, London: Pandora.

(charles), H. (1992) '"Whiteness" – The relevance of politically colouring the "Non"', in H. Hinds, A. Phoenix and J. Stacey, (eds) *Working Out: New directions for women's studies*, London: Falmer, pp. 29–35.

Cherry, D. (1986) *Painting Women: Victorian women artists*, Rochdale Art Gallery.

Cook, E. and Wedderburn, A. (eds) (1909) *The Works of John Ruskin*, vol. 36: *Letters*, London: Allen.

Dixon-Hunt, J. (1968) *The Pre-Raphaelite Imagination*, London: Routledge & Kegan Paul.

Doughty, O. and Wahl, J. (1965–7) *The Letters of Dante Gabriel Rossetti*, 4 vols, Oxford: Oxford University Press.

Greer, G. (1981) *The Obstacle Race*, London: Picador.

Hall, S. (1973) 'Encoding and decoding the TV message', CCCS pamphlet, University of Birmingham.

Jordanova, L. (1990) *Sexual Visions: Images of gender in science and medicine between the eighteenth and twentieth centuries*, Hemel Hempstead: Harvester Wheatsheaf.

Kellein, T. (1991) *Cindy Sherman*, Basel: Edition Cantz.

Laing Art Gallery (1989) *The Pre-Raphaelites: Painters and patrons in the north east*. Newcastle: Tyne and Wear Museum Services.

Marsh, J. (1984) *The Pre-Raphaelite Sisterhood*, London: Quartet.

Moi, T. (1990–1) 'Appropriating Bourdieu', *New Literary History*, 22: 1017–49.

Pearce, L. (1991) *Woman/Image/Text: Readings in Pre-Raphaelite art and literature*, Hemel Hempstead: Harvester Wheatsheaf.

Pearce, L. (forthcoming) '"I" the reader: text, context and the balance of power', in D. Reynolds and P. Florence (eds) *Media/Subject/Gender – Feminist Positions and Redefinition*, Manchester: Manchester University Press.

Pollock, G. (1988) *Vision and Difference: Femininity, feminism and the histories of art*, London and New York: Routledge.

Stacey, J. (1988) 'Desperately seeking difference', in L. Gamman and M. Marshment (eds) *The Female Gaze: Women as viewers of popular culture*, London: Women's Press.

Surtees, V. (1971) *The Paintings and Drawings of Virginia Surtees (1828–1832): A catalogue raisonné*, 2 vols, Oxford: Oxford University Press.

Tate Gallery Catalogue (1984) *The Pre-Raphaelites*, London: Penguin.

Williamson, J. (1978) *Decoding Advertisements: Ideology and meaning in advertising*, London: Marion Boyars.

Chapter 7

Working Girl: A Woman's Film for the Eighties

Female spectators and popular film

Julia Hallam

Working Girl (Mike Nichols, 20th Century Fox, United States 1988) was one of the top grossing box-office films of its year in the United States and reached number 4 in the popularity charts within days of its release in Britain in 1989.[1] The film aroused little by way of attention from the film critics, but was reviewed widely in the popular press, particularly on the women's pages, where it was used to focus debates around issues of the glass ceiling and female bosses working in traditionally male occupations.[2] In this article, I want to use the film and the discourse of interpretation that surrounds it as a means of looking at feminist interventions in academic film criticism and mainstream journalism. There has been a great deal of emphasis on ethnographic methods of research in recent work on textual interpretation; finding out what actual readers do with texts rather than claiming that texts position all readers in exactly the same way is a very necessary corrective to methods of interpretation that have ignored differences between film viewers (see Introduction). None the less, I will argue that feminist work on textual interpretation continues to be a necessary correlative to ethnographic methodologies because it is important that public discourses of textual interpretation include a feminist perspective. Film audiences do not interpret films in a vacuum, as recent work on the historical reception of films is beginning to show (Staiger, 1992). Furthermore, films still have the power to create a shared enjoyment of their themes, particularly when they are watched in the collective atmosphere of the cinema. This public aspect of film viewing and the discourses that surround it continues to be an important part of the marketing and promotional strategies that will decide the ultimate profitability of a film on the video rental market and its television sales value.

Recent ethnographic work is beginning to reveal how female readers and viewers can face a range of contradictory responses to texts which are a result of their own experiences interfacing with the narrational and formal strategies of textual organisation, as well as responding to textual content.[3] Feminist film theory has begun to elaborate frameworks in which this response can be explored. I have chosen four areas of this work which have enabled me to understand my own mixed response to *Working Girl* more clearly. Briefly, these can be summarised as issues of genre and classification, issues of representation and images of women, issues around textual positioning and the female spectator, and issues of reception and interpretation. I make no attempt here to examine all these areas in depth; rather, the abbreviated critical history given below is a reflection of my own intellectual interests, which have always been motivated by a desire to find out how femininity is culturally constructed, and how I am subjectively situated as a result of my interactions with that construction.

Films are not discrete fictional products that exist in isolation; nor are the strategies that are used to interpret them. Both exist in broader frameworks of socio-economic and cultural relations that transcend boundaries created, for example, by nation states. Hollywood films are bought and sold on the world market; their audiences are counted in millions. Getting the audience into the cinema depends on mass advertising campaigns, good press coverage and audiences enjoying the film and telling their friends about it – the industry has long been aware that recommendation by word of mouth is the surest way to advertise a film. Success is measured in terms of 'bums on seats' rather than critical acclaim in the quality press or in academic writing. The economics of the movie industry are well known to be a risky business for investors, but highly lucrative if a film is successful. This has created an inbuilt conservatism in the industry's financial entrepreneurs, the producers, who have a tendency to produce well-tried and tested formula films which are virtually guaranteed a return at the box office. Fiction films are amongst the most expensive leisure commodities our culture produces, a highly technical art form involving teams of highly skilled people in the creation of the finished product. The tendency for the financiers of films to want a product that they know will sell, often irrespective of the wishes of those who provide the creative input by way of screenwriting, directing, cinematography and so on, has been well documented.[4] The producer is often cast as the Hollywood bogeyman by those who see art and commerce as two irreconcilable opposites. The producer plays a central role in the selection of screenplays and procurement of financial backing, but it is the consumers of films who determine whether or not a producer stays in business. Tried and trusted formats re-dressed to suit contemporary themes and tastes are one way a producer can substantially reduce the risks.

OLD STORIES FOR NEW TIMES

The hallmarks of the commercial film are repetition and difference; each film is similar to its generic predecessor, but never completely identical. Well-known story formulae are constantly recycled, but each new version has a fresh twist to the tale, a different angle, that often draws on contemporary issues and debates. *Working Girl* is an exemplar of this type of film, drawing on two generic forms that were particularly popular in the 1930s and 1940s, the proletarian woman's film and the career-girl comedy. As Mary Beth Haralovich has argued, proletarian women's films enacted a struggle between feminine morality and the economic pressures of the times (Haralovich 1990). In these stories, the social and economic repression of working-class women was highlighted, along with issues of sexual harassment at work. The economic context of the Depression was exploited as the basis for their narrative content. Haralovich argues that the concern with economics in these films decentres the distinguishing characteristics of the woman's film, the domestic, familial and romantic. In the proletarian woman's film the problematic (of female subjectivity, agency and desire) is firmly tied to the social relations of power which derive from the intersection of gender and economics (Haralovich 1990: 173). These films positioned women's narrative choices within the fragile contours of a patriarchal capitalism in which the morality of womanhood struggled with economic pressures. In comparison, the career comedies of the late 1930s and early 1940s tended to foreground successful middle-class heroines who had broken into traditionally male professions, usually journalism and the law, and were engaged in witty 'battle of the sexes' repartee with their male colleagues; invariably they were either engaged or married to these men by the end of the film. *Working Girl*, as I shall discuss in detail below, reworks elements from both these genres to construct what could debatably be called 'a woman's film' for the 1980s.

Repetition and difference, recognition and surprise are keywords in the dialogue between audience and industry, as familiar stories and recognised codes are transformed and mutated to satisfy audience demands for something different – but not too different. A successful film tends to spawn others of a similar type, giving rise to generic cycles. At different times, certain kinds of stories are more popular than others; cowboy films, detective thrillers, science fictions and horror films, etc. have all waxed and waned in terms of their box-office success over the years. One way that genres can be distinguished from each other is by their narrative patterns. During the opening sequences of all narrative films, there is typically a disturbance of equilibrium, and an enigma is created which the film will then work to resolve. Enigmas tend to be generic; in the detective thriller, for instance, there is a murder which a main character, often in the form of a detective or private investigator, will set out to solve. These narrative patterns are worked out through the agency of their principal characters, and are presented to the film audience from that character's point of view. The woman's picture, however, has been defined not by its narrative characteristics, but by its leading female character of narrative agency. As Mary Anne Doane points out, the woman's film of the 1930s and 1940s was not a 'pure' genre as such, but was 'crossed and informed by a number of other genres or types – melodrama, *film noir*, the gothic or the horror film – and finds its unification ultimately in the fact of its address' (Doane 1987: 284). Designed by the industry to appeal to a female audience, these films featured female stars who were much more popular among women in the audience than among men. Fan culture in the 1940s was largely a female culture and was indicative of the intense involvement of (mainly young) women with their favourite stars. As I shall argue below, *Working Girl's* address to the audience is significantly different from this 1940s model, a result of changing patterns of cinema-going affecting the way that films are made, marketed and ultimately consumed.

A 1980s STORY OF SUCCESS

During the 1980s in Britain, stories of the rise of the poor girl from 'rags to riches' held particular currency in the context of the rise and rule of Margaret Thatcher. Thatcher's emphasis on 'enterprise' and individual success seemed to offer new opportunities for women as well as men. An explosion of books advising women on how to succeed in business appeared in the bookshops (for example *When a Woman Means Business* (Moore 1989) and *The Competitive Woman: A survival guide for the woman who aims to be boss* (Cameron 1989), along with numerous best-selling novels celebrating the meteoric rise of their principle fictional characters – Barbara Taylor Bradford's *A Woman of Substance* (Grafton, 1981), Shirley Conran's *Lace* (The Women's Press, 1981), and Lisa Althur's *Original Sins* (Penguin, 1983). All have leading female characters who rise to fame and fortune from fairly inauspicious beginnings (see Newman 1991; Tincknell 1991).

In a similar way, Working Girl draws on the Cinderella story and its many reworkings as the basis for a modern fairy tale of New York. In the film, a hardworking secretary from the poor side of town, Tess McGill (played by Melanie Griffiths), crosses the class barrier and becomes a boss; it is, however, the presence of the metaphorical 'ugly sister' in the shape of a stingingly successful WASP career woman, Katherine Parker (played by Sigourney Weaver), who adds contemporary zest to the story in the context of 1980s Britain. Rather than replaying the format of the career-girl comedies of the 1940s, where middle-class heroines played out a competitive, sexually charged dynamic with their male colleagues/lovers in careers like journalism and law (His Girl Friday (United States 1940), Adam's Rib (United States, 1949)), Working Girl's comedy turns on a battle between women of different social classes fighting for status and economic rewards. In this modern screwball comedy, winning the man is part of the prize for success, but he is not the reason for seeking it in the first place.

The film tells the story of an ambitious working-class woman striving to become a broker in the traditionally white male middle-class enclave of the New York stock market. Tess lives in a poor area of Staten Island, travelling daily by ferry to her job as a secretary in a downtown Manhattan stockbroking firm. She is intelligent and ambitious, having spent years at nightschool gaining the qualifications that would theoretically enable her to advance her career by taking her place as a dealer in her own right. She is, however, trapped by her sex and her class into a subservient servicing role, where she is subjected to indirect sexual harassment from the men she works for, who promise her promotion if she 'looks after' the needs of their business clients. Far from passively accepting this state of affairs, Tess reacts by using the office electronic newsboard to publish the fact that her boss is an 'arsehole'. Sternly admonished by the female head of personnel, she is offered a new position – her last chance – with a female boss, Katherine Parker. Katherine immediately gains Tess's respect and confidence when she assures her that they will work as a team. Seizing the opportunity this presents to prove her abilities, Tess presents Katherine with her ideas for a media take-over bid, based on her knowledge from reading the popular press. Katherine rejects the idea as unworkable, but secretly tries to set up the deal.

Katherine takes a skiing holiday, breaks her leg and Tess is left to handle her affairs. She discovers Katherine's double-dealing, and determines to find a way to make the deal herself. At the same time, Tess also discovers her steady boyfriend, the neighbourhood hunk, in bed with someone else.

She decides to take action, leaves her boyfriend and sets to work on her image, retraining her voice, restyling her hair and 'borrowing' Katherine's clothes in an attempt to take over Katherine's upper-class WASP identity. After a series of typically screwball incidents in which she meets and falls in love with Katherine's intended fiancé, aptly named broker Jack Trainor (Harrison Ford), she is almost ready to clinch the deal when Katherine returns and discovers what has been going on. Katherine finds out that not only has Tess taken control of the take-over deal, but that Trainor has been helping Tess and is no longer interested in the possibility of marrying her. At an important meeting, Katherine storms in on her crutches and attempts to expose Tess's duplicity so that she can regain control of the deal and her man, but fails miserably when she cannot explain how she put the deal together in the first place. Tess reveals how the gossip columns in the popular press had provided her with the necessary information. Convinced of Tess's authenticity, the men tell Katherine to 'get your skinny boney ass out of here'. She hobbles from the room, trying to summon the last vestiges of her dignity. Tess wins the deal, gets the man and starts a new job with her own office and a secretary. The film ends with Tess triumphant, on the phone to her old friends in the typing pool, who acknowledge her achievement with a unanimous cheer to the rousing strains of Carly Simon's song 'Let the River Run'.

Tess, then, is clearly the leading character in the film. The story is in a sense her story, and it is with her success that we, the women in the audience, can identify. Here is a story that tells of a woman's triumph over the twin adversaries of class and sexual exploitation, of a rise in social status achieved by Tess herself in spite of the prejudices of both male and female bosses. Tess gets the job and the man she wants in spite of the sexist attitudes of the men she has worked for and Katherine's classist assumptions of her 'natural' inferiority. She achieves this on the strength of her own initiative – there's no good fairy in this story – and without ending up mad, dead or married, as so many of her 1930s and 1940s counterparts did. The film, however, is a comedy; we find ourselves laughing, and in particular laughing at Katherine along with the men in the audience – Katherine, who represents one of the few women in a position of power in the traditionally male enclave of the stock market. The female audience is offered a position of identification with Tess, whilst also being offered a detached position of amused, sympathetic and superior knowledge through which they can laugh at Katherine and pleasurably despise her. This reaction, which was widely reported in the popular press, is a difficult one for feminist film criticism to address; writing in Spare Rib (April 1989), Lorraine Gamman commented that on one level the film seems to offer encouragement to working-class women to 'go for it' – but that narrow ideas about feminism inform the film, as do male fears of powerful women. What I want to try to map out as part of this reading are the problems for the feminist critic created by women's pleasure in popular entertainment forms. Trying to understand and analyse this pleasure has led to a move away from an 'images of women' approach to films which focused on issues of the representation of women, to a concern in feminist film criticism with the female spectator, textual positioning, and the cinema as a signifying apparatus.

FROM IMAGES OF WOMEN TO THE FEMALE SPECTATOR: SIGNS OF CHANGING TIMES

Feminist film criticism and theory have developed in the context of a film industry and a critical establishment overwhelmingly dominated by male film-makers, male reviewers and male critics. It seems to have found a distinctive voice in the late 1960s and early 1970s after a period of film production that Molly Haskell describes as 'the most disheartening in screen history' (Haskell 1987: 323). Between 1962/3 and 1973, violence and sexuality were substituted for romance on the screen and the roles and prominence accorded to women grew steadily worse and openly misogynistic. It is hardly surprising, given this atmosphere, that feminist critics saw little in mainstream cinema to inspire them and much to distress them. Some took direct action, picketing cinemas that were showing particularly gruesome examples of woman-hatred, where women were openly depicted as victims of rape and violence for the pleasure of a predominantly male audience.[5] Others, in the face of this overall climate of blatantly sexist and misogynistic treatment of women on the screen, tackled the male-dominated reviewing and critical establishments.[6] On all these fronts, the main issue at stake was the representation of women. Films were portraying women as sex objects, victims and brainless 'bimbos'; there were few examples of independent or strong-minded women and the vast majority of images were white and heterosexual. A growing number of feminist film critics exposed cinema (and Hollywood in particular) as an oppressive patriarchal bourgeois institution, and women as its victims (Byars 1988: 111). Mainstream film texts were dismissed as inherently patriarchal, with an all-encompassing ideology inscribed in the very mechanisms of cinema's technical apparatus, from the camera lens through to the projector. Attention began to turn away from analysing issues of content and representation to a focus on textual study and developing an emergent women's cinema.

Teresa de Lauretis sums up these two types of feminist film work which increasingly seemed to be at odds with each other:

> One was culled for immediate documentation for the purposes of political activism, consciousness raising, self expression and a search for 'positive' images of woman; the other insisted on rigorous, formal work on the medium – or better, the cinematic apparatus, understood as a social technology – in order to analyse and disengage the ideological codes embedded in representation. (de Lauretis 1989: 128)

In the latter enterprise, readings of popular films tended to become increasingly based on a post-structuralist approach, which emphasised the repression and displacement of female desire and experience into male wish fulfilment and fantasy. This 'reading against the grain' pointed out the contradictions, gaps and 'slips of the tongue' within the dominant Hollywood discourse, emphasising the complex signifying practices and multilayered narrative systems employed by mainstream fiction films. Women were virtually absent from positions of power at all levels in the film industry at this time, and invisible as contributors to the film-making process, in spite of the fact that, as Molly Haskell points out, 'women have figured more prominently in film than any other art, industry or profession (and film is all three) dominated by men' (Haskell 1987: 8). Stressing the 'cracks' in what had appeared to be a monolithic and coherent patriarchal discourse was an empowering one for feminist film critics. Unlike their sisters in literary criticism, feminist film critics have had no equivalent 'canon' of women film-makers in mainstream film to draw inspiration from. Women directors in Hollywood have been few and far between, the exception rather than the rule. Feminist critics have therefore had to base their mainstream critical practice on questions of representation and absence; by reading films 'against the grain' it became clear that cinematic images are not the mimetic reflections of real life that they can seem to be, but highly mediated artefacts that are open to a range of meanings and interpretations (Mayne 1988: 29).

Within this context, a convergence between feminist psychoanalytic accounts of gendered subject formation (e.g. Juliet Mitchell's *Psychoanalysis and Feminism*, 1974) and film theory in general raised the question of the relationship between representation and gendered subjectivity. In a keynote article written in 1975, Laura Mulvey used this theory to argue that mainstream film texts place male viewers in a dominant position of specularity, because women characters within the film are invariably objectified by the desiring looks of male characters. Female viewers could only identify masochistically with these objectified images of femininity, and had no actively desiring looks of their own. Cine-psychoanalysis asked new questions about the representation of women, such as how 'ideal readers' (spectators) are placed in relation to film texts. Theoretical work by feminist critics on a group of films that had been produced with a female audience in mind – in particular the woman's picture of the 1930s and 1940s – started to ask if there was a specific female or feminine spectator (Kuhn 1984). This question hinged upon the fact that these films had been made to address a female viewer. Did they create a gendered textual position that female audience members could adopt?

The question of address – how films hail or interpellate their readers into the film text, thereby creating character identification and a suspension of disbelief – is crucial to an understanding of how film texts position their readers. It is important to note at this point a clear difference in feminist film theory beween the audience as a social group and the spectator as the subject positioned by the processes of cinematic signification. 'A film may, through the modes of address it constructs, privilege a certain kind of spectator–text relationship. This, however, is no guarantee that every member of every audience for that film will react to it in precisely this way' (Kuhn 1984: 28). (For a discussion of the reader–text relationship, see Mills, Introduction, this volume.)

SEEING IS BELIEVING: FORMAL ANALYSIS AND FILM TEXTS

People go to the movies 'to be taken out of themselves', and one of the ways a film is judged as 'good' by an audience is the extent to which they become engrossed in it. As I said previously, one of the ways film does this is through the presentation of a narrative enigma, a disturbance of equilibrium and its resolution. The audience is drawn into the film's chain of cause and effect. Another is through the process of character identification, through which we feel that the characters and their world are in some way 'real' for the duration of the time we are watching the film. When we read what Colin McCabe has described as classic realist texts, much of our pleasure comes from taking up the position the narrator offers us because this position is the place from which the meaning of the text seems to emanate. 'The function of the narration, whether first person explicit or third person implicit, is to provide the unquestioned authority by which various claims (to truth) may be tested' (Lapsley and Westlake

1988: 171). McCabe claims that realism should not be defined by its content or capacity to mirror reality but by a certain textual organisation whose effect is to position the reader.

McCabe has identified the films produced by the studio era in Hollywood as 'classic realist texts'. By this he means, that, as with nineteenth-century realist novels, these films efface the means of their construction, presenting themselves as unproblematic representations of the material world. Narrative realism, however, depends on a great deal of artifice to conceal its construction. In a film like *Working Girl* realistic settings are an important part of creating the illusion, along with naturalistic acting, lighting, camera angles, continuity editing and sound. Mode of address, how the film presents itself to the film viewer, hinges on the combination of all these factors, but most importantly on how the film is shot and edited. The camera creates meaning by the way it shoots what is in front of it; a high angled shot, for instance, can make a character look large and threatening. Long shots, medium shots and close-ups determine the viewer's proximity to the image. Choices about angles, close-ups and shot lengths are made in the first instance when a film is in production, but are often modified when the film is assembled in the editing process. Editing places shots in relation to each other, setting up patterns of looking relations between characters in the film and creating the pace, the speed at which visual information is given to the audience. Changes in shot in the classic Hollywood narrative film are invariably motivated by character action; continuity editing ensures that the audience is always spatially orientated as it follows the action.[7] When watching these films, we are invariably presented with a viewpoint that matches that of a character; spatial relationships and character motivation work hand in hand via the camera to create point of view.

Whereas questions of narrative, genre and representation can be seen to apply to literature as well as to film, the question of address begs an answer in relation to the way films communicate primarily as visual media. In cinema, it is the image track rather than the soundtrack that shows us what 'really happens' because the spectator is sutured (stitched) into the visual field of the film through the system of looks relayed to the audience by the camera (Dayan 1976). The film audience tends to believe what is shown them rather than what they hear because the omniscient point of view is that of 'an absent other', the camera's eye. Usually, this third-person narrator position is closest to the viewpoint of the leading character, and it is through, and in relation to, this character that we are encouraged to make the events of the film intelligible. The shot/reverse shot format of continuity editing, where we see someone looking at something and are then placed as if we were looking at it ourselves from over their shoulder or through their eyes, creates an identification with the character that the camera is positioned closest to. We tend to believe what we see – what the camera places us to see – rather than what we hear, not least because of the large screen and the darkened auditorium, an environment that encourages us to suspend our disbelief and 'lose' ourselves in the film. Typically, we watch a disturbance of equilibrium within the world of the film, with the action centred on a particular character or group of characters who are presented in considerable psychological depth. Through these individual characters, the film's enigma will be played out until its final resolution. Part of our pleasure is invested in the process of narrative itself, and the reaching of a satisfactory conclusion to the enigma created by the disturbance of equilibrium. The extent of our pleasure is likely to depend on the degree of identification we feel with particular characters in the film and how satisfied we are with the way the film has manipulated the plot to restore equilibrium and effect satisfactory closure. In *Working Girl*, according to newspaper reviews of the film's reception in the United States, audience enjoyment was most intense amongst women (many of them secretaries) who identified with Tess, and audience dissatisfaction was highest amongst women (some of them feminists) who did not identify with Tess because they found her 'sickly sweet confection of femininity' decidedly unattractive.[8]

NO LOOK OF OUR OWN?

Identification and point of view have played a pivotal role in feminist analyses of mainstream narrative film. As I have noted, Laura Mulvey showed how narrative cinema excludes a female spectatorial viewpoint in its signifying system (Mulvey 1975). Mulvey claimed that the camera always creates a position for the male spectator in mainstream narrative cinema, never a position for the female. This does not mean, of course, that only men in the audience can take up that position, but that the structures of looking set up by the camera presuppose a male viewing position and a male view of the world, much as the use of the pronoun '*he*' in English has meant female readers read through an 'objective' human (male) viewpoint. Female members of the audience can adopt a spectatorial position offered to male viewers, just as black members of the audience can adopt white spectatorial positions, but this involves a re-imagining, a reconstitution of the self as an 'other'; in mainstream narrative films, this 'other' is invariably a white male fantasy figure.

Mulvey identified three relations of looking in the cinema that reduce the female image to the status of an object of the male gaze: the look of the camera at the image it was filming, the system of looking between characters in the film, and the look of the audience at the screen. Within this framework, the camera's privileging of male characters and their points of view situates the woman as a fetish, an object to be looked at. The camera invariably favours active male characters, recording their desiring looks at the female, who tends to stop the narrative flow of the film and becomes a spectacle for the male viewer through the relay of looking relations addressed to the male spectator. Female characters, rather than forwarding narrative action like their male counterparts, tend to be placed as spectacle in all genres except for the woman's picture, already identified as such by its female characters of narrative agency. In other Hollywood genres, for example the detective thriller or the gangster film, the film viewer is aligned with the male protagonist's point of view, a position that Mulvey identified as voyeuristic. The male spectator has a direct point of identification with the leading male character on the screen; he can unproblematically suspend his disbelief and partake in the fantasy, in much the same way as male readers can unproblematically assume the 'he' narrational position offered by many written texts. The female spectator is left without a look of her own; man is the bearer of the look, woman is there for her 'to-be-looked-at-ness'. Within this hierarchy of looking relations, the female spectator has two options: she can 'either betray her sex and identify with the masculine point of view, or, in a state of accepted passivity, she could be masochistic/ narcissistic and identify with the object of masculine representation' (Bovenschen 1977: 127).

Mulvey's work placed the female gaze at the centre of debate on gendered spectatorship in feminist film theory; her proposition, supported by cine-psychoanalysis, firmly placed 'the woman question' into a male theoretical film discourse, but removed the female spectator from any active role in the looking relations created by mainstream cinema. The female spectator was left without an active look of her own, her pleasure theorised as narcissistic or masochistic, condemned to ahistoricity, without possibility for change. This essentially negative view carried with it an underlying assumption that women are basically the passive dupes of a dominant patriarchal ideology inherent in the textual mechanisms of commercial cinema. Within this school of thought, women could only realise their oppression through a feminist film practice which would rethink the relations of narrative pleasure and looking, through the search for a feminist film aesthetic. Mulvey turned her attention to independent film-making, whilst feminists who were dissatisfied with the essentially negative place this theorising assigned to the female spectator continued to research questions of address centred on the woman's picture and its audience.

SPECTATOR POSITIONING: WORKING GIRL'S FORMAL STRATEGIES

By the beginning of the 1980s, it was clear that feminist film criticism had bifurcated and developed two different trajectories, a dualism that Annette Kuhn sees as marked by the binary oppositions of universalism and specificity within the discourses of film and television theory itself (Kuhn 1984). The universalising of psychoanalytic approaches seems to offer little scope for theorising subject formation in its cultural and historical specificity but does address the textual relationship between gender and subject formation. However, issues of difference between women as viewers of texts rather than only as textually constituted subjects are subsumed under the concept of the female spectator into a seemingly ahistorical uniformity that ignores specific differences such as race, class and age. More discrete approaches, which concentrate on conjectural analyses of the material conditions under which women have been cinema audiences in relation to the socio-historical and institutional conditions of the production, distribution and exhibition of films, are broadening our knowledge of the conditions of film consumption. Jackie Stacey's work with female fans of the 1940s is filling in part of the picture for the British context, as is Mary Beth Haralovich's work on the proletarian women's films of the 1930s in the United States (see Haralovich 1990; Stacey 1991). None the less, we still know very little about actual audiences for particular films, or the conditions of reception within specific viewing contexts.

The gendered reader in the 1990s is situated on the cusp of these two critical trajectories:

> the distinction between social audience and spectator/subject, and attempts to explore the relationship between the two, are part of a broader theoretical endeavor: to deal in tandem with texts and contexts. The distinction between social audience and spectator must also inform debates and practices around cultural production, in which questions of context and reception are always paramount. (Kuhn 1984: 28)

My approach to *Working Girl* will therefore attempt to explicate the relationship between these two approaches, although there can be no simplistic grafting of one onto the other. First of all, a close reading of the text will try to show how a female spectator (in the cine-psychoanalytic sense) is situated by this particular text, and then questions about the film's reception by the press will locate it within feminism's contemporary discourses on femininity, illustrating how the range of feminist approaches enlivens and stimulates debates around the meaning and interpretation of popular films.

In *Working Girl*, the point of view we are offered seems to belong to Tess. The title carries the promise that it will be her story, and it is her dissatisfactions which motivate the action. As viewers, however, we are often presented with point-of-view shots that present us with knowledge that Tess does not have. We know that Katherine is setting up the Trask deal long before Tess does, we know that Katherine has decided to marry Jack Trainor and we know that Katherine discovers what Tess is up to before Tess knows she knows. As viewers, we are placed in a position of omniscience, and much of the comedy hinges on what we know that the characters are unaware of, intensifying our sense of anticipation when they walk into confrontational situations. In the initial stages of Tess's relationship with Katherine, we are presented with shots of Tess from Katherine's point of view, a position that emphasises her gaucheness and gaudy clothes in relation to Katherine's sophisticated *haute couture* image. As Tess completes her transformation, however, and begins her association with Jack Trainor, his point of view increasingly dominates the film's looking relations. In an earlier sequence of the film, Tess is posing in black underwear to please her boyfriend; although she objects to parading in this way, she is none the less presented as a visual spectacle. In Mulvey's terms, the boyfriend's gaze offers an active/male spectatorial position of voyeuristic desire, whilst the spectacle of Tess and her verbal reticence offers a passive/female point of masochistic/narcissistic identification.

In the later sequences with Trainor, the boyfriend's overtly sexual gaze of desire is replaced with Trainor's more 'fatherly' gaze. He looks at Tess asleep in bed between white sheets, watches her talking to Trask about the merger, dressed in a neat white blouse and suit, sees her picking her possessions up off the floor in T-shirt and jeans. All these images suggest that Tess is being seen differently, that she has undergone a transformation; from being seen as sexually experienced to being seen as innocent and naive, from being a working-class desiring 'bad' girl to a middle-class virginal 'nice' girl. The 'dumb blonde' Tess is seen to be not quite so dumb after all, whilst dark-haired middle-class Katherine, in spite of her expensive white underwear, is a 1980s version of the female devourer who eats not only men, but poor innocent working-class girls too! Although, as textual subjects, it is easy to identify with Tess, we are not given any shots from Katherine's point of view which encourage a sympathetic view of her. We are shown Katherine's view of Tess as a lesser being, kneeling at her feet to fix her ski boots, sitting opposite her in cheap jewellery and gaudy make-up. Seeing Tess from Katherine's point of view makes explicit the class relations between the two women, but also opens up the possibility of identification with Katherine, a position that at least one female reviewer of this film took, delighting in Katherine's luxurious excess, success and total selfishness (see Suzanne Moore, New Statesman and Society, 7 April 1989, pp. 49–50).

Through this analysis of the system of looking relations within the film, several conclusions can be drawn about how it attempts to position viewers as textual subjects. In Working Girl, the spectator is sutured into Tess's point of view at particular instances in the film, but the omniscient viewpoint, where the camera situates the spectator as a third person watching the action unseen by the characters, tends to remain within a male scopic field.[9] Once Tess meets Jack Trainor, the camera places itself in a direct relationship to his view of both Tess and Katherine. Although he figures far less prominently in the narrative than Tess, once he enters it there is an overall feeling of his omniscience, since only he knows of his relationships with both Tess and Katherine, and he is the crucial figure in the success – or not – of the deal. The omniscient 'third eye' seems to have a closer relationship with him than either of the female viewpoints, even though the film is ostensibly about Tess.

As mentioned above, this overall point of view that privileges a male gaze and positions 'woman' in relation to it has long been recognised by feminist film critics as an all-pervasive characteristic of most narrative cinema, but whether audiences actually take up the ideal spectatorial positions on offer is open to question. Feminists, like many other marginalised groups in society, often resist the positions on offer and seek other meanings (cf. Pearce, this volume).[10] Film audiences are not homogeneous collections of people who uncritically accept the spectatorial positions on offer, but individual subjects who bring their own range of meanings to a film. Meanings are, however, culturally constructed; different groups in society attach different meanings to texts. Not only are all audiences composed of pre-existing social subjects, but they can be cine-literate subjects too, aware of the codes of classical cinema and how these codes mediate reality. In a 1950 study of the mid-1940s Hollywood audience, anthropologist and film critic Hortense Powdermaker noted a lack of gullibility amongst teenage girls, who described many of the films designed to attract a female audience as 'weak', 'corny' and 'unrealistic' (Walsh 1984). *Working Girl*, however, seems to have struck something of a different chord in its female audience according to a review that reported the film's reception in the United States: 'Weaver is not bothered by the violent reactions that Katherine has provoked in women cinema-goers' (*Today*, 9 January 1989). The film has clearly sold itself as an object for consumption by female cinema-goers, aided by its press coverage, and it is to the relations between the popular press, film and consumption that I shall now turn as a way of explicating the pleasure relationship between female audiences and the images of women that they consume.

REVIEWING *WORKING GIRL*: DISCOURSES OF INTERPRETATION

In the press book for *Working Girl*, a brief synopsis of the film's story concludes 'Tess soon realises that she's in a combat zone and she'll have to use commando tactics if she wants to survive.' The cover photo depicts Tess and Katherine either side of Jack Trainor with their hands on his chest. All three are smiling and looking directly at the camera. Tess is described in the press book as 'sweet but street smart', Trainor as 'a white-collared Prince Charming' and Katherine as 'a seductive piranha'. Before critics review a film, the promoters try to direct audience response by fixing a preconceived notion of what the film will be about in the mind of the reviewer. Press books are one way in which the film industry tries to control the circulating discourse of interpretation that surrounds a film's reception by attempting to fix meaning.

Looking at the reviews in the popular press, it is clear that many of the journalists have in fact followed the press-book line. There are numerous references to Trainor's chivalric qualities and Katherine's non-human character. What strikes me most about the journalists' accounts, however, is the distinctive gender division in the interpretative strategies they are using. This is partly a matter of context. Almost all the reviews on the arts pages were written by men, who consistently evaluated the film using traditional aesthetic terms of reference rooted in literature and fine art. Discourses of genre criticism, authorship and film form dominated these critical reviews. In *The Guardian* for example, Derek Malcolm commented that the film was 'too hollow to be a red-blooded woman's film'. *The Scotsman*'s critic adopted the *auteur* approach, situating the director Mike

Nichols as a film-maker following in the tradition of Capra, Hawkes and Wilder, whilst Iain Johnstone in The Sunday Times gave his readers a run-down of Nichols' career.

The film was also widely reviewed by female journalists writing on the women's pages, where an 'images of women' approach was used to focus on issues of female bosses in traditionally male occupations. In this approach, the film's reworking of the Cinderella story is often seen as part of a broader discourse of femininity which recasts white middle-class ideas around motherhood and work into a 'superwoman' mould. Superwoman is the successful woman of the 1980s; she manages to have a buoyant career, an equal relationship with her partner and bring up her children without detriment to her health and well-being. 'Superwoman' is a real possibility, an achievable goal, as women like Shirley Conran and Erica Jong have tried to prove. Advertisements are full of images of these women, as Joanna Thornborrow's reading of the Filofax advertisement in this volume demonstrates. The gross parody of the Katherine character as a single childless woman in a position of power who has taken control of her own life (including planning her marriage to Jack Trainor to satisfy her desire to have children) can be seen as part of this nexus of representations of woman circulating in the 1980s, a projection of fears and fantasies about women who reject the 'traditional' values of family life. As Bryony Coleman commented in The Guardian (16 February 1989), taking a broadly feminist stance towards the film, 'All the signs indicate that top women continue to be characterised as more ruthless, ambitious and manipulative than their male equivalents.' This, as Margaret Marshment points out in The Female Gaze, is a modern replay of an old theme:

> the history of female representation has a strong undercurrent of women who are bad and strong; from Medea to Lady Macbeth, from fairy tale stepmothers (and step sisters), to film noir heroines . . . when women are powerful and independent, they are evil. (Marshment 1988: 31)

The liberated career woman is the 'evil woman' of the 1980s, whether she is Alexis Colby of Dynasty, Alexis Forrest of Fatal Attraction or Katherine Parker in Working Girl.

Two other female critics took a similar approach to Coleman. Writing on the re-emergence of class as an issue in contemporary popular cinema for the New Statesman and Society, Suzanne Moore commented:

> Tess is a kind of heroine – a working-class woman made good. But heroine-worship comes at a price, and part of that includes being described as a working girl rather than a working woman. . . . My sympathies were with Katherine – so completely set up as a male fantasy of a ball-breaking career bitch – that it's hard not to fall in love with her. (7 April 1989: 50)

Moore is clearly resisting identification with Tess in favour of Katherine, in a feminist view somewhat similar to that of Lorraine Gamman's in *Spare Rib*: 'Tess failed to impress me – perhaps because her squeaky little voice operated to remind us all along that she was a working girl rather than a woman' (p. 22).

These reviewers all share an interest in feminist ideas and their representation, which, given the reader constituencies of *The Guardian*, *New Statesman and Society* and *Spare Rib*, is perhaps unsurprising. In *Mirror Woman*, however, the reviewer is plainly antagonistic to what she perceives as feminist values, claiming that 'This film will do more for secretaries than feminism ever did – they are shown as the life support system of the office.' She goes on to say: 'Everyone has come across a Katherine Parker type. All glossy incompetence, disguised in designer clothes.' *Mirror Woman* was not alone in its antagonism towards female managers. The *Daily Mail* (18 January 1989), in a lengthy article that describes the 'dirty tricks' played on female subordinates by their female bosses, warned its readers to 'Beware these career girl cobras. We thought we were sisters, working together in a male dominated world, but a controversial new film reveals the truth we always feared.' Here, the writer goes to considerable lengths to point out what she sees as feminism's faulty premise, that all women are (potentially) equal. *Miss London* (7 April 1989), however, also addressing secretaries, 'temps' and female office workers, took quite a different view: 'If you're a frustrated secretary you're going to love it . . . a neat feminist drama that shows women can sometimes be their own worst enemy.' Clearly, the label 'feminist' has different meanings for different people, as one might expect. In all the reviews written by women, a clear opinion was expressed about feminist political goals and feminism's ideas and values, showing that feminism as a (contradictory and unfixed) subject position is widely circulating as an interpretative strategy amongst female journalists. In addition, the reviewers who showed the clearest political affiliation to feminist ideas focused on issues of representation, one of the earliest strategies used by feminist film critics in their analysis of mainstream narrative films.

CONSUMPTION IS HOW A PRODUCER REMAINS A PRODUCER

As I mentioned at the beginning of this chapter, *Working Girl*'s commercial success means that many people have enjoyed the film, and they have told their friends about it; differences amongst audience members have been sufficiently subsumed under a shared enjoyment of its themes. Furthermore, as the press reviews revealed, there was a general assumption that many women would see the film, if not immediately at the cinema, then at some later point on video or television. As I have already pointed out in the formal analysis, the film tries to interpellate a female viewer into a particular relationship with its narrative and formal strategies, although in fact it falls short of being a 'woman's film' as that notion has been traditionally understood, because Jack Trainor, rather than Tess, is the only one who knows the truth, who is in a position of knowledge. None the less, it is safe to assume that the female audience for the film runs into millions, without even considering its video consumption.

In her analysis of the woman's film of the 1940s, Many Anne Doane points to a relationship between women as consumers of commodities and as consumers of images of women, in the context of the patriarchal positioning of women as a commodity, a relationship that blurs the subject/ object dichotomy. The spectatorial gaze set up by the cinematic apparatus and the consumer gaze constructed by late capitalist society are both articulated in the cultural construction of femininity. Doane goes on to point out that much feminist theory has envisaged women's relationship to commodities in terms of being one herself, 'she is the object of exchange, rather than its subject.' The female spectator, as a psychic entity, is invited when watching a film to witness her own commodification, and furthermore to buy an image of herself in so far as the female star is proposed as an ideal of feminine beauty (Doane 1987: 24). The seediness of Tess's Staten Island neighbourhood environment and the luxurious lure of Katherine's Manhattan apartment are constantly juxtaposed in the film, setting up the equation that equates a 'feminine ideal' of beauty and success with material goods and the status of owning them. Tess succeeds in her ambitions because she changes her image, she adopts Katherine's style. In consuming the film, female viewers also consume the image of Tess becoming like Katherine.

> The economy of the text (in a literal sense as an object of commodity exchange), its regulation of spectatorial investments and drives, is linked to the economy of (commodity purchasing), the logic of the female subject's relation to the commodity – her status as a consumer of goods and consumer of discourses. (Doane 1987: 25)

As a considerable amount of research has shown, narrative films address women as consumers playing a role in the cultural construction of femininity. Tie-in products, such as clothes, make-up and domestic goods, are often marketed through the star herself, or by direct means of association.[11]

The class relations in *Working Girl* clearly function in relation to commodities, since the plot turns on the theft of both property and ideas. As Andrea Walsh has pointed out, the appeal of the woman's picture of the 1930s and 1940s to the female audience was based on particular notions of feminine morality that focused on interpersonal relationships and responsibilities (Walsh 1984). Like its earlier generic counterparts, *Working Girl*'s main protagonists are women, and without doubt the film seeks to address a female viewer, but it lacks the 'sacrifice' element that was so common in many of these earlier woman's pictures. In these films, women frequently sacrificed their own welfare for that of their children (*Stella Dallas* (United States 1937), *Mildred Pierce* (United States, 1945)), relinquished their careers for love (*Lady in the Dark* (United States, 1944)), or gave up everything to fight for a good cause (*Mrs Miniver* (United States, 1942), *Madame Curie* (United States, 1944)). In *Working Girl*, however, far from being willing to give things up, both leading characters help themselves to what they want. One steals an idea to further her own career, whilst the other steals an identity to gain the status and economic success that she believes should be hers. This moral duplicity led actress Ellen Barkin to reject the part of Tess when it was offered to her, because she disliked the film's morality and regarded the relationship between the two leading women as a distortion of power relations in the workplace (interview on *Wogan*, BBC1, January 1990). Jo Spence's comments in relation to advertising addressed to women seem to sum up the situation succinctly:

> in publications aimed at women, the advertising industry seems happy to add the image of women as worker to its repertoire of images of wives and mothers and women's objectified sexiness. What these changes emphasise, though, is individual earning and consumption, not the collective practices inherent in the struggles within the women's movement and the labour movement. (Spence 1987: 53)

Working Girl promotes the fantasy that we can all be Tess if we change ourselves, we can all become 'superwoman' through our own individual – rather than collective – actions.

If the film is seen as part of a circulating discourse of certain kinds of ideas about femininity and working women current in the late 1980s, it is clear that these images are reworking earlier themes of female subordination to male values. The film does not tackle issues of sexual harassment or power relations in the workplace faced by women who try to break through the 'glass ceiling'. As the *Sunday Express* critic pointed out succinctly, 'embedded somewhere in the plot is a film about real hardships and just what it takes to overcome them faced by working girls with ambitions beyond their station' (2 April 1989). Janet Newman, in her analysis of popular 1980s career-advice books for women, points out that 'rules' are being set out which women must follow in order to succeed, but the basic structures of society are being left intact. Conflict at work has to be 'managed' at a personal level, and any identification with the needs and interests of other women must be abandoned if women want to get on (Newman 1991). *Working Girl* represents this individualistic enterprise ethos in a fictional form, presenting a comedy of class and power relations that, unlike women's films of the 1940s, places conflict between women at the centre of the plot.

A comparison between *Working Girl* and the 'woman's film' of the 1930s and 1940s brings out some changes in the format of films that seek female audience members. When we go to the cinema, we are both textual subjects, placed by the film through its signifying practices, and social subjects who bring our own meanings and values to films according to our own personal biographies and social experiences. *Working Girl's* mode of address and its popular appeal can be explained by the film industry's attempt to 'have it all', to address both women and men, perhaps because it is no longer economical for mainstream films to seek a predominantly female audience. Commenting on the film at the end of 1988, the *Village Voice* saw it as typically representative of films that are now being made to attract women without alienating their male friends or husbands, since these days women rarely go to the cinema alone or with other women. The implications of this marketing strategy on film texts that appear to address a female viewing subject have yet to be fully assessed by feminist critics.

Though ostensibly addressing women and offering points of identification for the female viewer in the figure of Tess (and, for some, Katherine), the film none the less presents women to be laughed at, figures of fun, spectacle and narrative entertainment. Although a woman is the character of narrative agency, the system of looking relations within the film places Tess as the object of the gaze of the two men who desire her, as a spectacle to be visually consumed by them, and therefore she is also consumed by a textual subject who identifies with the male point of view. Viewers who identify with Tess are arguably placed in a position of complicity and narcissistic identification with the film's omniscient view of her as spectacle and object of consumption, whilst those who identify with Katherine have to bear with her the indignities of her demise. When I watched the film with a friend, the pleasure experienced at Tess's success, but our ambivalence about the film in general, were a direct consequence of the way we felt we had been textually positioned as viewers. On the one hand, as mature students ourselves, we easily accepted the place offered by the text to identify with Tess and her success, but we had problems with her (for us) too feminine character. One the other hand, we identified with Katherine and found it difficult not to enjoy her ruthlessness even though our feminist selves were protesting.

As the review in the *New Statesman and Society* commented, the kind of femininity *Working Girl* suggests works best as nothing but a prop, a masquerade onto which we project our exhausted daydreams about what women are really like. If we accept the idea that femininity is a masquerade (an idea the film certainly plays with and articulates through Tess's donning of Katherine's identity), masquerading for self-gratification and personal purposes, rather than only for male visual pleasure, apparently speaks to an image of female desire that has figured prominently in representations of women in the 1980s across a range of media. This awareness of the self as an image, an awareness that the characters in the film play with through lines like Tess's best friend Cynth's 'You wanna be taken seriously, you need serious hair', is the point at which feminist ideas about the social construction of femininity can be seen to have informed the film and the discourses that surround it, although these feminist ideas have been appropriated and re-articulated to suit patriarchal constructions of the female imaginary. What I find interesting about *Working Girl* is not debates about its regressiveness or otherwise as a text (as I stated at the beginning, all mainstream commercial films have a tendency towards conservatism), but its reworking of genre – the woman's picture – in the light of contemporary issues around women and work.

Feminism has clearly had an influence on these debates at the popular level; many women now seem to accept the constructedness of femininity in a way that has not seemed so evident before. Although in some papers, for example *The Sunday Telegraph* (2 April 1989), male reviewers used the film as an opportunity to deride feminist values ('if Cinderella wants to catch Prince Charming, she shouldn't act like her ugly feminist sisters'), many of the reviews in the popular press were written by women for the 'women's pages', and these reviewers were consistently more critical of Griffiths' portrayal of a 'trembling lip' femininity and the ethics of the film than their male counterparts. *Mirror Woman* (30 March 1989) praised the film because it 'exposes the subtleties of the new stereotypes', whilst *The Guardian* (16 February 1989) critic called Katherine a 'superbitch, sexier and meaner than ever before'. This seems to indicate that not only has the collective female audience, in its many and varied forms, an understanding of the conventions of mainstream narrative film like its counterpart in the 1940s, but it also understands the constructedness of the female image itself, as a masquerade we all play out in its many and variant forms.

NOTES

1. *Screen International* produces comprehensive listings of top grossing films based on box-office takings. For *Working Girl* figures, see N644, 14 January 1989.
2. The 'glass ceiling' is a metaphorical term used to describe the situation faced by successful career women when they discover they are not being promoted above a certain level. The top jobs are in sight, but strangely unobtainable. In *Working Girl*, the issue is raised through the depiction of Katherine, the successful career woman, as an upper-class ambitious, ruthless, sexually manipulative 'bitch'. See Bryony Coleman, *The Guardian*, 16 February 1989, and *Mirror Woman*, 30 March 1989.
3. See, for instance, *Women Viewing Violence* (Schlesinger *et al.* 1992); *Women Watching Television* (Press 1991); *Remote Control: Television, audiences and cultural power* (Seiter *et al.* 1989); 'Framing experience. Case studies in the reception of *Oranges Are not the Only Fruit*' (Hallam and Marshment 1993). The vast majority of ethnographic work on moving images has been done, for practical reasons, with television and video. It must be emphasised, however, that the cinematic experience cannot be reduced to watching films on video, as any avid cinema-goer would not hesitate to point out.
4. The most recent contribution to the literature in this area is Nicolas Kent's *Naked Hollywood: Money, power, and the movies* (1991). For a personal account, see screenwriter William Goldman's *Adventures in the Screen Trade* (1984). For a more academic approach, see Thomas Schatz, *The Genius of the System: Hollywood film making in the studio era* (1989) and James Monaco, *American Film Now: The people, the power, the money, the movies* (1984).
5. A more recent example of this was the mass picketing of cinemas in the early 1980s that accompanied screenings of *Dressed to Kill* (Brian de Palma, United States, 1980), a film that graphically depicts the murders of several women.
6. See the writings of Kathi Maio, *Feminist in the Dark: Reviewing the movies* (1989), one of the first feminists of the second wave to become a well-known popular reviewer in the United States.
7. Continuity editing is a system of shooting and editing that enables film viewers to be continuously orientated in the visual space of the film. For example, most sequences begin with an establishing shot to create a sense of place, followed by a mid-shot which begins to focus the attention on a particular aspect of the place and/or characters, followed by a series of closer shots which direct our point of view to a particular series of events or exchanges between characters. For a detailed explanation of the formal conventions of continuity editing, see Bordwell and Thompson (1990: especially 218–30). For an explanation of how the term and the system it describes was conceptualised and developed in the classical Hollywood cinema, see Thompson, 'The continuity system' in Bordwell *et al.* 1985.
8. See *Today* (9 January 1989) and The *Daily Mail* (18 January 1989).
9. I use the term 'scopic' here as an associative one with scopophilia, which is defined as sexual pleasure gained from looking at things, particularly bodies. The scopic field of a film is the one in which desiring looks are circulating and articulated between the characters and relayed via the camera to the audience. Mulvey claimed that this pleasure was always male in classic Hollywood cinema, that there was no place for an active female desiring look. Female spectators had to identify with male characters to identify with active desire, a transvestite viewing

position that denied them a look of their own. For arguments that challenge Mulvey's view, see Gamman and Marshment (1988) and in particular Stacey's article 'Desperately seeking difference', which explicates a lesbian position.

10.   In a pioneering article written in 1986, Elizabeth Ellsworth analysed the context of reception surrounding the film *Personal Best*, comparing how lesbian feminist critics interpreted the film, against the distributing company's marketing strategy and the dominant (male) media response. Ellsworth argues that marginal groups use cultural forms in the process of defining themselves, claiming that material practices like conciousness-raising groups, women's studies courses and feminist film reviewing collectively develop interpretative strategies that make sense of their structures of feeling and move them into the sphere of public discourse by giving social and semantic form to anxieties and desires.

For a historical material approach to film reception and group identification see Staiger (1992).

11.   For a more detailed discussion on the social construction of femininity, see Brownmiller (1984). For a more academic approach, see Smith (1988: 37–59). For work that examines the relationship between film viewing and consumption see, for example, Haralovich (1990), LaPlace (1987), and Eckert and Turim in Gaines and Herzog (1990).

REFERENCES

Bordwell, D. and Thompson, K. (1990) *Film Art: An introduction*, New York: McGraw-Hill.

Bordwell, D., Staiger, J. and Thompson, K. (1985) *The Classical Hollywood Cinema: Film style and mode of production to 1960*, New York: Columbia University Press.

Bovenschen, S. (1977) 'Is there a feminine aesthetic?', *New German Critique*, 10: 111–37.

Brownmiller, S. (1984) *Femininity*, London: Paladin Grafton.

Byars, J. (1988) 'Gazes/voices/power: Expanding psychoanalysis for feminist film and television theory', in D. Pribram (ed.) *Female Spectators: Looking at film and television*, London: Verso, pp.110–31.

Dayan, D. (1976) 'The tutor code of classical cinema', in B. Nichols (ed.) *Movies and Methods*, London: University of California Press.

Doane, M. A. (1982) 'Film and the masquerade: Theorising the female spectator', *Screen*, 23, 3/4 (September/October): 74–89.

Doane, M. A. (1984) '"The woman's film", Possession and address' reprinted in C. Gledhill (ed.) (1987) *Home Is where the Heart Is: Studies in melodrama and the woman's film*. London: British Film Institute, pp. 283–98.

Doane, M. A. (1988) *The Desire to Desire: The woman's film of the 1940s*, London: Macmillan.

Ellsworth, E. (1986) 'Illicit pleasures: Feminist spectators and "personal best"', *Wide Angle*, 8, 2: 45–56.

Gaines, J. and Herzog, C. (eds) (1990) *Fabrications: Costume and the female body*, London: AFI/Routledge.

Gamman, L. and Marshment, M. (eds) (1988) *The Female Gaze: Women as viewers of popular culture*, London: Women's Press.

Goldman, W. (1984) *Adventures in the Screen Trade*, London: Macdonald.

Hallam, J. and Marshment, M. (1993) 'Framing Experience: case studies in the reception of *Oranges Are not the only Fruit*', paper to the Consoling Passions Feminist Television Conference, Los Angeles, California.

Haralovich, M. (1990) 'The proletarian woman's film of the 1930s', *Screen*, 3,2 (Summer): 172–87.

Haskell, M. (1987) *From Reverence to Rape: The treatment of women in the movies*, 2nd edn), Chicago and London: University of Chicago Press.

Kent, N. (1991) *Naked Hollywood: Money, power and the movies*, London: BBC.

Kuhn, A. (1982) *Women's Pictures: Feminism and cinema*, London and Boston: Routledge & Kegan Paul.

Kuhn, A. (1984) 'Women's genres: Melodrama, soap opera and theory', *Screen*, 25, 1 (Spring): 18–28.

LaPlace, M. (1987) 'Producing and consuming the woman's film', in C. Gledhill (ed.) *Home Is where the Heart Is*, London: British Film Institute, pp. 138–66.

Lapsley, R. and Westlake, M. (1988) *Film Theory: An introduction*, Manchester: Manchester University Press.

Lauretis, T. de (1989) *Technologies of Gender: Essays on theory, film and fiction*, London: Macmillan.

Maio, K. (1989) *Feminist in the Dark: Reviewing the movies*, Freedom, California: Crossing Press.

Marshment, M. (1988) 'Substantial women', in L. Gamman and M. Marshment (eds) *The Female Gaze: Women as viewers of popular culture*, London: Women's Press, pp. 27–43.

Mayne, J. (1988) 'The female audience and the feminist critic', in J. Todd (ed.) *Women and Film*, New York and London: Holmes & Meier.

Mitchell, J. (1974) *Psychoanalysis and Feminism*, Harmondsworth: Penguin.

Monaco, J. (1984) *American Films Now: The people, the power, the money, the movies*, New York: Zeotrope.

Mulvey, L. (1975) 'Visual pleasure and narrative cinema', *Screen*, 16, 3 (Autumn): 6–18.

Newman, J. (1991) 'Enterprising women: Images of success', in S. Franklin, C. Lury and J. Stacey (eds) *Off-centre: Feminism and cultural studies*, London: Harper-Collins.

Press, A. (1991) *Women Watching Television: Gender, class and generation in the American television experience*, Philadelphia: University of Pennsylvania Press.

Schatz, T. (1989) *The Genius of the System: Hollywood film making in the studio era*, New York: Simon & Schuster.

Schlesinger, P., Dobash, R. E., Dobash, R. P. and Weaver, C. K. (1992) *Women Viewing Violence*, London: British Film Institute.

Seiter, E., Barchers, H., Kreuzner, G. and Warth, E. M. (eds) (1989) *Remote Control: Television, audiences and cultural power*, London and New York: Routledge.

Smith, D. (1988) 'Femininity as discourse', in L. Roman, E. Christian-Smith and K. Ellsworth (eds) *Becoming Feminine: The politics of popular culture*, London and New York: Falmer.

Spence, J. (1986) 'Class and gender in images of women', in K. Davies, J. Dickey and T. Stratford (eds), *Out of Focus: Writings on women and the media*, London: Women's Press, pp. 51–3.

Stacey, J. (1991) 'Feminine fascinations: Forms of identification in star–audience relations', in C. Gledhill (ed.) *Stardom: Industry of desire*, London: Routledge. pp. 141–63.

Staiger, J. (1992) *Interpreting Films: Studies in the historical reception of American cinema*, Princetown NJ: Princetown University Press.

Tincknell, E. (1991) 'Enterprise fictions: Women of substance' in S. Franklin, C. Lury and J. Stacey (eds), *Off-Centre: Feminism and cultural studies*, London: HarperCollins, pp. 260–73.

Walsh, A. (1984) *Women's Film and Female Experience 1940–1950*, New York: Praeger.

Chapter 8

'The Glass of Gin'

Renegade reading possibilities in the classic realist text

Kay Boardman

The focus of this chapter is Eliza Meteyard's short story entitled 'The glass of gin', which was published in parts in *Eliza Cook's Journal* in 1849.[1]*Eliza Cook's Journal* was a cheap family periodical which was very much a product of the turbulent 1840s and contained the traditional fare of informative articles, features, fiction and poetry; but unlike the more expensive conservative competitors it also dealt with controversial contemporary debates such as child labour, slavery and women's education.[2] Although the issues surrounding the periodical as a genre are complex and interesting, they remain beyond the concerns of this chapter.[3] What does need to be considered here is that 'The glass of gin' appeared in a popular magazine which was addressed to a specific readership who were identified by class and by gender.

Eliza Cook's Journal was one of a group of publications which addressed themselves to a lower-middle-class and artisan readership.[4] The short story, as I will argue, is directed at middle-class women, who were becoming crucial consumers of fiction and periodicals at this time. Although 'The glass of gin' is written by a woman, it may not necessarily be astute to assume that women write in a specific way[5] (see Mills, this volume). What is important to this chapter is that the text is directed at women readers and it is the relationship between the woman reader and the text that is primarily of interest.

I have chosen 'The glass of gin' because it is a deceptively complex piece of popular fiction which utilises the generic properties of the romance alongside the didactic fervour of the tract; all of which is encased in the dominant fictional form of the nineteenth-century, classic realism. I intend to approach the text from a materialist position, on the assumption that the

199

social and economic conditions from which a text emerges play a role in the forging of the representations of gender and class within the narrative, and hence the reading relations fostered by the text.

The narrative is concerned with two sisters, Alice and Mary, who are forced to leave the country and seek employment in London. They symbolise the dichotomous representation of woman as either Madonna or Magdalen. Alice, who represents the pure woman, gains her reward in a fairy-tale marriage, and Mary, the fallen woman, pays the penalty of death and damnation for her social and sexual transgressions.

The relationship of sexual difference to the developing urban consciousness of the mid-century was one of dialectical flux which constantly presented itself through various cultural discourses and representations. A materialist understanding of social and economic history acknowledges that the struggle of the emergent middle class to gain economic power accompanied the struggle to represent ideal feminine behaviour.[6] Indeed, in this story, we can see how one particular example of the textual construction of the female subject manifests itself in and through an investigation of controversial contemporary issues such as female sexuality, class and temperance. 'The glass of gin' reveals that the classic realist text, the dominant fictional form of the nineteenth century, was often a site for ideological struggle; within its seemingly fluid narrative framework the struggle is manifested through the various, often conflicting, positions available to the reader. In order to approach the text in this way I have called upon Althusser's (1971) work on ideology and the subject and upon aspects of reader-response theory (Iser 1978) as a means to discovering how narrative strategies play a role in the social and textual construction of the subject.

TYPES OF READER

The work of Wolfgang Iser (1978) has been very influential in theorising the relationship between the reader and the text. Reader-response criticism, generally, sees the reader as the co-creator of meaning and not a passive dupe to an author who has sole control of the construction of meaning within the text (Tompkins 1980). In terms of the reader's active participation in the production of meaning, Iser has assigned to the reader the task of filling in the gaps and making sense of the indeterminacy in the text; in other words, when the reader fills in the gaps, then the act of communication begins (Iser 1978:111). An ideal reader is one who possesses the competencies expected by the author and who can bring this knowledge to the reading activity.[7] Thus, the author is able to discriminate about what needs to be made explicit and what can be left unsaid on the assumption that a certain level of understanding and competency has already been reached by the ideal reader. As Robert Allen points out in his critique of reader-response theory, the ideal reader is in fact a textual place and therefore a property of the text, rather than a truly hypothetical reader (Allen 1989: 89). In this process of the production of meaning, then, a complex interaction is taking place and, as noted in the Introduction to this book, the text, through the ideal reader, can structure the reader's response, at least to some extent. However, the real or material reader does not necessarily follow all of the cues offered by the text as her/ his relationship to the text is mediated by a number of factors. These include (1) the point of view or ideal reading position offered and indeed structured by the text, (2) other positions available within the text, (3) the reader as a complex social subject. There are, however, a number of issues to consider in relation to this third factor: (a) as Sara Mills states in this volume, the reader is, of course, not a unified subject and we must therefore be careful not to oversimplify discussions around this area; (b) the individuality of the reader's response is suspect and each reading undertaken is encrusted with previous ones (Allen 1989: 102–31); and (c) in the absence of empirical data we are faced with the problem of a virtually unknown and unknowable reader about whom we have little reliable information, apart from ungendered sales statistics. A number of recent studies have used empirical data to explore this complex relationship between the reading subject and the text (see also Radway 1987; Ballaster *et al.* 1991). But this type of empirical research is not possible when one is considering the historical reader, and this issue brings to the fore some of the problems associated with the mapping of modern reception theory onto nineteenth-century texts such as 'The glass of gin'.[8] If a readership cannot be constructed, then a model of generic possibility most certainly can be; yet despite this, it is probable that the reading possibilities that I proffer for the text may not be interpretations that a Victorian reader would be likely to devise. However, we can identify a set of patterns which are inscribed in the text (Poovey 1988: 89–90).

In the absence of empirical data, then, we must return to the two issues which are of main concern, namely point of view and reading positions available within the text. The real or material reader is aware that the dominant reading position offered to her/him through the ideal reader, for instance, may be contradictory and problematic and therefore s/he has the opportunity to take up other positions which are available through the text. The text can be seen as a site for competing interpretations, and the place of the ideal reader, as Allen points out, is just one of a number on offer (Allen 1989). In this complex web of narrative strategies, then, several messages may be struggling for precedence (see the Introduction to this volume). In this chapter, I will argue that there are three major positions available to the reader in 'The glass of gin': colluding, resisting and renegade.

'THE GLASS OF GIN'

As I mentioned earlier, 'The glass of gin' chronicles the plight of two sisters, Alice and Mary Clive, from rural England who are forced to leave their home on the death of their father. They move to London, the large metropolis which stands in stark contrast to the country life they have left behind. On their arrival in London they contact an acquaintance of the family, Lucy Phillip, who was once supported by Mr Clive after her own father's bankruptcy. However, they find Lucy unwilling to offer accommodation and even basic hospitality. Forced to rely on themselves they finally manage to procure humble but respectable lodgings. Both seek work, but it is the younger sister Alice who takes primary responsibility for making their home a cosy and welcoming haven. Mary very quickly falls victim to the evils of alcohol and Alice has to endure living with a sister who not only fails to make a contribution to the household economy but who also pawns and sells precious articles from the former family home to subsidise her dependence on gin. After suffering for some months and enduring the ultimate horror of a brutal attack on her by her sister, Alice finally finds the courage to leave. On setting up home on her own, Alice has the fortune to find a position as a nanny to the orphaned grandchildren of a wealthy former admiral. After she has nursed the younger sick child to recovery, the admiral is so overwhelmed by her natural warmth and devotion that he asks her to move in with the family and take up a permanent position. However, Lucy Phillip re-appears and informs Admiral Murray of Alice's tainted family connection and Alice is sent away in disgrace. In the meantime, Mary has fallen to the lowest state of degradation through her alcoholism and is committed to the workhouse. In her dying hour, Alice is called for and arrives just as Mary takes her last depraved gasp of life. Responding to the sheer horror of the situation, Alice swoons and is caught by the admiral's nephew, Mr Murray, who takes her home, apologises for the family's shabby treatment of her, and subsequently proposes to her.

The story ends with the happy couple returning to Alice's former home, which, as a surprise, has been bought for her by her husband.

The story is presented in two parts, the first dealing with Mary's alcoholism and the second with Alice's connection with the Murrays and her marriage. The two parts are very different in terms of the way they deal with particular issues: part I grappling with the temperance problem through the figure of the dissolute elder sister and part II concerning itself with the development of the romance and the resolution of the problems set up in the first section (for a discussion of plot resolution, see Hallam, this volume).

CLASSIC REALISM

In the nineteenth century, classic realism dominated prose writing and through it the notion of the subject as the origin of understanding. As Colin McCabe points out, classic realism also provides a seemingly unproblematic representation of the material world (McCabe 1985). 'The glass of gin' has all the hallmarks of a classic realist text including, as I will show, hierarchy of discourse, illusionism and closure (Belsey 1980). Another device of classic realist fiction is to interpellate the reader and address itself to her directly and, in doing so, offer the reader the position from which the text is most obviously intelligible. These elements contribute to a tacit understanding of the text as unified. The notion of the unified reading subject is important, as it is the product of a liberal humanist philosophy that works on the assumption that human identity is whole, consistent and without contradiction. These texts are conventionally read as having a fixed and unified meaning which emanates from a 'common-sense' reading, which assumes that there is a 'voice of truth' inscribed in the narrative. In *Critical Practice*, Catherine Belsey describes the contribution common-sense readings of literary texts have made and calls for a critical practice that is aware of the influence of ideology on the social formation and the subject (Belsey 1980). Belsey's work is of seminal importance to the consideration of classic realist texts like 'The glass of gin' in that it brings into focus issues not only about types of readers and readings but also of the ideological underpinning of this type of representational practice.

'The glass of gin' operates successfully as a classic realist text. There is a hierarchy of discourse in the overriding message that gin is the harbinger of evil, moral corruption and, more importantly, moral and sexual degradation. The story vividly charts Mary's decline from a respectable middle-aged spinster to a filthy drunken thief who finally drinks herself to death. But as the narrative develops Mary's story becomes the subplot of a main plot concerned with Alice's rise from near destitution to a higher social position through marriage. Alice's story, unlike Mary's, demonstrates that virtue is rewarded and that good finally triumphs over evil. Hierarchy of discourse is demonstrated most explicitly through the privileging of the narrator's point of view in the use of both direct address (see Mills, this volume) and upper-case lettering to signal the horror of the events as they occur. Illusionism, another technique of classic realism, presents the story as if it were real and attempts to conceal its fictionality by glossing over narrative contradiction or conflict. 'The glass of gin' presents the illusion that the narrative events mirror real life and constitute a fair, true, and just representation of real social events.

One of the pleasures of the classic realist text is its narrative closure. In this short story Mary the alcoholic dies without redemption whilst Alice improves gender and class status by her marriage to Mr Murray. Marriage is a typical classic realist device for closing a narrative and the reader is seemingly left content in the knowledge that the heroine has received her just deserts; patience and virtue are rewarded and good triumphs over evil, as the narrator says: 'Good and evil are not imaginary things; and such as, like you have done, pursue the steady way of virtue through trial and temptation, like you, shall find reward!' (p.137).

In *Critical Practice*, Belsey calls for a productive critical practice which specifically draws upon an Althusserian model of ideology to inform an understanding of the inscription of the subject within the text (Belsey 1980). What is particularly useful about the Althusserian model is that it views the unified self of the classic realist text as a product of an ideology which purports to be unified and consistent. According to Althusser, it is the role of ideology to construct people as subjects and it does so through the process of interpellation (see the Introduction to this volume).

For the feminist critic, this process is particularly interesting as it deals with the way individuals misrecognise themselves and play subordinate roles apparently unwittingly. If the critic's main concern is with literature, then the model of interpellation can be used to discuss the positioning of readers as subjects by texts. Developing an understanding of how women come to texts as readers and how, in an active participation with the text, they read against the grain and produce rereadings, makes concrete and pragmatic use of reader-response theory and validates the feminist critics' claims for an acknowledgement of the importance of gender as a crucial determinant in the production and consumption of literature (see Mills, this volume). For Belsey, the new critical practice does not simply reject the classic realist text as inadequate but rather works towards foregrounding its contradictions in order to be able to read it radically, against the grain.

> The solution, then, must be not only a new mode of writing but also a new critical practice which insists on finding the plurality, however 'parsimonious', of the text and refuses the pseudo-dominance constructed as the 'obvious' position of its intelligibility by the forms of classic realism. As readers and critics we can choose actively to seek out the process of production of the text: the organization of the discourses which constitute it and the strategies by which it smooths over the incoherences and contradictions of the ideology inscribed in it. (Belsey 1980: 129)

It is precisely within this space smoothed over by the contradictions, the gaps, slides and inconsistencies of the text that the reader can produce readings which are against the grain (for a fuller discussion, see Macherey 1978). In 'The glass of gin' the hierarchy of discourse constructs a gendered reader which colludes with the dominant reading of the text that spells out the penalties of the refusal to accept conventional gender roles. We must be aware that literature both produces and reproduces ideology and therefore the various readings wrought from the story will inevitably be ideological constructs, something from which we can never totally escape. This concern with the signifying practice in process, the act of reading that is, is one of importance in relation to literature as an ideological construct in that the text only comes into existence through the process of being read.

THE COLLUDING READER

The common-sense reading of 'The glass of gin' witnesses the decline of the fallen woman and celebrates the constancy of the Victorian ideal of femininity. This common-sense reading is synonymous with the first of the reading positions available within the text, that of the colluding reader. However, it must be made clear that, as with the other reading positions, the place of the colluding reader as the dominant reading cannot simply be equated with passivity. Nor, as Pearce and Hallam also point out in this volume, are any of the readers' textual negotiations performed in a vacuum.

The most obvious and indeed textually explicit position open to the reader, then, is that of the colluding reader. In 'The glass of gin' the omniscient and intrusive narrator invites the colluding reader to share in the horror of Mary's self destruction and degradation. Although anonymous, the narrator speaks from an unambiguously middle-class position; s/he does not foreground her/his gender, but it is hard not to assume that s/he is a woman, as the narrative works so hard to forge a sisterly sharing of values between the narrator and the reader. The narrator makes fairly extensive use of direct address, which is an obvious strategy to bring the place of the reader into focus, and it is consistently used to foreground the excess of Mary's actions. For instance, to sustain her addiction, Mary gradually sells or pawns all the possessions that she shares with Alice. Episode by episode the narrator reveals the extent of Mary's actions, 'THE BEAUTIFUL SILVER TEA-SERVICE, TEAPOT, SUGAR-BASIN, EWER, WERE GONE FOR ACCURSED GIN (emphasis in original, p. 91), and one by one their material possessions and family heirlooms are sold. The use of upper case foregrounds the signal that this behaviour is deemed to be shocking by the narrator and that it will be accepted as such by the reader.

It is no coincidence, then, that in Mary's campaign of self-destruction, she not only undermines her moral reputation, but also her rights to class membership; this is shown by her disregard for the last material trappings of middle-class respectability that the sisters share, as well as a disregard for ethical responsibilities, such as thrift and self-help. One by one their material possessions and family heirlooms are sold and the horror of this is compounded by Mary's inability to show remorse. Indeed, in a later scene Mary returns home and forces Alice to go to her room:

> Afraid of an altercation, and thus making this miserable sorrow known, Alice complied; but what sleep, or even rest, could there be, with such sorrow in the very chamber? – a sorrow not to be shut out, but one recognised by all the senses. Rest? It is desecration to name this sweetest right of nature, in the remotest relation to such a scene! For if there be a hell on earth, if there be one form of degradation more unseemly than another, one companionship more loathsome, one atmosphere more foul, it is in the chamber, and in necessitated association, with a drunkard! (p. 72)

With regard to indirect address to the reader in the form of rhetorical questions and the presentation of 'common-sense' knowledge, we can see that although it breaks the veil of artifice and negates the idea of the unseen narrator, it helps to make explicit the dominant reading and creates a position for a colluding reader to insert herself/himself (see Mills, and Thornborrow, on indirect address, this volume).

Another factor of importance in the endeavour to explore collusive reading stategies is protensive tension which is the expectation a reader has as to what is coming next. This is relevant to the consideration of any reading process but is of particular importance in relation to serialised fiction. 'The glass of gin', therefore, not only utilises protensive tension at the end of each instalment but through the use of point of view, in this case Alice's, the reader is invited to empathise with her plight as each episode progresses. Another strategy which invites the reader to engage actively in the build-up of narrative events is the fact that the reader is frequently presented with knowledge that Alice does not have (see Hallam, this volume). For instance, the reader is aware of Mary's addiction before Alice and in the first episode there are hints about Mary's future demise through her lazy and selfish manner. At the end of the second instalment, when Alice and Mary have moved to cheaper accommodation and Mary has pledged to reform, the narrator ends on this note: 'But had Alice been more learned in the philosophy of drunkenness, or less loving, or less blind, she would have soon discovered, in the sudden hilarity, or sullenness, preferable alone to drink, how little was this sobriety real!' (p. 73). Indeed, as the story progresses the colluding reading position is continually made available through these strategies and the shift in the use of the individual 'I' to the collective 'we' explicitly makes the textual place of the ideal reader open to the colluding reader.

THE RESISTING READER AND THE RENEGADE READER

What are the possibilities for the reader who does not take up the colluding position offered to her/him through the dominant reading of the text? This question has been taken up by Judith Fetterley in her study of American literature, where she demonstrates that many female readers of classic American texts like *The Great Gatsby* are pushed into the position of reading as men (Fetterley 1978; see Mills, and cf. Christie, this volume). In other words, there is no space within the text to read as a woman; thus women become resisting readers and resist the male subject position offered to them by the text. Fetterley's resisting reader is in many ways like Walker Gibson's reader who rebels in her/his rejection of the role offered to her/ him through the mock reader, 'A bad book, then, is a book in whose mock reader we discover a person we refuse to become, a mask we refuse to put on, a role we will not play' (Gibson, in Tompkins 1980: 5). The notion of the resisting reader is really the apogee of the practice of reading against the grain, but it is only the first step in the production of a reading strategy that makes active use of what Macherey terms the 'unsaid' of the text (Macherey 1978). So what does the resisting reader do when she sees a role that she refuses to play? What active use of the gaps and inconsistencies does she make? In 'The glass of gin', gender and class positions are established very early in the text. As already stated, the ideal reader is constructed as female and middle class, but there are points within the narrative framework where class and gender positions slide and displacement occurs between the way the ideal reader is meant to respond and the way the real or material reader may respond.

This is not the interaction of collusion where the reader takes the routine position of the subject specifically designated by the text. Here the place of the ideal reader set up by the text, that is, white, female and middle class, has been usurped by what I shall term a 'renegade' reader who takes up the position of a number of possibilities revealed by the contradictory gaps in a common-sense reading of the text, but who certainly does not collude with the textual pointers that are directed to the ideal reader. An illustration of a similar process can be seen in Annette Kuhn's work on film narrative (1982), where Kuhn draws on cinema and the popular technique of classic realism to demonstrate what she terms the process of suture:

> This definition draws back to the point that in histoire, the source of cinematic enunciation is typically absent from, or invisible in, the text. Suture is the process whereby the gap produced by that absence is filled by the spectator, who thus becomes the 'stand in', the subject-in-the-text. (Kuhn 1982: 53)

The process of subjectivity in cinema is seen as both ongoing and dynamic in that the subject is constantly being 'sewn-in' to, or caught up in, the film's enunciation (see also Hallam, this volume). Comparisons can be made between the suture of the spectator of film narrative and the renegade reader of literary narrative, although the sutured subject is more passive than the renegade subject, who makes active use of the gap in the signifying process and produces alternative readings of the text.

I have developed the term 'renegade reader' to sustain the notion of multiple subject positions offered by any one text; this reading position goes one step further conceptually than Fetterley's resisting reader in its acknowledgement of the potency of hierarchy of discourse in the unified reading of the classic realist text, which is, by definition, often the most persuasive common-sense understanding of the fiction on offer. The renegade reader not only resists and reads against the grain, but actively constructs a number of alternative readings available from within the text.

The narrator in 'The glass of gin' has a particular class position and she not only affirms this by identifying with her readership through the narrative, but she also uses it as a device to develop a relationship with her reader which is based upon their assumed similarities. For example, as she relates the tale of the two sisters through an exposé of their lives and problems, both narrator and ideal reader reach mutually shared conclusions regarding temperance, class, respectability and the woman question. It is only with the renegade reading of the text that the repressed message of the text seeps through. The purpose of the remainder of this chapter is to identify those points within the narrative where renegade reading possibilities emerge and alternative subject positions appear as a key to the 'unsaid' of the text. There are three important thematic concerns that are part of this key: they are class, temperance and sexuality.

In the common-sense reading of 'The glass of gin', class is dealt with on two levels: firstly it appears on a simple level as a contemporary discussion of social mobility and the hypocrisy of the *nouveau riche*; and secondly, through the character of Mary, it forms an implicit link to the assumptions that both the working class as a group and women as a group are to be controlled. In this way, women and the working class as marginalised groups, both politically and socially, function as threats to the natural order and male middle-class hegemony. The threat that independent women in particular pose (in this instance Alice and Mary when they arrive in London) represents the vulnerability of middle-class women when their particular class status is threatened by engaging in paid work.

However, the character who represents the disadvantages of social mobility to those who are not noble enough to accept the ensuing paternalistic responsibilities is Lucy Phillip. She, as I mentioned earlier, had received help from the sisters' father, but when the sisters arrive in London she refuses them hospitality and accommodation. Lucy represents the lazy and ungrateful upper classes, who are not prepared to acknowledge the contribution of the industrious newly emergent middle class who were making England 'the workshop of the world'. After being refused accommodation by Lucy and her husband, the sisters finally procure lodgings and the narrator says:

> the power to call it their own, to rest in it undisturbed, to find that it would and could shelter them, conferred on it a sanctity I can scarcely describe. . . . It is these contrasts, and the rare pleasures annexed, which makes the lives of the rich so poor beside those of struggling thousands. Experience can alone afford this class of pleasures; to imagine them is as impossible as to ride the winds. (p. 56)

The colluding position is offered here and it rests on the assumption that if the reader is not rich s/he will at last have some sympathy with the idea that there is some nobility to be gained from suffering.

The second instance of the way class is dealt with is by far the most interesting and indeed the most relevant to a discussion of alternative reading positions. At this level, class issues are extremely complex and the difference between class as a social group and a gendered understanding of class needs to be identified. In much Victorian literature, there are clear connections to be made between the representation of the working classes and the representations of Victorian woman as a subject identified primarily through her sexuality/gender.[9] Both groups were denied political voice and both groups were understood as being incapable of taking responsibility for political choice. This claim is controversial and undoubtedly complex but recent studies of representation such as those collected by Mendus and Rendall (1989) have argued persuasively that marginalised and subordinate groups who were identified through differences of class, race and gender were indeed denied full participation in social and political life by their very difference.[10] In this particular instance there are representations of femininity which revolve around women's precarious relationship to class respectability not only through the marriage market, but also through the less attractive option of independence which automatically made them sexually vulnerable. The growth of scientific rationalism was partly responsible for this particular relationship between class and gender, as the division of the world into mind and matter meant that women were assigned to this realm along with beasts, the working class and people of other races (Mendus and Rendall 1989).

But it is through Mary's association with alcohol that the thematic concerns about class and sexuality in the text really take on significance. Temperance was an important social issue in the mid-nineteenth century and was the subject of tracts, novels, tales, poems and even plays. The National Temperance Society was formed in 1842 and it offered the prospect of a higher degree of security in return for abstinence from drink. Excessive drinking was seen to be the contemporary malaise and it was an issue not unconnected with class concerns (see Harrison 1971). The debate about temperance became the site of a fierce evangelical battle of social control. Indeed, alcohol became metonymically connected to indulgence; its abuse was viewed as indicative of the inability of the working classes to gain access to 'self-help', and it was seen to be as much a question of control as a medical problem.[11] The most common image of the drunkard was the one of the working man who frittered his wages away in the gin palace whilst his wife and children slowly starved in a squalid garret. The temperance problem was often used by working-class radicals to explain the pressures on the poor and to indicate the depth of their need. However, proponents of the self-help philosophy used the opposite argument, stating that alcohol and its abuse was the reason why they were living in such degrading conditions.

The development of a storyline based around a female character who becomes an alcoholic was not a completely new idea, but where Mary's character is particularly interesting is in her relationship with her sister. The two sisters arrive in London looking for work after the death of their father. The reality for women was such that if there was no father, brother or husband to support them, they were forced to earn a living. The problems facing independent women were enormous, and the options open to middle-class women, who were under far more pressure to display 'respectability' than their working-class counterparts, were very limited. Apart from going into domestic service or doing needlework, which were not options for middle-class women, their only realistic chance of finding work was in becoming governesses.[12] Mary's problem is that, lacking the moral fibre of Alice, she is unable to cope with the move from the country to the city and with the responsibility of independence; she thus turns to drink as a way of solving her problems.[13].

The dominant message of a common-sense reading of the story, however, is that drinking quite obviously is not the solution to female poverty but marriage quite clearly is, a fact borne out in Alice's ideal match with Mr Murray. This is of course demonstrated through the closure. However, the temperance question is used to demonstrate in graphic detail the vulnerability of individuals who do not conform to the 'natural' pattern of existence and in this way 'The glass of gin' is unequivocally didactic. Formulaic texts such as this, as Whelehan argues in this volume, should not be ignored because they are 'negative' works of fiction. Undoubtedly, Victorian readers, like any other readers, were reflective and able to 'unpack' aspects of this type of exemplary fiction. A renegade reading of the text uncovers a voyeuristic pleasure in the excesses of Mary's behaviour and refusal to conform to the contemporary stereotype of respectable femininity. In this way, the overriding message of the text is a further example of the contemporary need for control of female sexuality through the regulation of desire.[14]

The first reference to gin in the narrative is when Alice discovers Mary in a collapsed state and believes she is ill. It is the narrator who informs the reader that Mary is drunk and Alice has to call her landlady for help before she is told the horrible truth about her sister:

> She hurried to the bed, and kneeling down, tried to arouse her – tried with passionate caresses, passionate words, to arouse her from what seemed a deadly stupor; but no endearing words, no purity of love, no tenderness, no pity, could free one so guilty, from the wilful leprosy and curse of GIN! (p. 71)

In this section of the story and specifically at this point in the plot, when Mary's drunken state is revealed, the tone of the narrative voice switches from composure to hysteria. On each subsequent revelation of Mary's outrageous deeds, the narrator takes on a hectoring tone. This uncompromising revelation of the cause of Mary's behaviour demonstrates graphically the narrator's position on the subject. The ideal reader is invited to join in with the horrified exhortations about the evil of alcohol abuse and eradicate this evil by bringing it to public attention.

When Alice finally becomes aware of Mary's drink problems we see the lamentations of the narrator point to the fact that alcoholism is compounded by its manifestation in a woman. After Alice has left Mary she sees her one day as she is passing a gin-palace:

> She tried to pass on, and could not; and turning to look, as if impelled by some species of fascination or charm, she beheld, through the opened doors of the gin-palace, set wide apart for the gratification of the gaping multitude, a Highland piper standing, playing his bagpipes in the middle of the floor, an old blind leering fellow seated on the end of a form against the brass bound counter, scraping a violin; whilst Mary (it was her in all hideous certainty), with her bonnet off, her bit of bedizened cap, scarcely covering her half gray matted hair, her gown half torn from the waist, and rent in a wide gash across the bosom, was dancing round the piper, with such indecent gestures, as raised the hootings, and the reckless laughter of the mob. (p. 123)

After witnessing this scene, Alice attempts to leave, but before doing so is brutally attacked by her sister. The ideal reader is not invited to empathise with Mary, and the narrator shows quite unambivalently that she is biased in favour of Alice by frequently expressing her point of view and never that of Mary. But from the quotation it is clear that it is the latent renegade reading possibilities that facilitate a reading of the subtextual levels of pleasure and thrill at the fantasy of decadence and excess.

But why was alcohol so stigmatised? Did moral concerns about its abuse outweigh the medical ones? Certainly, in 'The glass of gin' the concern is with the morally degrading effects of the loss of control in drunkenness. But there was also another reason: middle-class concern about intemperance was as much about the work ethic as about fear of loss of control. The Smilesian self-help doctrine was very much the foundation stone of the development of capitalism through the work ethic; indulgence in afterwork drinking sessions was anathema to the proponents of thrift and self-regulation. In this respect, Mary can be seen as an allegory of the working class under the guardianship of the middle class in the form of Alice. What leads from this allegorical function of Mary as representative of the working class is the elision of sexuality and class as in need of regulation.

A discussion of the problematic relationship between the sisters at a subtextual level will help to illustrate this elision. What happens between

Alice and Mary is what can best be described as an instance of gender-role displacement. After Mary has turned to drink, she takes on seemingly masculine attributes. Through her characterisation, we see a break with the traditional representation of femininity that not only shatters the Victorian stereotype of female restraint but also crosses over gender and class boundaries to masculine and implicitly working-class values and behaviour. It is at this point that the relationship between the two sisters begins to become problematic. When Mary has sunk to the lowest depths of alcoholism, they no longer function as sisters, but almost as husband and wife. Mary is dominant, Alice is submissive; Mary is violent, strong and aggressive, whereas Alice is weak and vulnerable. In the first instalment of the story, Mary is set up as a moody and rather sullen character and does not possess the cheerful disposition of her younger sister. However, in the next instalment, we learn that they are step-sisters and that they share the same father. In a common-sense reading of the text, this would be loaded with significance, demonstrating that Alice's mother was 'good' and Mary's was 'bad', confirming the adage that 'like begets like'.

As the narrative develops, Mary becomes more and more masculine in her attitude and behaviour and represents excess in both body and spirit. For instance, on one of her drunken rampages, she knocks her dinner to the floor, strikes Alice and then storms out. The omniscient narrator then intervenes and reveals, 'I must draw a veil over that night's further scene; . . . Oh, God! nothing in thy great earth is more sorrowful, or more awful to behold, than this, thy desecrated image, in the fairest form thou has assigned to it, that of WOMAN!' (p. 72). The fact that Mary is a woman is clearly intended to make the horror of the situation even more alarming. However, for the renegade reader, the veiling of that night's events reveals one of the pointers to the unsaid; in this instance, the repressed sexuality represented through Mary's gender-role displacement. In the next instalment, the horror of Mary's behaviour is developed further as Alice takes Mary to task for pawning some of their few beloved possessions: 'And as she spoke, [Mary] raised her hand, and dashed it with brutal ferocity in the young girl's face. Whilst the blood poured down in a stream, Mary pushed her into the bed-room and locked the intervening door' (p. 91). This is shocking not only because of its violence but because of its significance as only the beginning of a brutal assault on Alice, who, whilst having previously complained about Mary's unreasonable behaviour, meekly sits making a cap of artificial flowers for her sister:

> Alice still not replying, she snatched the flowers from her hand, deliberately tore them to a thousand shreds, and scattered them upon the rug at her feet. This done,

she again repeated her question; but no answer being made, she seized Alice by the throat, who in vain attempting to avoid her iron grasp (for Mary was much taller and stronger than herself) was at last thrust down upon the sofa. (p. 91)

Concerned neighbours then rush in to the room to save Alice from being strangled. Mary's strength and capacity for violence on the one hand denotes her inability to fit into the role of helpless victim and therefore explains why she, in the logic of the text, must finally die; but also in her role as aggressor she becomes Alice's oppressor. Alice, like the abused wife, has to suffer the violent mood swings of her partner before she finally finds the strength to emancipate herself by leaving. It is ironic that Alice's liberation only comes with her marriage.

Throughout the narrative, Mary is clearly associated with moral contagion and not only represents a threat to her sister through her violence but also through association. Alice's fairy-tale romance is threatened once when Lucy Phillip re-appears and informs the Murrays of Alice's connection with Mary. On Mary's death, the narrative is partially resolved; it remains for the marriage to close the text perfectly. It is only at the end of the story that we can finally assess the role of the fallen woman in the romantic resolution of conflict. The fallen woman represents women's precarious relationship to the society in which they live. Marriage was the only safe option, and Mary, in her wholesale rejection of marriage, not only suffers at the hand of fate but remains as a reminder of the social and moral degradation of the fallen woman. In Mary the gin/sex elision is resolved, albeit problematically through her class and gender-role displacement. The final equation works thus,

middle class	GIN	working class
self control		animal needs
good woman/angel		bad woman/whore

The juxtaposition of a common-sense reading of 'The glass of gin' alongside examples of renegade readings has demonstrated that the task of the feminist critic who wants to make possible alternative subject positions for the female reader is to reject the unity of the text and instead seek its omissions and contradictions and to ignore closure and stress the development of the narrative *before* the textual resolution (see Whelehan, this volume). To deconstruct the text, to offer new ways of reading allows the feminist reader to question the possibility of a transcendent signified and explode the myth of the unified subject. A renegade reading practice exposes the gaps in the text and attributes significant agency to the reader in the production of meaning and thus breaks through and shatters the spurious 'truth' of the classic realist text.

NOTES

1. 'The glass of gin' appeared in the first volume in six instalments, from 26 May to 30 June 1849.
2. *Eliza Cook's Journal* (1849–54), a 1½d weekly, had a peak circulation of 60,000 and its editor, Eliza Cook, became a household name through both the success of her journal and her poetry.
3. The collection of essays in Brake *et al.* deals with the study of the periodical as a genre in its own right.
4. Two other popular publications were *Chambers' Journal* and *Household Words*.
5. It is significant, however, that writing was one of a growing number of professions becoming open to women in this period. Eliza Meteyard was a single, self-supporting professional writer who published a prolific amount of fiction concerning women's issues. For more information on Meteyard, see Mitchell (1981).
6. See Armstrong and Tennenhouse (1987), Mendus and Rendall (1989) and Poovey (1988) for excellent examples of this type of theory at work.
7. In *Channels of Discourse* (1989), Robert Allen describes 'the bewildering array of readers' proposed by reader-response theorists.
8. A different type of empirical research can be found in Dearko Suvin's essay 'The social addressees of Victorian fiction: A preliminary enquiry' (1982: 11–40), where historical readerships are defined by using a variety of data.
9. For an interesting discussion of representations of female sexuality see Nead (1988).
10. See especially the essay by de Groot '"Sex" and "race": The construction of language and image in the nineteenth century', in Mendus and Rendall (1989: 89–128).
11. Samuel Smiles' book *Self Help* was a best seller and had an enormous impact on the public when it appeared in 1859. Although 'The glass of gin' is ten years earlier, Smiles articulated what had been a popular philosophy since the early Victorian period.
12. See Poovey (1988) for a useful discussion of Victorian representations of governesses.
13. Williams (1973) is still the seminal work on literary perceptions of the changing urban landscape and the disruptions entailed by this type of shift from country to city.
14. The legislation of the Contagious Diseases Acts of 1864, 1866 and 1869 was designed to control female prostitution.

REFERENCES

Allen, R. C. (1989) 'Reader-oriented criticism and television', in R. C. Allen (ed.) *Channels of Discourse*, London: Routledge, pp. 74–112.

Althusser, L. (1971) *Lenin and Philosophy*, London: New Left Books.

Armstrong, N. and Tennenhouse, L. (eds) (1987) *The Ideology of Conduct: Essays in literature and the history of sexuality*, London: Methuen.

Ballaster, R., Beetham, M., Frazer, E. and Hebron, S. (1991) *Women's Worlds: Ideology, femininity and the woman's magazine*, London: Macmillan.

Belsey, C. (1980) *Critical Practice*, London: Methuen.

Brake, L., Jones, A. and Madden, L. (eds) (1990) *Investigating Victorian Journalism*, London: Macmillan.

Fetterley, J. (1978) *The Resisting Reader: A feminist approach to American fiction*, Bloomington: Indiana University Press.

Harrison, B. (1971) *Drink and the Victorians: The temperance question in England, 1815–1872*, London: Faber & Faber.

Iser, W. (1978) *The Act of Reading: A theory of aesthetic response*, London: Routledge & Kegan Paul.

Kuhn, A. (1982) *Women's Pictures: Feminism and cinema*, London: Routledge.

McCabe, C. (1985) *Theoretical Essays*, Manchester: Manchester University Press.

Macherey, P. (1978) *A Theory of Literary Production*, London: Routledge & Kegan Paul (first published 1966).

Mendus, S. and Rendall, J. (eds) (1989) *Sexuality and Subordination: Interdisciplinary studies in gender in the nineteenth century* London: Routledge.

Mitchell, S. (1981) *The Fallen Angel: Chastity, class, and women's reading*, Bowling Green, OH: Bowling Green University Press.

Nead, L. (1988) *Myths of Sexuality: Representations of women in Victorian Britain*, Oxford: Blackwell.

Poovey, M. (1988) *Uneven Developments:The ideological work of gender in mid-Victorian England*, Chicago: University of Chicago Press.

Radway, J. (1987) *Reading the Romance: Women, patriarchy and popular literature*, London: Verso (first published 1984).

Suvin, D. (1982) 'The social addressees of Victorian fiction: A preliminary enquiry', *Literature and History* 8: 11–40.

Tompkins, J. (ed.) (1980) *Reader-response Criticism: From formalism to post-structuralism*, Baltimore: Johns Hopkins University Press.

Williams, R. (1973) *The Country and the City*, London: Chatto & Windus.

Chapter 9

Feminism and Trash
Destabilising 'the reader'

Imelda Whelehan

> Some people are trying to make an honest woman out of the feminist critic, to claim that every 'worthwhile' department should stock one. I am not terribly interested in whether feminism becomes a respectable part of academic criticism; I am very much concerned that feminist criticism become a useful part of the women's movement. (Robinson 1986: 19–20)

This chapter began life as a lecture and, in common with many of my lectures, became more of an argument with myself. It draws partly upon my experiences as a lecturer in English, teaching women's writing and feminist criticism, and was prompted by a nagging suspicion that feminist criticism still carries far too much of the baggage of traditional concepts of literary value, especially in relation to studies of contemporary women's writing. Such values thrive largely unexamined despite their obvious conflict with feminist political aims; and I shall attempt to explore such tensions by considering how the inclusion of popular fiction or 'trash' might enhance current feminist textual criticism.

I am particularly concerned with the role of the reader in feminist criticism. It may be true that, to some extent, criticism is always 'about' the exchange of opinions: the institution of criticism has always paid lip service to the notion that each reader brings to bear upon her/his interpretations the wealth of individual 'experience'. For mainstream criticism, this is clearly consonant with the bourgeois ideology of abstract individualism that sustains it, and appears compatible with the status of the author as a unique individual *par excellence*. F. R. Leavis' appeal to readerly consensus – 'This is so, isn't it?' – still suggests that there are boundaries already inscribed within literary critical discourse which a reader broaches at her/his peril.[1] To respond, 'No, it's not!' to such blandishments would not only appear impolite: it is almost unthinkable – exposing the fact that the implied reader is one who readily accepts the critical parameters presented to her/him. The question is not really a question after all.

Feminist criticism derives impetus from both feminist politics and mainstream literary criticism, and certain tensions arise from this dual inheritance. One effect is that feminist criticism addresses an implied reader who is conscious of 'woman' as a crucial political category denoting an oppressed and culturally marginalised group (see Mills, this volume); but one who – as a student of 'literature' – has been inculcated into the mysteries of literary value and the hierarchies it sustains. The implied feminist reader is largely a mirror image of the 'mainstream' feminist critic: she is white, middle class, heterosexual and knows a 'good' book when she reads one. This model reader is a willing participant in feminist critical resisting rereadings; but having decanonised certain readings of 'classic' female texts, other readings and other texts are arguably canonised in their place.

When teaching male-authored texts, feminists evoke the word 'canon' as a convenient shorthand to catalogue the numerous subtle phallocentric practices which have resulted in the marginalisation of women in literature. The term 'canon' has become a pejorative one in the mouths of feminist and radical theorists alike; and once situated as a means by which 'unconscious' prejudices are perpetuated, satellite words such as 'literary', 'great' and 'English literature' can be interrogated in new and challenging ways. Feminism has crucially added a political dimension to this debate, perceiving women writers as either occupying the margins of high culture or becoming tokenistic figures within it, mirroring broader ideological and cultural exclusionary practices in our society. Ever since Virginia Woolf, feminist writers have remarked upon the incongruity of 'woman writer': the two terms sit uneasily together in much the same way as 'woman executive' do – and both *as women* are subjected, we imagine, to 'an intellectual measuring of bust and hips' (Ellmann 1979: 29).

However, feminist approaches to female-authored texts risk ultimately underpinning the patriarchal logic of literary studies by producing a female canon which re-affirms time-honoured notions of literary aesthetic value, since it is itself exclusionary. In the face of the impossibility of ever doing justice to the variety of women's writing available, there is an urge to select the 'best' – not least to combat the still-prevailing popular mythology that women spew out their experiences on the page with little concern for 'art' (Battersby 1990). Yet how one arrives at such a selection is rarely explicitly addressed. In teaching a course devoted to contemporary women's writing, I am at liberty to select material; and a course which begins in the 1960s seems relatively free from the lure of the few 'canonical' women writers available.[2] Despite this, I distinctly feel my unconscious 'litera. prejudices creeping in – in the sense that critical acclaim has a way of making some writers appear essential. Mentally, I picture certain authors jockeying for position, declaring themselves central to the integrity of such a course. Sylvia Plath, Jean Rhys, Toni Morrison and Jeanette Winterson figure strongly, ostensibly because of their 'serious' treatment of 'women's issues'; but underlying my apparent personal convictions is an awareness that I could trawl up a reasonable amount of secondary material for my students' use.

This course has, as part of its brief, a commitment to provide an overview of as many genres as possible. However 'genre' itself generates two possible interpretations, signifying broad formal literary divisions (epic, tragedy, the novel, etc.), as well as carrying connotations of a popular, 'non-literary' nature. Genre writing, such as crime, romance or science fiction, is often viewed derisively as formulaic, conservative, appealing to popular taste, and, all in all, rather 'Art'-less. The term 'pulp fiction' implies trash – with its connotations of disposability and transitoriness; just as 'Literature' implies good-quality serious art 'for all time'.

The rather unwieldy category of women's writing, which delimits only on the basis of authorial gender, exposes tensions between art and trash. Literature implies a privileged status to which few women writers gain access: historically, women writers have colonised the popular domain in face of their exclusion from the celestial heights of literature. The binary opposition highbrow/lowbrow becomes analogous to the masculine/ feminine one, as Anne Cranny-Francis has pointed out (1990: 1–28). Where, then, do the writers I have already cited *really* fit in? Although few would describe Sylvia Plath's *The Bell Jar* as pulp, it appears to me that Plath as poet occupies a modern literary mainstream, while simultaneously (as novelist) inhabiting that rather grey area between high and lowbrow dubbed the 'women's book' – commonly regarded as confessional, formless and experiential. Meanwhile, Plath's 'vital statistics' glare luridly at us from a recent Faber cover of *Johnny Panic and the Bible of Dreams*, as if to complete the intellectual measurement of her worth, and confirm Ellmann's assertion that even as 'literature', women's work is subject to quite different critical criteria. Men's books invite access to the febrile workings of the author's mind; women's books are, in contrast, intellectually ransacked for evidence of the body behind the work – often its tragic demise in face of the creative urge. Many students of Plath follow the critical lead and look to her 'life' for textual illumination. Her suicide gives her a mythological status akin to Marilyn Monroe's – an analogy made more powerful by Faber's decision to depict her as a bikini-clad and smiling 'cover girl'.

If certain contemporary women's texts receive a disproportionate amount of feminist scholarly attention, I suspect that it is because the critical 'malestream' encourages such a concentration on the select few. Feminist criticism must necessarily pursue two potentially conflicting aims. The first is to combat the misconception that women writers rarely qualify as genius because they are the intellectual inferiors of men: therefore 'superior' texts are singled out for attention, and an alternative tradition of female excellence is sought, although the criteria used clearly derive their meaning from a patriarchal view of literary value. Elaine Showalter's *A Literature of their Own* (1982) is perhaps the most famous example of such a position. The second aim links criticism to politics, attempting to expose the continued exclusionary practices rife within the institution, which confine women's (and gay and black) writing to the margins of a phallo/ethno/heterocentric literary tradition. The role of the reader/critic as an active one is thereby foregrounded; and is taken to be a position of intervention and interrogation of dominant meanings generated at the heart of English Studies. From this political perspective, mainstream canonical/critical processes, and the means by which hegemonic ideological positions are sedimented within critical practice, are themselves subject to scrutiny.

Both aims, though contradictory, still have a place on a feminist agenda for the 1990s. It is politic to capitalise upon students' knowledge of the female 'greats', whilst it might be more 'political' to combine such studies with a consideration of popular fiction, rather than dismissing it as largely conservative and anti-feminist. A comparative study, undertaken regardless of literary kudos, can manifest evidence of a wide cross-fertilisation of ideas and textual strategies, some of which may appear more 'feminist' than others, but many of which have derived impetus from the writings of the Women's Movement. This helpfully problematises many students' initial belief that doing feminist criticism means learning and pursuing a 'party line' – a belief often strengthened by the implied feminist reader who appears to be addressed (see Mills, this volume). A women's writing course celebrates the popularity of women's texts, at the same time that its very existence affords a critique of the inequities of Literature – even though it, of necessity, uncomfortably resides within the boundaries of English Studies itself. The business of discovering a female literary tradition, while revealing the perpetuation of a male elite, involves feminist academics in an evident double bind.

Even now women's writing is often perceived as 'trivial' in relation to male-authored texts; however, some escapes the trashcan and moves in more cultured circles, as if to 'prove' that male-orientated criticism has shed its patriarchal excesses. The institution of English Studies fosters the view that to study literature is to re-affirm hierarchies of value, and those women who are deemed worthy of mainstream attention are seen as exceptional and unique, whereas feminist politics prioritises the examination of collective female experience. It is difficult to avoid imposing a (patriarchal) pedagogical logic upon our feminist intentions, which assumes that our particular selection of writings is the 'best' within a certain period or genre. Although I personally favour a focus on *connections* between texts, rather than single textual analysis, I remain aware that all processes of selection reveal an agenda – unconscious or not – and 'Even those of us who reject the authority of the canon are inevitably involved, in our teaching and writing, in making choices according to some principle of invidious comparison' (Greene in Kauffman 1989: 82). Despite my personal intentions to combine literature and trash in a mutually enhancing fashion, I find myself foregrounding 'canonical' women writers as worthy of attention for their singularity, whereas romance and crime writers come to represent *tendencies* within their genre. On the one hand, I re-activate the cult of the author as authority; on the other, I celebrate the means by which genre fiction writers can and do transcend the limits of formula, to produce texts which enable students to develop their own critical faculties, freed from the spectre of the author as purveyor of truth and meaning. Biographical criticism of writers such as Plath and Rhys hampers textual interpretation, by inventing a coherent authorial psychology, whereas genre texts are often approached 'cold'.

The combination of literature and 'trash' on my course proved to be a happy one. Nowhere is discussion more lively and far-reaching than when we analyse texts where a feminist/literary consciousness is either invisible or minimal; and nowhere are the themes of the debates more 'feminist'. It is as if the students' innate sense of a high/lowbrow divide affects their belief of what it is proper to say about books which occupy one or the other category. Literature demands a 'literary approach' – a consideration of formal and thematic devices particular to the text, and peculiar to the individual author. Whereas 'trash', perhaps because its formal qualities are ever on display, and its conventions are already familiar to students from other media, facilitates appraisal of the political implications of literary study itself. The reader is less likely to feel passive under the weight of 'canonical' criticism and more able actively to intervene in feminist debate, rather than attempt to rehash a rote-learned feminist 'position'.

There is perhaps something dangerous and exciting about studying trash

– the very notion seems to be a contradiction in terms. The general view is that it is written with instant gratification in mind, to be consumed and disposed of. The massive sales of bestsellers enable publishers to maintain a backlist of slow- but steady-selling works of 'Literature', implying a symbiotic relationship between the two – a relationship that I would assert extends to the cross-fertilisation of textual strategies. Trash is particularly challenging for women, since they are the targets for much of it, and even if the majority appears to incite 'false consciousness' among its readers, when women read them, they often find women's 'ordinary' lives the centre of narrative attention, a position that might be interpreted as one of strength (Radford 1986; Radway 1987). Even if the narrative closure returns us to a patriarchal *status quo* (e.g. marriage), the central character has often transgressed feminine behavioural 'norms'. Such works are by no means straightforwardly 'positive', but under the scrutiny of the feminist reader they yield contradictions which invite a re-appraisal of dominant feminist literary critical practice itself. In this light, it becomes impossible to dismiss a genre such as the romance as 'invented by women cherishing the chains of their bondage' (Greer 1971: 180); and in recent years several feminists have argued that genre fiction can be liberating for its readers, however conservative the 'message' appears to be (cf. Pearce, this volume).[3] However, feminist literary critics generally remain reluctant to extend their gaze towards the lowbrow, leaving this field to cultural critics; as a result feminism's political thrust is compromised. To stick to the highbrow, even if you 'politicise' it by addressing questions of gender, perpetuates an unmodified assumption that art serves a qualitatively different social/intellectual purpose from pulp.

It would be unnecessarily harsh to castigate feminist literary critics for perpetuating prejudices which are endemic to the discipline of English, considering the advances made by dint of their work from within the institution. Women's writing courses exist where before there was a vacuum; feminist publishers thrive and prosper; students discover a new dimension to literary study where gender matters. There is now a plethora of engaging and invaluable material which has not only unearthed a 'lost' tradition of writing by women, but itself has facilitated further critical debate. I am more concerned that, in face of a degree of institutional acceptance of feminist studies, there is a pressing need to take such projects further, in order to defy absorption or depoliticisation. Once feminism becomes an accepted part of a discipline (however marginal), it is tempting to ask who is changing whom. Many women's texts are now 'respectable', but is respectability a workable political position within education? Education is of course a site of privilege and an ideological breeding ground;

in English Studies this means nurturing a popular consciousness of why literature is worthy of serious study at all. Is it therefore enough to situate some writers as feminist role-models at the expense of arguing that all texts are susceptible to feminist readerly appropriation, even (or especially) those which most fervently deny feminism any currency?

Feminism has been particularly successful in stirring the guilt of the academy, introducing women's writing options as a vital component of English Studies; and this itself has changed the terms of feminist debates within the academic institution. At one time feminists were arguing for the inclusion of women's writing within the curriculum, and struggling for academic credibility; now we have no option but to fight from within, and debate focuses upon methods of resistance against incorporation and dilution of feminist ideas into 'just one more way of talking about books' (Ruthven 1984: 8). Contrary to popular belief, few feminists would regard theory as amounting to doctrine, but rather as presenting a series of positions which are fluid enough to respond to a changing political/social environment. None the less, the academic institution encourages doctrinal tendencies, where courses can be codified and concretised within the discipline – itself an attempt to defuse the threat of a wholesale destabilising of the meaning of 'English'. Feminists have long since pinpointed education as a primary site of socialisation into preferred forms of behaviour: in addition to combatting such values from a political perspective, one must be able to resist dominant archetypes of enduring aesthetic value. The assumption that offering feminist readings makes one immune to investment in such values is a complacent one. Feminism comprises a plurality of oppositional discourses, and requires a pedagogical approach which celebrates such diversity, while enabling students to scrutinise the means by which mainstream criticism seeks to impose preferred readerly identities: none the less, it is quite capable of imposing 'preferred' identities of its own. Admittedly, some of these identities are constructed by the reader who imagines a feminist stance to comprise a fairly concrete position, but this is itself never adequately addressed by critics.

In order to afford a necessary degree of academic acceptance, feminist thought has made compromises at one level, whilst remaining uncompromising at another. Its interventions into male canonical writings have, along with other radical critical positions, denied the fixity of textual hermeneutics, and undermined the putative neutrality of gendered objectivity, in a celebration of subjectivity and historical specificity. Work on both female- and male-authored texts has unearthed contradictions and focused upon gaps and silences, to announce the power of the unsaid within writing, which topples the notion of ideological certainties, and unseats the primacy of the 'preferred reading' (see Mills, Boardman, and Christie, this volume). However, the concept of a preferred reading includes an implied acceptance of what we should 'prefer' to read. Such a position consolidates the high/lowbrow at the expense of examining the conditions of possibility of such a division, neglecting more women's writing in the genre field than it establishes as 'literature'.

It is tempting to suggest that since the mid-1980s, feminist criticism has itself become highbrow, turning away from the deliberately accessible anti-elitist writings of the 1970s, and becoming unnecessarily obstructive to students who come fresh to the subject. None the less, feminist theory has been central to the development of feminist praxis in the classroom, as well as exposing entrenched patriarchal investments in the stronghold of the academic institution as a whole. I do not share the anti-theory sentiments of early Second Wave feminist writers, but I am uncomfortably aware that such theory appears arcane to some students, or as just one more branch of that mysterious body of thought known as Critical Theory – which has shown a marked interest in feminist research *as theory*, but is less keen to stomach redefinitions of the 'political' that go with it.[4]

In the last analysis, theory is never as inaccessible as it appears; but there is a tendency to view it as the apolitical wing of feminist thought. It is constantly at risk of co-option; of being regarded as a learnable 'technique' which might bear little resemblance to the way one experiences the contradictory pulls of 'femininity' in the material world. Since the late 1980s a new 'generation' of feminist critics has emerged, who address popular culture more or less exclusively (e.g. Gamman and Marshment 1988; Carr 1989; Dudovitz 1990; Hawkins 1990; Munt 1992). They have argued that there are 'puritan' streaks in established feminist critical positions and have questioned whether criticism in such an environment metamorphoses into outmoded orthodoxy, more prescriptive than it is 'liberating'.[5] It is the case that any concentration upon women's 'literature' still privileges white, bourgeois, heterosexual women as writer/reader, and therefore leaves issues of race, class and sexual orientation as optional considerations within feminism.

Although feminist work in popular culture has many interfaces with feminist literary criticism, the two fields bifurcate because literary studies rarely involves a substantial investigation into genre fiction. To bring the two aspects together within English Studies is, of course, not always a viable option, given the rigidity of institutional disciplinary boundaries. I suspect that after the upheavals and resulting ideological clashes within English over the past decade and more, the acceptance of radical critical perspectives including feminism is an effort to re-affirm a 'discipline' – to absorb such tendencies into a slightly modified curriculum which is, at heart, English of the old school. Women's writing courses are perhaps both safe and subversive. Safe, in that they potentially establish feminist/female 'classics' and maintain an unproblematical division between superior/ inferior art (one woman's insightful perceptions into the female condition opposed to 'simplistic'/stereotypical representations of women in formulaic writing). Subversive, in that even the existence of new 'classics' problematises literary movements dominated by males, foregrounding hitherto 'minor' texts, and offering modes of critical enquiry which bear little relation to those adopted in other areas of English.

Early Second Wave politics (e.g. Koedt *et al.* 1973; Millett 1977; Firestone 1979; Feminist Anthology Collective 1981) endeavoured to show how female potential extended far beyond the constraints of the culturally constructed 'feminine'. Authenticity and experience thus became a crucial part of early feminist vocabulary; and when critics such as Kate Millett and Mary Ellmann alerted their readers to inauthentic representations of female experience within male-authored texts, the implication was that women writers wrote correspondingly authentic narratives. Just as political writings reproduced narratives of 'real' female experience, politically engaged fiction was presumed to contribute to the quest for 'true' female identity (usually in the singular). The term 'authenticity', used to indicate the search for the 'real' female secreted behind feminine bad faith, can inaccurately suggest a commitment to producing one 'correct' political and personal stance to which women must conform – if they are to be 'permitted' to call themselves feminists.

In this sense, it might be assumed that any feminist analysis of representational practices in popular culture might be considered futile or one-dimensional, yielding only negative results (by way of negative images of women), whereas 'good' women's writing unproblematically yields up true and positive representations that are empathetic regardless of a reader's social/cultural roots. In order to resist such readerly presuppositions, it is important to rethink what the notion of the 'authentic' actually allows feminist critics to do. I would assert that 'authenticity' is actually intended to be a byword for the act of re-envisaging one's social realities rather than another suffocating model of conformity; but on occasions it takes some judicious reading of feminist texts to arrive at this conclusion. With this view in mind, it becomes apparent that cultural criticism which takes 'negative' portrayals of femininity seriously, enables the feminist reader to understand better how representation has an ideological currency which directly impinges upon female experience. This practice might productively provide points of overlap with feminist literary criticism, forestalling the very understandable tendency among readers to equate 'positive' women's texts with the 'real', whilst simultaneously facilitating an evaluation of how representation, taken in a wider context, makes persuasive appeals to, and influences, our lived social realities. In the sphere of women's writing, merely conflating the 'real' and the fictional risks confirming that women's texts are predominantly confessional, with little engagement with narrative experimentation. Moreover, if authenticity is used as a measuring stick for authorial 'feminist' consciousness, how do we extend this model to accommodate conflicting strands of feminism, and what do we do with texts that have no such obvious political investment? (See Mills, and Pearce, this volume.)

Feminism of the 1970s did contain unexamined prescriptive tendencies, not least in the feminist 'mainstream' blindness to the differing experiences of non-white, working-class or lesbian women, exhorting women to embrace a feminist identity that obscured factors of racial and class privilege. Most women cannot simply make a new set of 'choices' in their lives, and femininity as construct is a minefield, since patriarchy manifestly does not offer one single model or option. In the 1980s and 1990s this has become clearer; fiction, film, television advertisements and magazines have responded to the threats/challenges to established order offered by feminism, albeit in ways that could not have been predicted (see Thornborrow, this volume).

As the Women's Movement wanes, feminism as an intellectual tendency has thrived within the establishment, but offers little response to such new challenges as the dawning of 'post-feminism'. Feminist literary criticism arguably remains on the margins, tolerated because it obeys the chief rules of the master discourse; feminist cultural criticism, on the other hand, takes seriously the effect of ostensibly 'liberated' media images of women, which seem to offer a range of feminine identities to put feminism's 'options' to shame. Such critics confront the possibility that these mainstream representations are more attractive as affirmations of sexual equality than what appears to many as the rigid orthodoxy of feminism (see Hallam, this volume). Rather than regarding women as simply duped or trapped by such forms of representation, feminist cultural critics see these areas as ripe for intervention and consequent subversion. This is itself a development of 'images of women' feminist criticism, but engages with the diverse meanings such images offer, rather than simplistically attributing them to the continued social/sexual exploitation of women. Readers/viewers are not merely conceived of as passive consumers acting out bad faith, but are regarded as using such images as symbols of female strength – or representations they themselves hold up for critical scrutiny (see Bradby, this volume).

I believe that there ought to be closer links between feminist literary and cultural criticism – and that the distinction I make between the two 'strands' above could be rendered ultimately fallacious. At present feminist literary analysis still concentrates on two main aspects: (a) women's writing as a category and resulting individual textual studies: and (b) revisionary critiques of male-authored texts, or male-dominated literary movements. Although mainstream women novelists under study are not all feminist writers, the emphasis is upon those whose 'literary' credentials are impeccable; popular forms of fiction which either target a female audience or attract a 'mass' readership by virtue of the genre they occupy are usually overlooked.[6] Even some important contemporary fictional explorations of modern feminist thought are inexplicably neglected. Such texts as Marilyn French's *The Women's Room*, Lisa Alther's *Kinflicks* and Erica Jong's *Fear of Flying* became international bestsellers, probably far more widely read among women than Germaine Greer and Kate Millett ever were; yet they rarely merit a mention from feminists, implying that their contribution to feminist consciousness raising is deemed to be, if anything, negative. Rosalind Coward asserts that, regardless of the novels' political commitment, 'the commercial world has recognized these novels as a genre of sexual writing' (Coward 1984: 179) – ironically, it seems to be their explicit sexual content that renders feminists speechless.

If feminist critics continue to devote their attention to 'quality' work (in the case of women), and sometimes 'overrated' work (in the case of men) their challenge to mainstream English will be progressively diluted. In the changing face of higher education, where courses have increasingly to adapt to modular or credit-accumulation systems, the pressure upon all academics is to produce saleable items, and women's studies courses have proved themselves marketable commodities; though with this acceptance, it is possible that political credibility wanes. Critics, such as Toril Moi, maintain that 'the principal objective of feminist criticism has always been political; it seeks to expose, not to perpetuate, patriarchal practices' (Moi 1985: xiv). I would agree; but the sense in which the word 'political' is being used in the context of her or other literary theorists' work is hard to establish – the implication is that it merely involves a choice between vying feminist positions such as radical, socialist, black or lesbian. English has become adept at absorbing opposition; if feminist academics are now fast becoming the vanguard of the Women's Movement, we need to exploit institutional 'acceptance' and turn it to our own advantage.

This issue is not a new one, and it may be argued that the worst 'literary' excesses of feminist criticism are a product of a tendency which has been largely superseded by a community of more theoretically sophisticated feminist academics. However, I would assert that the literary/trash distinction still effectively operates within feminist criticism, if only by virtue of being ignored. Literary critical texts (e.g. Sellers 1991) continue the invaluable work of broaching the theory/text divide offering readings of literary texts in a wider socio-historical context; yet the novice feminist reader might be forgiven for being unable to identify a 'political' agenda common to both literary and cultural criticism. What is needed to bridge seeming methodological gaps is more attention to the *common political aims* of both enterprises, rather than an assumption that both branches address different implied readers ('English' versus 'Cultural Studies'), or that the implied feminist reader is naturally adept at making the necessary connections herself.

It is easy to get carried away by the sophistication of our own critical rhetoric at the expense of making feminist readings engaging and accessible to a new cohort of English students, or recognising that some critical work seems to forestall rather than invite active debate. Feminist cultural critics, in their focus upon representation, encourage readers/viewers to unpack the signifying systems that seduce the receiver into a preferred reading of the text. In doing so, they pinpoint contradictions and tensions upon which such representation is founded, and interrogate the means by which ideological subject positions 'hail' the viewer/reader (see Boardman, and Mills, this volume). Students can question whether all depictions of reality are unstable and changeable, and 'authenticity' of the image is fore-grounded as fluid and negotiable. The reader or viewer, rather than a passive absorber of whatever ideological position the text appears to favour, interacts with the image so that neither viewer nor image wholly define each other. Cultural criticism suggests that women do not merely posit themselves as 'victims' of the image, but can find means actively to reject or recast it. Even fictional narratives deemed 'conservative' from a feminist point of view can be resisted by interrogating the text's closure in the light of more unstable sub-narrative forces, which suggest its artificiality and instability (see Pearce, this volume).

Once high/lowbrow textual divisions are suspended, the logic of this opposition, and the unequal value attributed to all such binaries can be problematised. Cultural criticism freely engages with any cultural artefact regardless of its aesthetic status, recognising that such value is the product of a discursive system which itself devalues female contributions. That higher education still fetishises white bourgeois male experience as the centre of Englishness and culture becomes abundantly manifest in recent debates about 'political correctness' here and in the United States. A recent article in *The Independent* painfully hits this home, in its description of 'bias' on a university English course. It asks, 'Were books being put on the lists because they were written by women or homosexuals? Was the canon of accepted literary texts, particularly the plays and poems of Shakespeare, being surreptitiously reduced?[7] The tone is that of espionage, of groups of undesirables (women and homosexuals) attempting clandestinely to chisel away at the foundations of 'our' culture. While we cling to 'highbrow' assumptions inherent in patriarchal literary criticism, we are fuelling the fire for such debates and allowing such cultural exclusionism to continue.

Many dominant forms of cultural expression – whether films, soap operas, advertisements or pulp fiction – have been busily 'quoting' feminism since the 1970s. It is inadequate to observe complacently with righteous indignation that such quoting is in fact misquoting, unless we intervene in order to demonstrate that feminism does not resemble its popular persona very closely. Feminism's quotability is a backhanded tribute to the fact that it is still perceived as a threat; and that threat is only removed when feminists choose respectability, in favour of renewed political challenge.

I have spent a great deal of time criticising 'highbrow' tendencies in feminist literary criticism, but as yet have said little about how one might redefine feminist criticism within English Studies. I have implied that a primary objective should be to extend the range of textual material used, so that popular genre fiction is explored as a matter of course. It is likely that a tendency to favour close study of individual texts does not serve the political interests of feminism very well, since by viewing them in various relations to each other one might ask quite different questions, and discover some surprising 'answers'. Crossing generic boundaries allows readers to debate seriously the issue of what endows one text with a quality marker, while another is consigned to the trashcan; in addition many points of comparison can be established – for example, the function of 'mirror' imagery in *The Bell Jar*, *Wide Sargasso Sea*, *The Invisible Cord* (Catherine Cookson) and *Mirror Image* (Melinda Cross, Mills & Boon). Feminist criticism, strictly speaking, knows of only one boundary: that its object of study is women as writers and/or readers; and we have yet to capitalise fully upon this fact.

'Images of women' criticism has been revamped in cultural studies to allow for the heterogeneity of female identity/experience, and therefore avoid unpopular (not to say racist, heterosexist, etc.) homogenising tendencies of earlier critical works. Isolating the virgin/whore dichotomy as central to the meaning of the 'feminine' gained critics a foothold in re-evaluating male portrayals of women, but originally little account was taken of the multifarious ways women spectators/readers position themselves in relation to such depictions. It is still the case that the strong, autonomous, promiscuous female character is demonised in books, films and television, and that, generally speaking, she is punished or tamed in the end. The end result may be a 'negative' image, but in structural terms such 'demonic' women are the most compelling ingredient of the plot; in fact, the narrative dynamics often centres on their machinations – from *King Lear* to *Dynasty* (see Boardman, this volume, on closure). The good women in such texts are static: all they can do is represent 'femininity' visually (as object/objectification) and by 'silence' (to speak is to be 'shrewish'). Neither portrayal of the female is positive in feminist terms, but both display the instability of a patriarchal *status quo*, where the demonic woman turns 'nature' on its head, not by her actions, but by the fact that they are performed by a female. The maintenance of the *status quo* is effected by coercion (death, punishment, taming) and announces its own unnaturalness quite effectively.

Cultural critics (e.g. Gamman *et al.* 1988) address the thorny question of women's pleasure in viewing such 'demonic' images. Their ambiguity (they are 'bad' but they are strong) is seductive, and countless women enjoy and consume such 'conservative' texts as a matter of choice (see Pearce, and Boardman, this volume). Romance texts are largely conservative in the final choices they seem to offer their female characters, despite the fact that in the initial stages of the narrative the heroine might appear to be something of a proto-feminist. But although such texts are 'formulaic', they are by no means static, and have absorbed, if perverted, some central feminist ideas. I would therefore argue that it is not simply misguided to ignore 'negative' works of fiction; it is dangerous. In addition, it is offensive and simplistic to dismiss the reading/viewing activities of such a vast group as merely collusive, without investigating the ways that they can and are read to resist the social *status quo* – not least because in everyday life such representations can hardly be avoided (see Hallam, this volume). This also has ramifications for how feminist critics should perceive their potential readers, in that more students now come to higher and adult education with non-standard qualifications, and to assume a specific form of grounding in English Studies is often misguided (Milloy and O'Rourke 1991). In any case, the implied feminist reader of women's writing bears little relation to the average reader, who, as part of her/his daily reading practice, consumes newspapers, television programmes, magazines and genre fiction. A fusion of the tenets of cultural and literary criticism might enable the reader of women's writing better to reconcile these seemingly distinct activities with the 'political activity' of feminism.

I have already suggested that 'high art' tends to re-affirm 'objective' observations that women, by virtue of their almost wholesale exclusion from such a category, must be naturally intellectually inferior to men and therefore 'explains' their concentration in mass-market genre fiction. For feminists to ignore such work and its readership is to leave such divisions ironically intact as natural and inevitable. Some women writers have for example appropriated the 'formulae' of the crime/thriller, science fiction/ utopia genres, and have exploited readerly expectations for feminist purposes. A study of such fiction in relation to their more conservative sisters demonstrates that narrative strategies are themselves political tools, but ones which capitalise on readerly enjoyment rather than moral didacticism. Such writers deconstruct the ideological values endemic in such formulae more effectively than any critical study could. If the danger of studying trash is to insert it into a bourgeois discursive arena, and thereby re-affirm its 'trashiness', this is a calculated risk feminists in the academy must take. It is only by extending feminism's critical gaze that further scrutiny of the patriarchal investment in cultural value can be undertaken, and that the woman reader becomes acknowledged as a cultural reader, rather than simply an interrogator of the 'literary'.

Feminist cultural critics have extended the range of objects of study we can and should use for political purposes; in this they have certainly benefited from pathfinding feminist work in literary and film studies. Likewise, feminists working in English can benefit from shedding some of its more tenacious tenets, not least its self-appointed privilege to sort the great from the trash. Genre fiction often relegates the status of author as subordinate to genre, and the activity of reader as consumer is thereby foregrounded. Necessarily 'thematic' issues explored in feminist criticism could be similarly expanded to facilitate discussion of broader feminist political debates: for example, a study of representations of the family in *King Lear*, *Oranges Are not the Only Fruit*, *The Munsters*, a Catherine Cookson novel, *The Thorn Birds*, *Fear of Flying* and *Pride and Prejudice*. All reflect anxiety about family organisations, and all offer critiques – even the 'conservative' ones. One could further analyse the relations between the high and lowbrow to investigate what happens to women's 'literary' texts when they are rendered popular through the medium of television or film – for example, *The Handmaid's Tale*, *Oranges Are not the Only Fruit* or *The Company of Wolves*.

To address the plurality of responses a single text or inter-textual comparison can yield is to make a sustained political attempt to break down the boundaries between theory, writing and politics, so that theory functions as a useful tool for the reader, rather than as a tyrant. There are all too many people willing to attribute feminism's 'failure' to the tyranny of orthodoxy, and who would agree with Sally Minogue's view:

> Feminist criticism has begun to assume a punitive, narrowing aspect. In telling us which authors we should and should not read, and what areas of those authors we should or should not approve, and what aspects of behaviour of female characters we should and should not take as models of identity, it narrows our area of interest in literature in a distorting manner. (Minogue 1990: 11)

Minogue's critique appears in a volume of essays intent on rescuing some of the more established literary lions (Shakespeare, Eliot, Dickens, Milton, Charlotte Brontë and Lawrence) from the worst excesses of feminist vandalism, and, as a recent publication, is a salutory warning about the possible fate of feminism within the academy today. Where do we place such female critics, who debate 'feminist orthodoxy' from an 'objective' and 'neutral' stance? The volume's cover places them within the category of 'literature/literary theory/women's studies', and so, for the enquiring reader, they are one of 'us'. Here, the danger is of stasis and complacency, co-option and dilution, when on a wider political arena, the 'failure' of feminist politics to shake society's foundations indicates feminism's need to identify itself(selves) as work in progress.

The high/lowbrow divide is reinforced from many sides – publishing strategies, mainstream literary studies and feminist literary studies. A cheerful admixture of art and trash opens up new possibilities of comparison, and politicisation of fiction itself, denying the centrality of literature as an art form which teaches us about 'life'. Feminist politics exploded the public/private divide, arguing that women's assumed social inferiority is the condition of existence of both in their present form. Likewise denying the veracity of the art/trash binary acknowledges the means by which all cultural products can re-affirm or challenge the *status quo* – or even do both simultaneously. To take seriously the effect of women's relation to popular culture allows us to make some headway in unpacking the mixed messages that constantly bombard us in our public/ private lives – from Madonna to the television serial *The Manageress*. They may present illusions which seem to deny the tribulations of lived social experience; but illusion and reality is one more opposition which demands investigation. Fantasies can contain utopian possibilities: the fantasy tradition within women's writing itself challenges the commonplace preconception that feminist writing is a new form of moral didacticism.

Feminism in the 1990s, as I have already implied, encounters threats in very different guises from the errant sexism that could still have currency in the late 1960s. It has been recognised by many that a marked shift in politics during the 1980s and 1990s has meant that radical politics and theories are being suppressed by force (Evans *et al.* 1986). This has transformed the expectations of the students we now teach: many of the women simply do not feel the need to identify as feminists, and there is no use attributing this to political inertia. If the popular student consciousness of feminist criticism is of something 'punitive' and puritanical, we must ascribe this partly to our failure in fully liberating readers who can take and scrutinise their textual pleasures seriously. Many women (not necessarily 'unenlightened' ones) read romance, fantasy or bestsellers for 'pleasure' or 'escape', though they tend to internalise literary prejudices that situate such texts as unworthy objects of scholarly study. To deny the role of pleasure that one can take in seemingly repetitious and hackneyed formulae is to inject that element of prudishness which implies that there are proper books to read, as well as proper reading practices, although such propriety is never clearly delineated.

Alison Light observes:

> Feminist literary criticism is, as we know, quite capable of creating its own canons and schools, which can intimidate and exclude new writers and thinkers, tying them up in knots of deference and immobilising them as effectively as kowtowing to crusty professors did in the bad old days. . . Being a feminist, as I understand it, should not be like being in church: there are no blasphemies, no ritual incantations, no heretics and no saints. (Light, in Carr 1989: 28)

The prospect that we might be alienating more readers of women's fiction than we 'convert' is a chilling one; as Light points out, we risk immobilising a new generation of writers and thinkers upon whom our institutional survival depends – if feminism is not to be the preserve of 'crusty professors'. Such sentiments are being produced with increasing regularity, suggesting to me that the time for feminist critics to re-energise their activities and look to the popular is well overdue. I do not make this assertion simply because trash is trendy: if 'the personal is political', then so are our private pleasures.

NOTES

1. See Terry Eagleton's discussion of the critical model which informed *Scrutiny* in *The Function of Criticism* (1984: 69–84).
2. Paulina Palmer has observed that 'fiction by contemporary women writers often plays a minimal or non-existent role in the curriculum. It is marginalized or erased in favour of works of fiction from earlier periods' (Palmer 1989: 3). On the whole, I agree with her; but the available material on contemporary writers tends to be

predictable in its selection of authors. In fact, Palmer's own book is refreshing because of the range of modern writers to which she refers.

3. Lillian Robinson is a rare example of an early feminist critic, who in her essay, 'On reading trash' (1986; first published 1978), called for a more sophisticated analysis of trash and its readers:

> To attack the reactionary image of women and the ideology about our nature and roles that such novels present – as, for example, Germaine Greer has done – is to mistake the thing on the page for experience itself. A fully feminist reading of women's books must look at *women* as well as at books, and try to understand how this literature actually functions in society. (Robinson 1986: 205)

See also Radway (1987), Ann Rosalind Jones, 'Mills & Boon meets feminism' (in Radford 1986) and Leslie W. Rabine, 'Romance in the age of electronics: Harlequin enterprises' (in Newton and Rosenfelt 1985).

4. Kate Millett arguably initiated this aspect of feminist criticism in her call for 'defining a theory of politics which treats of power relationships on grounds less conventional than those to which we are accustomed' (Millett 1977: 24); and feminists have extended possible definitions of the political since.

The issue of feminism's co-option by other theories has recently been foregrounded in debates around feminism's relation to postmodernism. Susan Bordo identifies a trend in postmodern thought to transcend gender dualities, but forcefully remind us that 'like it or not, in our present culture, our activities *are* coded as "male" or "female" and will function as such within the prevailing system of gender–power relations' (in Nicholson 1990: 152).

5. Shelagh Young asserts that 'many feminist women do perpetuate a sort of alternative puritanism which can be very boring indeed' (Gamman and Marshment 1988: 178).

6. As Jane Gallop suggests, such an oversight has serious consequences for feminism because 'when feminist literary criticism devotes itself to geniuses like Emily Dickinson and Virginia Woolf, it contradicts feminism by preferring the woman who is different from and better than other women' (Gallop 1992: 138).

7. Sandra Barwick, 'English as she should be taught?', *The Independent*, Saturday 13 June 1992.

REFERENCES

Battersby, C. (1990) *Gender and Genius: Towards a feminist aesthetics*, London: Women's Press.

Carr, H. (ed.) (1989) *From My Guy to Sci-fi*, London: Pandora Press.

Coward, R. (1984) *Female Desire*, London: Paladin.

Cranny-Francis, A. (1990) *Feminist Fiction: Feminist uses of generic fiction*, Cambridge: Polity Press.

Dudovitz, R. (1990) *The Myth of the Superwoman: Women's bestsellers in France and the United States*, London: Routledge.

Eagleton, T. (1984) *The Function of Criticism*, London: Verso.

Ellmann, M. (1979) *Thinking about Women*, London: Virago.

Evans, J., Hills, J., Hunt, K., Meehan, E., ten Tusscher, T., Vogel, U. and Waylen, G. (1986) *Feminism and Political Theory*, London: Sage.

Feminist Anthology Collective (eds) (1981) *No Turning Back: Writings from the women's liberation movement*, London: Women's Press.

Firestone, S. (1979) *The Dialectic of Sex*, London: Women's Press (first published 1971).

Gallop, J. (1992) *Around 1981: Academic feminist theory*, London: Routledge.

Gamman, L. and Marshment, M. (eds) (1988) *The Female Gaze: Women as viewers of popular culture*, London: Women's Press.

Greer, G. (1971) *The Female Eunuch*, London: Paladin.

Hawkins, H. (1990) *Classics and Trash*, Hemel Hempstead: Harvester Wheatsheaf.

Kauffman, L. (ed.) (1989) *Feminism and Institutions: Dialogues on feminist theory*, Oxford: Blackwell.

Koedt, A., Levine, E., and Rapone, A. (eds) (1973) *Radical Feminism*, New York: Quadrangle.

Millett, K. (1977) *Sexual Politics*, London: Virago (first published 1971).

Milloy, J. and O'Rourke, R. (eds) (1991) *The Woman Reader: Learning and teaching women's writing*, London: Routledge.

Minogue, S. (ed.) (1990) *Problems for Feminist Criticism*, London: Routledge.

Moi, T. (1985) *Sexual/Textual Politics*, London: Methuen.

Munt, S. (ed.) (1992) *New Lesbian Criticism*, Hemel Hempstead: Harvester Wheatsheaf.

Newton, J. and Rosenfelt, D. (eds) (1985) *Feminist Criticism and Social Change*, London: Methuen.

Nicholson, L. (ed.) (1990) *Feminism/Postmodernism*, London: Routledge.

Palmer, P. (1989) *Contemporary Women's Fiction*, Hemel Hempstead: Harvester Wheatsheaf.

Radford, J. (ed.) (1986) *The Progress of Romance: The politics of popular fiction*, London: Routledge.

Radway, J. (1987) *Reading the Romance: Women, patriarchy and popular literature*, London: Verso (first published 1984).

Robinson, L. S. (1986) *Sex, Class, and Culture*, London: Methuen (first published 1978).

Ruthven, K. K. (1984) *Feminist Literary Studies*, Cambridge: Cambridge University Press.

Sellers, S. (ed.) (1991) *Feminist Criticism: Theory and practice*, Hemel Hempstead: Harvester Wheatsheaf.

Showalter, E. (1982) *A Literature of their Own*, London: Virago.

Conclusion

Generally, concluding chapters attempt to tie down the unruly strands of arguments which have woven themselves throughout the book, in order to present an image of the overall conception of the book. This is not the aim of this conclusion; rather the concerns of this short concluding section are to tease out some of those arguments which have been articulated throughout the course of this book, in order to demonstrate that the subject of gender and reading is one we have found it more productive to dispense with as a stable ground for argument. This is not a nihilistic or postmodern position, nor is it a position of simplistic relativism, since all of these positions can lead to political inertia and the inability to say *anything*. Feminist theory, for us, is concerned with bringing about changes in material conditions and also in consciousness. What we have been arguing for in these chapters is for an interdisciplinary arena, in which debates about reading can be voiced. Each of us has taken a particular position, not for the sake of simple exemplification ('I will do classic reader response today, and feminist linguistic analysis tomorrow') but because that is where we have reached in terms of our argumentation at the moment. We have listened to each others' arguments and have discussed these ideas with colleagues and friends. No doubt, each of us will develop these arguments over time and attempt to synthesise other approaches into our existing frameworks of reference, in order to produce more adequate models of the reading process. These essays should therefore be seen as a series of 'staging posts' in the process of theorising the relation between reader and gender.

As we mentioned in the Introduction, there are several issues which concern all of the essays, but which each of them has approached in a slightly different way. One issue of central importance is the very question of gender itself as a term. We feel that it is necessary for feminist studies to concentrate on gender rather than the term 'woman' in isolation. For all of us, in our different ways, whether we are analysing male-authored

236

texts or female-authored texts, male-directed texts or female-directed texts, these terms can only make sense to us if they are considered within a *system* of difference, that is, if they are treated as *relational* rather than *essential* terms. That is to say, the term 'woman' makes no sense on its own, just as the term 'man' needs always to be related to a context of meanings against which it serves as an opposing term. Using the term 'gender' opens out certain possibilities for us; it allows us to analyse the differences within the term 'women': the system of relational differences which intersect and struggle for precedence within that term. This allows us to examine the conditions for specific categories of female identity, and it also allows for change within and across those categories, at both a socio-historical and a personal level. This does not mean that all we can analyse are 'persons': individual accumulations of intersecting factors such as gender, disability, race, age and so on. If these elements mean anything, which we are convinced they do, they mean in a relational way. For example, if we only analyse 'women's writing' or the 'woman reader' we do not analyse 'men's writing' or the 'male reader', nor do we analyse the system of difference whereby these latter elements are constituted as 'strange' to us. If we consider the question of 'race', concerning ourselves only with black writing, then we will erase the very 'racialness' of white writing. If we consider 'sexual orientation' and only analyse lesbian and gay writing, then the constructedness of heterosexuality will be passed over. Thus, rather than the use of the term 'gender' signalling an inability to centre ourselves within feminist political analysis, and rather than it leading to us being unable to ground our arguments, we feel that the use of the term gender can significantly enliven debate in feminist theory. It is clear to us that using the term gender can mean that male and female difference may be treated as if they were the same and equal, but this is not our aim. We feel that it is necessary to maintain a distinction between the different oppressions that women and men suffer and struggle against (and there are times when we seem to be categorised as women and men, despite the differences within those terms), whilst setting these terms in a wider discussion of the influences of other factors apart from sex difference.

The other important issue which these essays have discussed is that of reading. We have all tried to work with models of the reading process which have stressed the fact that texts have more than one position of intelligibility. We have all found this much more difficult than the conventional critical position which aims to provide a 'super-reading' in direct competition with other readings. None of us has found it useful to produce a final reading of the texts which we have analysed; rather we have tried to examine the ways that readers negotiate positions for themselves within the constraints that the texts impose. In some of the essays, the stress has been on the way certain texts preclude any liberatory reading positions for the feminist; in other essays, there has been an emphasis on the way that feminist readers can tease out elements of pleasure and strength in even the most recalcitrant texts, ignoring the supposed resolution that the text imposes, with all the ideological dangers that closure implies. Writing these essays has called for a fundamental analysis of the reading process, so that we, as readers, do not take any element for granted and must hear other theoretical voices in the process of trying to establish theoretical positions for ourselves. This hetereogeneity of gender positions and reading positions has led us to heterogeneous theoretical positions. In discussing these essays with each other, our work has assumed the quality of a series of dialogues. Reading, gender and theory have all become far more complex to analyse and far more productive as interacting terms.

Bibliography

Allen, R. C., 'Reader-oriented criticism and televison', in R. C. Allen (ed.) *Channels of Discourse*, London: Routledge, 1989, pp. 74–113.

Allen, R. C., 'Audience-oriented criticism and television', in R. C. Allen (ed.) *Channels of Discourse Reassembled: Television and Contemporary Criticism*, 2nd edn, London: Routledge, 1992, pp. 101–38.

Althusser, L., 'Ideology and ideological state apparatuses', *Lenin and Philosophy*, London: New Left Books, 1971, p. 121–73.

Althusser, L., *Essays in Ideology*, London: Verso, 1984.

Anderson, B., *Imagined Communities: Reflections on the origin and spread of nationalism*, London: Verso, 1983.

Ang, I., *Watching Dallas: Soap opera and the melodramatic imagination*, London: Methuen 1989.

Ang, I., 'Wanted: Audiences', in E. Seiter, H. Borchers, G. Kreutzner and E. M. Warth (eds) *Remote Control*, London and New York: Routledge, 1989, pp. 96–115.

Armstrong, N. and Tennenhouse, L. (eds), *The Ideology of Conduct: Essays in literature and the history of sexuality*, London: Methuen, 1987.

Assiter, A., *Althusser and Feminism*, London: Pluto, 1990.

Ballaster, R., Beetham, M., Frazer, E. and Hebron, S., *Women's Worlds: Ideology, femininity and the woman's magazine*, London: Macmillan, 1991.

Barthes, R., *S/Z*, London: Cape, 1975.

Barthes, R., *Image–Music–Text*, London: Fontana, 1977.

Barthes, R., 'The death of the author', in R. Barthes, *The Rustle of Language*, Oxford: Blackwell, 1986, pp. 49–55.

Battersby, C., *Gender and Genius: Towards a feminist aesthetics*, London, Women's Press, 1990.

Bauer, D., *Feminist Dialogics: A theory of failed community*, Albany, NY: SUNY, 1988.

Belsey, C., *Critical Practice*, London: Methuen, 1980.

Benton, M., Teasey, J., Bell, R. and Hurst, K., *Young Readers Responding to Poems*, London: Routledge, 1988.

Berger, J., *Ways of Seeing*, London: BBC/Pelican, 1972.

Betterton, R. (ed.), *Looking on: Images of femininity in the visual arts and media*, London: Pandora, 1987.

Bobo, J., '*The Color Purple*: Black women as cultural readers,' in D. Pribram (ed.) *Female Spectators: Looking at film and television*, London: Verso, 1988, pp. 90–109.

Booth, W., *The Rhetoric of Fiction*, Chicago: University of Chicago Press, 1961.

Bordwell, D. and Thompson, K., *Film Art: An introduction*, New York: McGraw-Hill, 1990.

239

Bordwell, D., Staiger, J. and Thompson, K., *The Classical Hollywood Cinema: Film style and mode of production to 1960*, New York: Columbia University Press, 1985.

Born, G., 'Women, music, politics, difference: Susan McClary's *Feminine Endings: Music, gender and sexuality,*' *Women: A cultural review*, 3, 1 (1992): 79–86.

Bourdieu, P., *Distinction: A social critique of the judgement of taste*, trans. R. Nice, London: Routledge & Kegan Paul, 1984.

Bourdieu, P. and Passeron, J., *Reproduction in Education, Society and Culture*, London and Beverly Hills: Sage, 1977.

Bovenschen, S., 'Is there a feminine aesthetic?' *New German Critique*, 10 (1977): 111–37.

Bowles, G. and Klein, R. (eds), *Theories of Women's Studies*, London: Routledge, 1983.

Bradby, B., 'Do-talk and don't-talk: The division of the subject in girl-group music', in S. Frith and A. Goodwin (eds) *On Record: A rock and pop reader*, New York: Pantheon; London: Routledge, 1990, pp. 341–68.

Bradby, B., 'Like a virgin-mother: Materialism and maternalism in the songs of Madonna', *Cultural Studies*, 6, 1 (1992): 73–96.

Bradby, B. and Torode, B., 'Pity Peggy-Sue', *Popular Music*, 4 (1984): 183–206.

Brake, L., Jones, A. and Madden, L., *Investigating Victorian Journalism*, London: Macmillan, 1990.

Brown, M. E. and Fiske, J., 'Romancing the rock: Romance and representation in popular music videos', *OneTwoThreeFour*, 5 (1987): 61–73.

Brownmiller, S., *Femininity*, London: Paladin Grafton, 1984.

Brunsdon, C., '*Crossroads*: Notes on a soap opera', *Screen*, 22, 4: 32–7.

Brunsdon, C. and Morley, D., *Everyday Television: Nationwide*, London: British Film Institute, 1978.

Buckingham, D., *Public Secrets: Eastenders and its audience*, London: British Film Institute, 1985.

Buckingham, D., 'What are words worth: Interpreting children's talk about television', *Cultural Studies*, 5, 2 (1991): 228–45.

Burgin, V., 'Seeing sense', in H. Davis and P. Walton (eds) *Language, Image, Media*, Oxford: Blackwell, 1983, pp. 226–44.

Butler, J., *Gender Trouble: Feminism and the subversion of identity*, London: Routledge, 1990.

Byars, J., 'Gazes/voices/power: Expanding psychoanalysis for feminist film and television theory', in D. Pribram (ed.) *Female Spectators: Looking at film and television*, London: Verso, 1988, pp. 110–31.

Cameron, D., *Feminism and Linguistic Theory*, London: Macmillan, 1985.

Cameron, D., McAlinden, F. and O'Leary, K., 'Lakoff in context: The social and linguistic functions of tag questions,' in J. Coates and D. Cameron (eds) *Women in their Speech Communities*, Harlow: Longman, 1988, pp. 74–93.

Carr, H. (ed.), *From My Guy to Sci-Fi*, London: Pandora Press, 1989.

(charles), H., '"Whiteness" – the relevance of politically colouring the "Non"', in H. Hinds, A. Phoenix and J. Stacey (eds) *Working Out: New directions for women's studies*, London: Falmer, 1992, pp. 29–35.

Cherry, D., *Painting Women: Victorian women artists*, Rochdale Art Gallery, 1986.

Christie, C., 'Relevance theory and the analysis of audience response', PhD thesis, Strathclyde University, 1993.

Coates, J., *Women, Men and Language*, London: Longman, 1986.

Coates, J., 'Gossip revisited: Language in all-female groups', in J. Coates and D. Cameron (eds) *Women in their Speech Communities*, Harlow: Longman, 1988, pp. 94–122.

Coates, J. and Cameron, D. (eds), *Women in their Speech Communities*, Harlow: Longman, 1988.

Cook, E. and Wedderburn, A. (eds), *The Works of John Ruskin*, vol. 36: *Letters*, London: Allen.

Cook, S., 'The career and times of Irene Castle: Revolutions in music and manners', *World Beat: An international journal of popular music*, 1 (1991): 34–44.

Coward, R., *Female Desire*, London: Paladin, 1984.

Cowie, C. and Lees, S., 'Slags or drags', *Feminist Review*, 9 (Autumn 1981): 17–31.

Cranny-Francis, A., *Feminist Fiction: Feminist uses of generic fiction*, Cambridge: Polity Press, 1990.

Crawford, M. and Chaffin, R., 'The reader's construction of meaning: Cognitive research on gender and comprehension', in E. A. Flynn and P. P. Schweickart (eds) *Gender and Reading*, Baltimore and London: Johns Hopkins University Press, 1986, pp. 3–30.

Culler, J., *Structuralist Poetics: Structuralism, linguistics and the study of literature*, Ithaca: Cornell University Press, 1975.

Culler, J., *The Pursuit of Signs: Semiotics, literature, deconstruction*, London: Routledge & Kegan Paul, 1981.

Culler, J., *On Deconstruction: Theory and criticism after structuralism*, Ithaca: Cornell University Press, 1982.

Culler, J., 'Reading as a woman', in *On Deconstruction: Theory and criticism after structuralism*, Ithaca: Cornell University Press, 1982.

Davies, K., Dickey, J. and Stratford, T. (eds), *Out of Focus: Writings on women and the media*, London: Women's Press, 1987.

Davis, L. J., *Resisting Novels: Ideology and fiction*, London: Methuen, 1987.

Dayan, D., 'The tutor code of classical cinema', in B. Nichols (ed.) *Movies and Methods*, London: University of California Press, 1976.

Dixon-Hunt, J., *The Pre-Raphaelite Imagination*, London: Routledge & Kegan Paul, 1968.

Doane, M. A., 'Film and the masquerade: Theorising the female spectator', *Screen*, 23:3/4 (September/October, 1982): 74–89.

Doane, M. A., 'The "woman's film", possession and address' reprinted in C. Gledhill (ed.) *Home Is Where the Heart Is: Studies in melodrama and the woman's film*, London: British Film Institute, 1987, pp. 283–98.

Doane, M. A., *The Desire to Desire: The woman's film in the 1940s*, London: Macmillan, 1988.

Doughty, O. and Wahl, J., *The letters of Dante Gabriel Rossetti*, 4 vols, Oxford: Oxford University Press, 1965–7.

Drummond, P. and Patterson, R. (eds), *Television and its Audiences*, London: British Film Institute, 1988.

Dudovitz, R., *The Myth of the Superwoman: Women's bestsellers in France and the United States*, London: Routledge, 1990.

Durant, A. and Fabb, N., *Literary Studies in Action*, London: Routledge, 1990.

Dyer, G., *Advertising as Communication*, London and New York: Routledge, 1982.

Eagleton, T., *Literary Theory: An Introduction*, Oxford: Blackwell, 1983.

Eagleton, T., *The Function of Criticism*, London: Verso, 1984.

Eagleton, T., *Ideology: An introduction*, London: Verso, 1991.

Eco, U., *The Role of the Reader: Explorations in the semiotics of text*, Bloomington: Indiana University Press, 1979.

Ellman, M., *Thinking about Women*, London: Virago, 1979.

Ellsworth, E., 'Illicit pleasures: Feminist spectators and "personal best"', *Wide Angle*, 8, 2 (1986): 45–56.

Evans, J., Hills, J., Hunt, K., Meehan, E., Tusscher, T. ten, Vogel, U. and Waylen, G., *Feminism and Political Theory*, London: Sage, 1986.

Fabb, N. and Durant, A., 'Ten years on in the linguistics of writing', *Prose Studies*, 10, 1 (1987).

Fairclough, N., *Language and Power*, London: Longman, 1989.

Fairclough, N. (ed.), *Critical Discourse Analysis*, London: Longman, 1992.

Feminist Anthology Collective (eds), *No Turning Back: Writings from the women's liberation movement*, London: Women's Press, 1981.

Feminist Review, The Past before Us: Twenty-five years of feminism, No. 31, 1989.

Fetterley, J., *The Resisting Reader: A feminist approach to American fiction*, Bloomington: Indiana University Press, 1978.

Fetterley, J., 'Reading about reading', in E. A. Flynn and P. P. Schweickart (eds) *Gender and Reading*, Baltimore and London: Johns Hopkins University Press, 1986, pp. 147–64.

Feuer, J., 'Dynasty', paper presented at International Television Studies Conference, London, 1986.

Firestone, S., *The Dialectic of Sex*, London: Women's Press, 1979 (first published 1971).

Fish, S., *Is There a Text in this Class? The authority of interpretive communities*, London and Cambridge, MA: Harvard University Press, 1980.

Fiske, J., *Reading the Popular*, London: Unwin Hyman, 1989.

Flynn, E. A. and Schweickart, P. P. (eds), *Gender and Reading: Essays on readers, texts and contexts*, Baltimore and London: Johns Hopkins University Press, 1986.

Foucault, M., 'The subject and power', in H. Dreyfus and P. Rabinow (eds) *Michel Foucault: Beyond structuralism and hermeneutics*, Hemel Hempstead: Harvester Wheatsheaf, 1982, pp. 208–26.

Fowler, B., *The Alienated Reader: Women and popular romantic literature in the twentieth century*, Hemel Hempstead: Harvester Wheatsheaf, 1991.

Fowler, R., *Linguistic Criticism*, Oxford, Oxford University Press, 1986.

Fowler, R., *Language in the News*, London: Routledge, 1991.

Fowler, R., Hodge, R., Kress, G. and Trew, T., *Language and Control*, London: Routledge & Kegan Paul, 1979.

Franklin, S., Lurie, C. and Stacey, J. (eds), *Off-centre: Feminism and cultural studies*, London: HarperCollins, 1991.

Freeman, D. (ed.), *Essays in Modern Stylistics*, London: Methuen, 1981.

Freund, E., *The Return of the Reader: Reader-response criticism*, London: Methuen, 1987.

Frith, G., 'Transforming features: Double vision and the female reader', *New Formations*, 15 (Winter 1991): 67–81.

Frith, S., 'Why do songs have words', in S. Frith (ed.) *Music for Pleasure: Essays in the sociology of pop*, Oxford: Polity, 1988, pp. 105–28.

Frith, S. and McRobbie, A., 'Rock and sexuality', *Screen Education*, 29 (1979): 3–19.

Fuss, D., *Essentially Speaking: Feminism, nature and difference*, London: Routledge, 1989.

Gaines, J. and Herzog, C. (eds), *Fabrications: Costume and the female body*, London: AFI/Routledge, 1990.

Gallop, J., *Around 1981: Academic feminist theory*, London: Routledge, 1992.

Gamman, L., 'More Cagney and Lacey', *Feminist Review*, 37 (1991): 117–21.

Gamman, L, and Marshment, M. (eds), *The Female Gaze: Women as viewers of popular culture*, London: Women's Press, 1988.

Garratt, S., 'How I learned to stop worrying and love Madonna', *Women's Review*, 5 (March 1986): 12–13.

Gledhill, C., 'Pleasurable negotiations', in D. Pribram (ed.) *Female Spectators: Looking at film and television*, London: Verso, 1988, pp. 65–89.

Goddard, T., Pollock, J. and Fudger, M., 'Popular music', in J. King and M. Stott (eds) *Is This Your Life? Images of women in the media*, London: Virago, 1977, pp. 143–59.

Goffman, E., *Gender Advertisements*, London: Macmillan, 1976.

Goldman, W., *Adventures in the Screen Trade*, London: Macdonald, 1984.

Goodwin, M. H., 'Directive–response speech sequences in girls' and boys' task activities,' in S. McConnell-Ginet, N. Borker and N. Furman (eds) *Women and Language in Literature and Society*, New York: Praeger, 1980, pp. 157–73.

Gray, A., 'Behind closed doors: Video recorders in the home', in H. Baehr and G. Dyer (eds) *Boxed In: Women and television*, London: Pandora, 1987, pp. 38–54.

Greer, G., *The Female Eunuch*, London: Paladin, 1971.

Greer, G., *The Obstacle Race*, London: Picador, 1981.

Grice, H. P., 'Logic and conversation', in P. Cole and J. Morgan (eds) *Syntax and Semantics*, vol. 3: *Speech Acts*, New York: Academic Press, 1975.

Hall, S., 'Encoding and decoding the TV message', CCCS pamphlet, University of Birmingham, 1973.

Hall, S., 'Encoding/decoding', in S. Hall, D. Hobson, A. Lowe and P. Willis (eds) *Culture, Media, Language*, London: Hutchinson, 1980, pp. 128–38.

Hallam, J. and Marshment, M., 'Framing experience: case studies in the reception of *Oranges Are not the only Fruit*', Los Angeles, California: paper to the Consoling Passions Feminist Television Conference, 1993.

Halliday, M. A. K., 'Linguistic function and literary style: An enquiry into the language of William Golding's *The Inheritors*', in D. Freeman (ed.) *Essays in Modern Stylistics*, London: Methuen, 1981, pp. 325–60.

Halliday, M. A. K., *An Introduction to Functional Grammar*, London: Edward Arnold, 1985.

Halliday, M. A. K. and Hasan, R., *Cohesion in English*, London: Longman, 1976.

Haralovich, M., 'The proletarian woman's film of the 1930s', *Screen*, 31, 2 (Summer 1990): 172–87.

Harris, S., 'Questions as a mode of control in magistrates' courts', *The International Journal of the Sociology of Language*, 49 (1984): 5–27.

Harrison, B., *Drink and the Victorians: The temperance question in England, 1815–1872*, London: Faber & Faber, 1971.

Haskell, M., *From Reverence to Rape: The treatment of women in the movies*. 2nd edn, Chicago and London: University of Chicago Press, 1987.

Hawkins, H., *Classics and Trash*, Hemel Hempstead: Harvester Wheatsheaf, 1990.

Herrman, A., *An/Other Self: The dialogic and difference*, New York, Columbia University Press, 1989.

Herzog, C. C. and Gaines, J. M., '"Puffed sleeves before tea-time": Joan Crawford, Adrian and women audiences', in C. Gledhill (ed.) *Stardom: Industry of desire*, London: Routledge, 1991, pp. 74–91.

Hinds, H., Phoenix, A. and Stacey, J. (eds), *Working Out: New directions for women's studies*, London: Falmer, 1992.

Hobby, E. and White, C. (eds), *What Lesbians do in Books*, London: Women's Press, 1991.

Hobson, D., *Crossroads: The drama of a soap opera*, London: Methuen, 1982.

Hodge, B. and Tripp, D., *Children and Television: A semiotic approach*, Cambridge: Polity, 1986.

Holland, N., *Five Readers Reading*, New Haven: Yale University Press, 1975.

Howard, J. and Allen, C., 'The gendered context of reading', *Gender and Society*, 4, 4 (December 1990): 534–52.

Hurford, J. and Heasley, B., *Semantics: A coursebook*, Cambridge: Cambridge University Press, 1983.

Hymes, D., 'On communicative competence', reprinted in V. Lee (ed.) *Language Development*, London: Croom Helm, pp. 36–62.

Ingarden, R., *The Literary Work of Art*, trans. G. C. Grabowitz, Evanston, IL: Northwestern University Press, 1973.

Iser, W., *The Act of Reading: A theory of aesthetic response*, London: Routledge & Kegan Paul, 1978.

Jardine, A. and Smith, P. (eds), *Men in Feminism*, London: Methuen, 1987.

Jenkins, H., '"Strangers no more, we sing": Filking and the social construction of the science fiction fan community', in L. A. Lewis (ed.) *The Adoring Audience: Fan culture and popular media*, London: Routledge, 1992, pp. 208–36.

Jensen, K. B., 'Reception analysis: Mass communication as the social production of meaning', in K. B. Jensen and N. Jankowski (eds) *A Handbook of Qualitative Methodologies for Mass Communication Research*, London: Routledge, 1991, pp. 135–48.

Jensen, K. B. and Jankowski, N. (eds), *A Handbook of Qualitative Methodologies for Mass Communication Research*, London: Routledge, 1991.

Jordanova, L., *Sexual Visions: Images of gender in science and medicine between the eighteenth and twentieth centuries*, Hemel Hempstead: Harvester Wheatsheaf, 1990.

Jordin, M. and Brunt, R., 'Constituting the television audience: A problem of method', in P. Drummond and R. Patterson (eds) *Television and its Audiences*, London: British Film Institute, 1988, pp. 231–49.

Kaplan, E. A. (ed.), *Women in Film Noir*, London: British Film Institute, 1980.

Kaplan, E. A., *Rocking around the Clock: Music, television, postmodernism and consumer culture*, London: Methuen, 1987.

Kaplan, E. A., 'Feminism/Oedipus/postmodernism: The case of MTV', in E. A. Kaplan (ed.) *Postmodernism and its Discontents*, London: Verso, 1988, pp. 30–44.

Kauffman, L. (ed.), *Feminism and Institutions: Dialogues on feminist theory*, Oxford: Blackwell, 1989.

Kellein, T., *Cindy Sherman*, Basel: Edition Cantz, 1991.

Kennard, J., 'Ourself behind ourself, a theory for lesbian readers', in E. A. Flynn and P. P. Schweickart (eds) *Gender and Reading: Essays on readers, texts and contexts*, Baltimore and London: Johns Hopkins University Press, 1986, pp. 63–80.

Kent, N., *Naked Hollywood: Money, power and the movies*, London: BBC, 1991.

Koedt, A., Levine, E. and Rapone, A. (eds), *Radical Feminism*, New York: Quadrangle, 1973.

Kuhn, A., *Women's Pictures: Feminism and cinema*, London and Boston: Routledge & Kegan Paul, 1982.

Kuhn, A., 'Women's genres: Melodrama, soap opera and theory', *Screen*, 25, 1 (1984): 18–28.

Laing Art Gallery, *The Pre-Raphaelites: Painters and patrons in the north east*, Newcastle: Tyne and Wear Museum Services, 1989.

Lakoff, R., *Language and Women's Place*, New York: Harper & Row, 1975.

LaPlace, M., 'Producing and consuming the woman's film', in C. Gledhill (ed.) *Home Is where the Heart Is*, London: British Film Institute, 1987, pp. 138–66.

Lapsley, R. and Westlake, M., *Film Theory: An introduction*, Manchester: Manchester University Press, 1988.

Lauretis, T. de, *Alice Doesn't: Feminism, semiotics, cinema*, Bloomington: Indiana University Press, 1984.

Lauretis, T. de, *Technologies of Gender: Essays on theory, film and fiction*, London: Macmillan, 1989.

Laws, S., *Issues of Blood: The politics of menstruation*, London: Macmillan, 1990.

Leech, G., *The Principles of Pragmatics*, Harlow: Longman, 1983.

Lees, S., *Losing Out: Sexuality and adolescent girls*, London: Hutchinson, 1986.

Leith, D., *The Power of Address: Explorations in rhetoric*, London: Routledge, 1989.

Levinson, S., *Pragmatics*, Cambridge: Cambridge University Press, 1983.

Lewis, L. A. (ed.), *The Adoring Audience: Fan culture and popular media*, London: Routledge, 1992.

Linker, K., 'Representation and sexuality', in B. Wallis (ed.) *Art after Modernism: Rethinking representation*, New York: The New York Museum of Contemporary Art Publications, 1984, pp. 391–415.

Lotman, Y., 'The text and the structure of the audience', *New Literary History*, 14 (1982): 81–7.

Lovell, T., *Consuming Fiction*, London: Verso.

Lucas, C., *Writing for Women: The example of woman as reader in Elizabethan romance*, Milton Keynes: Open University Press, 1989.

McCabe, C., 'Realism and cinema: Notes on some Brechtian theses', in T. Bennett, S. Boyd Bowman, C. Mercer and J. Woollacott (eds), *Popular TV and Film*, London: Open University/British Film Institute, 1981, pp. 216–35.

McCabe, C., *Theoretical Essays*, Manchester: Manchester University Press, 1985.

MacDonell, D., *Theories of Discourse*, Oxford: Blackwell, 1986.

Macherey, P., *A Theory of Literary Production*, London: Routledge & Kegan Paul, 1978 (first published 1966).

McConnell-Ginet, S., Borker, N. and Furman, N. (eds), *Women and Language in Literature and Society*, New York: Praeger, 1980.

McRobbie, A., 'Dance and social fantasy,' in A. McRobbie and M. Nava (eds) *Gender and Generation*, London: Macmillan, 1984, pp. 130–61.

Maio, K., *Feminist in the Dark: Reviewing the movies*, Freedom, California: Crossing Press, 1989.

Manuel, P., 'Black women in British TV drama – a case of marginal representation', in K. Davies, J. Dickey and T. Stratford (eds) *Out of Focus: Writings on women and the media*, London: The Women's Press, 1987, pp. 42–50.

Marsh, J., *The Pre-Raphaelite Sisterhood*, London: Quartet, 1984.

Marshment, M., 'Substantial women', in L. Gamman and M. Marshment (eds) *The Female Gaze: Women as viewers of popular culture*, London: Women's Press, pp. 27–43.

Masterman, L., *Teaching the Media*, London: Comedia, 1985.

Mayne, J., 'The female audience and the feminist critic', in J. Todd (ed.) *Women and Film*, New York and London: Holmes & Meier, 1988, pp. 22–40.

Mendus, S. and Rendall, J. (eds), *Sexuality and Subordination: Interdisciplinary studies in gender in the nineteenth century*, London: Routledge, 1989.

Millett, K., *Sexual Politics*, London: Virago, 1977 (first published 1971).

Milloy, J. and O'Rourke, R. (eds), *The Woman Reader: Learning and teaching women's writing*, London: Routledge, 1991.

Mills, S., 'The male sentence', *Language and Communication*, 7 (1987): 189–98.

Mills, S., 'Feministiche close reading,' trans. Martina Mitchell, *T/extasy: Feministische Perspektiven in Grossbritannien: Feministische Studien*, 8, 2 (1990): 70–87.

Mills, S., *Discourses of Difference: Women's travel writing and colonialism*, London: Routledge, 1991.

Mills, S., 'Knowing y/our place: Marxist feminist contextualised stylistics', in M. Toolan (ed.) *Language, Text and Context: Essays in stylistics*, London: Routledge, 1992, pp. 182–208.

Mills, S., 'Negotiating discourses of femininity,' *Journal of Gender Studies* 3, 3 (May 1992): 271–85.

Mills, S. (ed.), *Language and Gender*, Harlow: Longman, forthcoming.

Mills, S., *Feminist Stylistics*, London: Routledge, forthcoming.

Mills, S., Pearce, L., Spaull, S. and Millard, E., *Feminist Readings/Feminists Reading*, Hemel Hempstead: Harvester Wheatsheaf, 1989.

Minogue, S. (ed.), *Problems for Feminist Criticism*, London: Routledge, 1990.

Mitchell, J., *Psychoanalysis and Feminism*, Harmondsworth: Penguin, 1974.

Mitchell, S., *The Fallen Angel: Chastity, class and women's reading*, Bowling Green, OH: Bowling Green University Press, 1981.

Modleski, T., *Loving with a Vengeance: Mass-produced fantasies for women*, London: Methuen, 1984.

Modleski, T., 'Feminism and the power of interpretation: Some critical readings', in T. de Lauretis (ed.) *Feminist Studies/Critical Studies*, Bloomington: Indiana University Press, 1986, pp.121–38.

Modleski, T., *Feminism without Women: Culture and criticism in a 'postfeminist' age*, London: Routledge, 1991.

Moi, T., *Sexual/Textual Politics*, London: Methuen, 1985.

Moi, T., 'Appropriating Bourdieu', *New Literary History*, 22 (1990–1): 1017–49.

Monaco, J., *American Films Now: The People, the power, the money, the movies*, New York: Zeotrope, 1984.

Montgomery, M., *An Introduction to Language and Society*, London: Methuen, 1986.

Montgomery, M., 'DJ Talk', *Media, Culture and Society*, 8, 4 (October 1986): 421–40.

Montgomery, M., 'Direct address and audience', *Parlance: Journal of the Poetics and Linguistics Association*, 1, 2 (Winter 1989), pp. 35–55.

Montgomery, M., 'Media discourse in the 1987 General Election: Ideology, scripts and metaphors', *English Language Research Journal: Language and ideology*, 3 (1989).

Montgomery, M., Durant, A., Fabb, N., Furniss, T. and Mills, S., *Ways of Reading*, London: Routledge, 1992.

Moores, S., 'Texts, readers and contexts of readings', in P. Scannell, P. Schlesinger and C. Sparks (eds) *Culture and Power: A media, culture and society reader*, London: Sage, 1992, pp. 127–57.

Morley, D., *The 'Nationwide' Audience: Structure and decoding*, London: British Film Institute, 1980.

Morley, D., *Family Television: Cultural power and domestic leisure*, London: Comedia, 1986.

Morley, D., 'Changing paradigms in audience studies,' in E. Seiter, H. Borchers, G. Kreutzner and E. M. Warth (eds) *Remote Control: Television audiences and cultural power*, London and New York: Routledge, 1989, pp. 16–43.

Mulvey, L., 'Visual pleasure and narrative cinema', *Screen*, 16, 3 (Autumn 1975): 6–18.

Mulvey, L., 'Afterthoughts on "Visual pleasure and narrative cinema"', *Framework*, 15–16 (1981): 12–15.

Munt, S. (ed.), *New Lesbian Criticism*, Hemel Hempstead: Harvester Wheatsheaf, 1992.

Myers, K., 'Understanding advertisers', in H. Davis and R. Walton (eds) *Language, Image, Media*, Oxford: Blackwell, 1983, pp. 205–23.

Nead, L., *Myths of Sexuality: Representations of women in Victorian Britain*, Oxford: Blackwell, 1988.

Newman, J., 'Enterprising women: Images of success' in S. Franklin, C. Lury and J. Stacey (eds) *Off-centre: Feminism and cultural studies*, London: HarperCollins, 1991, pp. 241–59.

Newton, J. and Rosenfelt, D. (eds), *Feminist Criticism and Social Change*, London: Methuen, 1985.

Nicholson, L. (ed.), *Feminism/Postmodernism*, London: Routledge, 1990.

O'Connell, M., 'Ordinary girls unpack Madonna's extraordinary gloss', (A = interview transcript; B = analysis), unpublished project, Department of Sociology, Trinity College, Dublin, 1987.

Olins, R. and Rafferty, F. F., 'No to the sexy sell', in *Daily Telegraph*, 10 February 1990, p. 5.

O'Sullivan, T., Hartley, J., Saunders, D. and Fiske, J., *Key Concepts in Communication*, London: Routledge, 1978.

Owens, C., 'The Medusa effect or the spectacular ruse', in *We Won't Play Nature to Your Culture: Works by Barbara Kruger*, London: ICA, 1983.

Palmer, P., *Contemporary Women's Fiction*, Hemel Hempstead: Harvester Wheatsheaf, 1989.

Parkin, F., *Class Inequality and Political Order*, London: Paladin, 1973.

Pateman, T., 'How is understanding an advertisement possible?', in H. Davies and P. Walton (eds) *Language, Image, Media*, Oxford: Blackwell, 1983, pp. 187–204.

Pearce, L., *Woman/Image/Text: Readings in Pre-Raphaelite art and literature*, Hemel Hempstead: Harvester Wheatsheaf, 1991.

Pearce, L., 'Feminism and dialogism', in H. Hinds, A. Phoenix and J. Stacey (eds) *Working Out: New directions for women's studies*, London: Falmer, 1992, pp. 184–93.

Pearce, L., *Dialogic Theory and Textual Practice*, Sevenoaks: Edward Arnold, forthcoming.

Pearce, L., '"I", the reader: Text, context and the balance of power', in D. Reynolds and P. Florence (eds) *Media/Subject/Gender – Feminist Positions and Redefinition*, Manchester: Manchester University Press, forthcoming.

Pêcheux, M., *Language, Semantics and Ideology*, London: Macmillan, 1982.

Pollock, G., *Vision and Difference: Femininity, feminism and the histories of art*, London and New York: Routledge, 1988.

Poovey, M., *Uneven Developments: The ideological work of gender in mid-Victorian England*, Chicago: University of Chicago Press, 1988.

Pratt, M., 'Linguistic utopias', in N. Fabb, D. Attridge, A. Durant and C. MacCabe, (eds) *The Linguistics of Writing*, Manchester: Manchester University Press, 1987.

Press, A., *Women Watching Television: Gender, class and generation in the American television experience*, Philadelphia: University of Pennsylvania Press, 1991.

Pribram, D. (ed.), *Female Spectators: Looking at film and television*, London: Verso, 1988.

Radford, J. (ed.), *The Progress of Romance: The politics of popular fiction*, London: Routledge, 1986.

Radway, J., *Reading the Romance: Women, patriarchy and popular literature*, London: Verso, 1987 (first published 1984).

Raving Beauties (eds), *No Holds Barred: New poems by women*, London: Women's Press, 1985.

Richards, I. A., *Practical Criticism*, London: Kegan Paul, 1929.

Riffaterre, M., *Text Production*, New York: Columbia University Press, 1983.

Rivkin, J., 'Resisting readers and reading effects: Some speculations on reading and gender', in J. Phelan (ed.) *Narrative Poetics: Papers in comparative studies*, vol. 5, 1986–7, pp. 11–23.

Roach, J. and Felix, P., 'Black looks', in L. Gamman and M. Marshment (eds) *The Female Gaze*, London: Women's Press, 1988, pp. 130–42.

Robinson, L. S., *Sex, Class and Culture*, London: Methuen, 1986, (first published 1978).

Ruthven, K. K., *Feminist Literary Studies*, Cambridge: Cambridge University Press, 1984.

Said, E., *The World, The Text and the Critic*, Cambridge, MA: Harvard University Press, 1983.

Scannell, P., Schlesinger, P. and Sparks, C. (eds), *Culture and Power: A media culture and society reader*, London: Sage, 1992.

Schatz, T., *The Genius of the System: Hollywood film-making in the studio era*, New York: Simon & Schuster, 1989.

Schlesinger, P., Dobash, R. E., Dobash, R. P. and Weaver, C. K., *Women Viewing Violence*, London: British Film Institute, 1992.

Scholes, R., 'Reading like a man,' in A. Jardine and P. Smith (eds) *Men in Feminism*, London: Methuen, 1987, pp. 204–18.

Seiter, E., *Rethinking TV Audiences*, Chapel Hill: University of North Carolina, 1987.

Seiter, E., Borchers, H., Kreutzner, G. and Warth, E. M. (eds), *Remote Control: Television, audiences and cultural power*, London and New York: Routledge, 1989.

Sellers, S. (ed.), *Feminist Criticism: Theory and practice*, Hemel Hempstead: Harvester Wheatsheaf, 1991.

Showalter, E., 'Feminist criticism in the wilderness,' in E. Abel (ed.) *Writing and Sexual Difference*, Hemel Hempstead: Harvester Wheatsheaf, 1982, pp.9–35.

Showalter, E., *A Literature of their Own*, London: Virago, 1977.

Showalter, E., 'Critical cross-dressing: Male feminists and the woman of the year', in A. Jardine and P. Smith (eds) *Men in Feminism*, London: Methuen, 1987, pp. 116–32.

Shuttle, P. and Redgrove, P., *The Wise Wound: Menstruation and Everywoman*, Harmondsworth: Penguin, 1980.

Smith, D., 'Femininity as discourse', in L. Roman, E. Christian-Smith and K. Ellsworth (eds) *Becoming Feminine: The politics of popular culture*, London and New York: Falmer, 1988, pp. 37–59.

Smith, D., *Texts, Facts and Femininity: Exploring the relations of ruling*, London: Routledge, 1990.

Spelman, E., *Inessential Woman: Problems of exclusion in feminist thought*, London: Women's Press, 1988.

Spence, J., 'Class and gender in images of women', in K. Davies, J. Dickey and T. Stratford (eds) *Out of Focus: Writings on women and the media*, London: Women's Press, 1986, pp. 51–3.

Sperber, D. and Wilson, D., *Relevance: Communication and cognition*, Cambridge, MA: Harvard University Press, and Oxford: Blackwell, 1986.

Stacey, J., 'Desperately seeking difference', in L. Gamman and M. Marshment (eds) *The Female Gaze: Women as viewers of popular culture*, London: Women's Press, 1988, pp. 112–29.

Stacey, J., 'Feminine fascinations: Forms of identification in star–audience relations,' in C. Gledhill (ed.) *Stardom: Industry of desire*, London: Routledge, 1991, pp. 141–63.

Stacey, J., 'Star gazing: Hollywood cinema and female spectatorship in 1940s and 1950s Britain', unpublished PhD thesis, 1992, London: Routledge, forthcoming.

Staiger, J., *Interpreting Films: Studies in the historical reception of American cinema*, Princeton, NJ: Princeton University Press, 1992.

Suleiman, S. and Crossman, I. (eds), *The Reader in the Text: Essays on audience and interpretation*, Princeton: Princeton University Press, 1980.

Surtees, V., *The Paintings and Drawings of Virginia Surtees* (1828–1882): A catalogue raisonné, 2 vols, Oxford: Oxford University Press, 1971.

Suvin, D., 'The social addressees of Victorian fiction: A preliminary inquiry', *Literature and History*, 8 (1982): 11–40.

Sweetman, R., *On Our Backs*, London: Pan, 1979.

Tannen, D., *You just Don't Understand: Women and men in conversation*, London: Virago, 1991.

Tate Gallery Catalogue, *The Pre-Raphaelites*, London: Penguin, 1984.

Taylor, J. and Laing, D., 'Disco–pleasure–discourse', *Screen Education*, 31 (Summer 1979): 43–8.

Thornborrow, J., 'Discourse, power and ideology: Some explorations of critical discourse analysis', unpublished PhD thesis, University of Strathclyde, 1991.

Thornborrow, J., 'Orderly discourse and background knowledge', *Text*, 11, 4 (1991): 581–606.

Tincknell, E., 'Enterprise fictions: Women of substance', in S. Franklin, C. Lurie and J. Stacey (eds) *Off-Centre: Feminism and cultural studies*, London: HarperCollins, 1991, pp. 260–73.

Todd, J. (ed.), *Women and Film*, New York and London: Holmes & Meier, 1988.

Tong, R., *Feminist Thought*, London: Unwin/Hyman, 1989.

Tompkins, J. (ed.), *Reader-response Criticism: From formalism to post-structuralism*, Baltimore: Johns Hopkins University Press, 1980.

Toolan, M. (ed.), *Language, Text and Context: Essays in stylistics*, London: Routledge, 1992.

Treneman, A., 'Cashing in on the curse: Advertising and the menstrual taboo', in L. Gamman and M. Marshment (eds) *The Female Gaze: Women as viewers of popular culture*, London: Women's Press, 1988, pp. 153–65.

Tulloch, J., *Television Drama: Agency, audience and myth*, London: Routledge, 1990.

Wales, K., *A Dictionary of Stylistics*, London: Longman, 1989.

Wallis, B. (ed.), *Art after Modernism: Rethinking representation*, New York: The New Museum of Contemporary Art Publications, 1984.

Walsh, A., *Women's Film and Female Experience 1940–1950*, New York: Praeger, 1984.

Wareing, S., 'Women in fiction – stylistic modes of reclamation', *Parlance*, 2, 2 (1990): 72–85.

Warhol, R. and Herndl, D. (eds), *Feminisms: An anthology of literary history and criticism*, Baltimore: Rutgers University Press, 1991.

White, H., 'The value of narrativity in the representation of reality', in W. Mitchell (ed.) *On Narrative*, Chicago: University of Chicago Press, 1980, pp. 1–23.

Wicomb, Z., 'Tracing the path from national to official culture', in P. Mariani (ed.) *Critical Fictions*, Seattle: Bay Press, 1991, pp. 241–50.

Willemen, P., 'Notes on subjectivity', *Screen*, 19, 1 (1978): 41–69.

Williams, R., *The Country and the City*, London: Chatto & Windus, 1973.

Williamson, J., *Decoding Advertisements: Ideology and meaning in advertising*, London: Marion Boyars, 1978.

Williamson, J., 'The making of a material girl', *New Socialist* (October 1985): 46–7.

Wittig, M., *The Straight Mind and Other Essays*, Hemel Hempstead: Harvester Wheatsheaf, 1991.

Wolff, J., *The Social Production of Art*, London: Macmillan, 1981.

Wren-Lewis, J., 'The encoding/decoding model: Criticisms and redevelopments for research on decoding', *Media, Culture and Society*, 5 (1983): 179–97.

Notes on Contributors

Kay Boardman is a lecturer in English in the Department of Cultural Studies, University of Central Lancashire. She teaches on post-Renaissance literature and cultural studies and is currently working on constructions of femininity in nineteenth-century periodicals.

Barbara Bradby is a lecturer in sociology and women's studies at Trinity College, Dublin, Ireland. She is interested in popular music as a site of production of meanings around sexuality and gender in contemporary culture and has published articles using both song analysis and audience research as approaches. She has two daughters, one long outgrown Madonna and the other (6) a practising fan.

Christine Christie has recently completed a PhD with the Programme in Literary Linguistics, University of Strathclyde. Her work applies current linguistic and cognitive theories of inferencing to the study of audience response, and tests out methodological issues in empirical studies of audience interpretation.

Julia Hallam teaches in the Department of Communications, University of Liverpool, and is a doctoral student in women's studies at the University of Warwick. Her doctoral research explores the relationship between popular fictional texts and women's work, concentrating on issues of representation, identification and subjectivity in nursing.

Sara Mills is a senior lecturer in linguistics and critical theory in the Department of English and Drama, University of Loughborough. She works on feminist linguistic/literary theory and feminist colonial discourse theory. Together with Lynne Pearce, Sue Spaull and Elaine Millard, she wrote *Feminist Readings/Feminists Reading* (1989) and has recently published an analysis of women's travel writing: *Discourses of Difference: Women's travel writing and colonialism* (1991). She is currently working on a book entitled *Feminist Stylistics* and is editing a collection of essays entitled *Language and Gender*.

Lynne Pearce is a lecturer in English and women's studies at Lancaster University. After several years focusing on nineteenth-century art and literature (and the relationship between them), she has now turned her attention to contemporary women's writing and is especially interested in a feminist re-appraisal of the romance genre. She is co-author of *Feminist Readings/Feminists Reading* (1989) and author of *Woman/Image/Text* (1991). She is currently completing a book on dialogic theory which has a particular focus on questions of gender and readership.

251

Joanna Thornborrow is a lecturer in the English Language Programme at Roehampton Institute, teaching courses in stylistics and language in its social context. Her research interests range through the fields of discourse analysis, including critical discourse theory, aspecs of media discourse and issues relating to language and gender. She has published articles in *Text* (1991) and *Discourse and Society* (1993), and has contributed to a collection of essays on critical discourse analysis (forthcoming).

Imelda Whelehan is a senior lecturer in English at De Montfort University, Leicester. She teaches Shakespeare, nineteenth-century fiction, contemporary women's writing and feminist politics, and has recently completed her doctoral thesis on Second Wave Anglo-American feminisms. Her main research areas are women's writing and feminist theory, and she is currently involved in projects dealing with 'feminist bestsellers' and the role of the feminist within the academic institution.

Zoe Wicomb teaches English at the University of the Western Cape, South Africa, and also writes fiction. She works on feminist theory and South African literature and cultural studies.

Index

253